Transnational Corporations and Human Rights

Also by Jedrzej George Frynas

OIL IN NIGERIA: Conflict and Litigation between Oil Companies and Village Communities

Also by Scott Pegg

INTERNATIONAL SOCIETY AND THE DE FACTO STATE

Transnational Corporations and Human Rights

Edited by

Jedrzej George Frynas
Lecturer in International Management
Birmingham University
UK

and

Scott Pegg
Assistant Professor of Political Science
Indiana University Purdue University Indianapolis
USA

First published 2003 by
PALGRAVE MACMILLAN
Houndmills, Basingstoke, Hampshire RG21 6XS and
175 Fifth Avenue, New York, N.Y. 10010
Companies and representatives throughout the world

PALGRAVE MACMILLAN is the global academic imprint of the Palgrave Macmillan division of St. Martin's Press, LLC and of Palgrave Macmillan Ltd. Macmillan® is a registered trademark in the United States, United Kingdom and other countries. Palgrave is a registered trademark in the European Union and other countries.

ISBN 0–333–98799–3

This book is printed on paper suitable for recycling and made from fully managed and sustained forest sources.

A catalogue record for this book is available from the British Library.

Library of Congress Cataloging-in-Publication Data
Transnational corporations and human rights / edited by
Jedrzej George Frynas and Scott Pegg.
    p. cm.
  Includes bibliographical references and index.
  ISBN 0–333–98799–3
    1. International business enterprises – Social aspects. 2. International business enterprises – Social aspects – Case studies. 3. Human rights. 4. Social responsibility of business. I. Frynas, Jedrzej George. II. Pegg, Scott.
  HD2755.5.T6745 2003
  323–dc21   2003041433

10 9 8 7 6 5 4 3 2 1
12 11 10 09 08 07 06 05 04 03

Printed and bound in Great Britain by
Antony Rowe Ltd, Chippenham and Eastbourne

Jedrzej George Frynas would like to dedicate this book to victims of human rights abuses anywhere.

Scott Pegg would like to dedicate this book to Reverend Moses Nyimale Lezor and Patrick Naagbanton, two local heroes with first-hand experience of how transnational corporations affect human rights.

Contents

Acknowledgements

We would like to thank all the contributors to this volume for their efforts. Our biggest debt of gratitude is to Alison Howson, our editor at Palgrave Macmillan. Alison was a pleasure to work with and her support was essential to us in completing this volume. We would also like to thank Kerry Coutts and everyone else at Palgrave Macmillan involved in this project. Barbara Slater did an outstanding job copy-editing the book. Finally, we would like to thank Roger Moody and Randy Persaud for putting us in touch with some of our contributors.

Jedrzej George Frynas would like to thank Rosemarie Broadbent for her support throughout this project.

Scott Pegg would like to thank Tijen for her love and support. He would also like to thank his current colleagues in the Department of Political Science at Indiana University Purdue University Indianapolis and his former colleagues in the Department of International Relations at Bilkent University for providing supportive environments in which to work on this book. Didem Ekinci, Paul Kay, Jensine Larsen and Gizem Sucuoğlu also contributed in various ways to this project. Thanks.

JEDRZEJ GEORGE FRYNAS, London

SCOTT PEGG, Indianapolis

Notes on the Contributors

Richard Boele is a founding director of the Australian Institute of Corporate Citizenship (AICC). He has worked as a corporate social responsibility consultant and social auditor with a range of clients including Amnesty International, BHP Billiton, the British government, BP, Normandy Mining and the Novo Group. He previously held key positions at The Body Shop International (UK) and human rights organizations, both in Australia and Europe. Richard is a Visiting Associate at the Graduate Centre of the Environment at Macquarie University, Sydney, Australia and holds an Industrial Fellowship with the Centre for Stakeholding and Sustainable Enterprise at the Kingston University Business School in London, UK.

Heike Fabig is a PhD candidate in Corporate Responsibility at the Graduate Research Centre for the Comparative Study of Culture, Development and Environment at the University of Sussex, UK. Her research examines the engagement of The Body Shop (a multinational skin and hair-care company) with the campaign for social and environmental justice of the Ogoni people in Nigeria. She worked previously as a human rights campaigner for a Flemish non-governmental organization focusing on the collective human rights of indigenous peoples, as a researcher and consultant for The Body Shop International and a tutor at the University of Sussex School of African and Asian Studies.

Jedrzej George Frynas received his PhD in Management, Economics and Politics (MEP) from the University of St Andrews. He is a Lecturer in International Management at Birmingham Business School, Birmingham University, and the author of *Oil in Nigeria: Conflict and Litigation between Oil Companies and Village Communities* (2000). His research focuses on the activities of transnational corporations in developing countries and he has published articles in *Third World Quarterly, African Affairs, Review of African Political Economy* and *Social & Legal Studies*, among others.

Ronie Garcia-Johnson received her PhD in Political Science from the University of Michigan. She is an Assistant Professor of Environmental Policy at the Nicholas School of the Environment and Earth Sciences, Duke University. Dr Garcia-Johnson is the author of *Exporting*

Environmentalism: U.S. Multinational Chemical Corporations in Brazil and Mexico (2000), which won the 2001 Harold and Margaret Sprout Award from the International Studies Association. She is working in the Duke Project on Social and Environmental Certification to understand the emergence, evolution, diffusion and effectiveness of various forms of certification. The team published its first article on certification in *Foreign Policy*.

Stuart Kirsch received his PhD in Anthropology from the University of Pennsylvania. He is a Visiting Assistant Professor in the Department of Anthropology at the University of Michigan and previously taught in the Department of Sociology and Anthropology at Mount Holyoke College. Dr Kirsch has published journal articles in *Current Anthropology, Critique of Anthropology, Social Anthropology* and *The Contemporary Pacific*. He has consulted widely on environmental issues and indigenous land rights in the Pacific.

William H. Meyer received his PhD in Political Science from the University of Iowa. He is an Associate Professor in the Department of Political Science and International Relations at the University of Delaware and the author of *Human Rights and International Political Economy in Third World Nations: Multinational Corporations, Foreign Aid, and Repression* (1998) and *American Foreign Policy in a New Millennium: Security, Economics and Morality* (2003).

Scott Pegg received his PhD in Political Science from the University of British Columbia. He is an Assistant Professor in the Department of Political Science at Indiana University Purdue University Indianapolis and previously taught in the Department of International Relations at Bilkent University in Ankara, Turkey. Dr Pegg is the author of *International Society and the De Facto State* (1998) and he has published journal articles in *The Washington Quarterly, Security Dialogue* and *Third World Quarterly*.

Alex Wawryk received a First Class Honours degree in Economics and a PhD in Law from the University of Adelaide, Australia. She is a barrister and solicitor of the Supreme Court of South Australia, and is currently lecturing in the law department at the University of Adelaide. Dr Wawryk has published articles in the *Journal of Energy and Natural Resources Law*, the *Australasian Journal of Natural Resources Law and Policy*, the *Environmental and Planning Law Journal* and the *Melbourne University Law Review*.

Morton Winston received his PhD from the University of Illinois. He is a Professor of Philosophy at the College of New Jersey. He is the author or editor of several books, including *The Philosophy of Human Rights* (1989), *Society, Ethics, and Technology* (2000), and *On Chomsky* (2001). Dr Winston has received two Fulbright Scholarships; to South Africa (1992) and to Thailand (1999–2000). He is also a long-time human rights activist with Amnesty International where he was a member of Amnesty International USA's national Board of Directors from 1991–97, and Chair of the Board from 1995–97. He is currently the Chairman of AIUSA's Business and Economic Relations Group. Dr Winston is also a member of the Advisory Board of Social Accountability International.

List of Abbreviations

ACC	American Chemical Council
AI	Amnesty International
AIP	Apparel Industry Partnership
API	American Petroleum Institute
ATCA	Alien Tort Claims Act
BC	British Columbia
CCC	Clean Clothes Campaign
CEC	Commission on Environmental Cooperation, NAFTA
CEO	Chief Executive Officer
CERES	Coalition for Environmentally Responsible Economies
CJM	Coalition for Justice in the *Maquiladoras*
CSR	Corporate social responsibility
eNGOS	Environmental non-governmental organizations
ETI	Ethical Trading Initiative
FCPA	US Foreign Corrupt Practices Act
FLA	Fair Labor Association
FSC	Forest Stewardship Council
FTAA	Free Trade Area for the Americas
HRQ	*Human Rights Quarterly*
ICA	International Coffee Agreement
ICCA	International Council of Chemical Associations
ICCPR	International Covenant on Civil and Political Rights
ICESCR	International Covenant on Economic, Social and Cultural Rights
ICO	International Coffee Organization
ILO	International Labor Organization
IMF	International Monetary Fund
iNGOs	Indigenous rights non-governmental organizations
IR	International relations
MFN	Most-favored nation trading status
MSV®	Management systems verification
MOSOP	Movement for the Survival of the Ogoni People
NAAEC	North American Agreement on Environmental Cooperation
NAALC	North American Agreement on Labor Cooperation
NAFTA	North American Free Trade Agreement

NAOs	National Administrative Offices, NAFTA
NDDC	Niger Delta Development Commission
NGOs	Non-governmental organizations
NLNG	Nigeria Liquefied Natural Gas
NNOC	Nigerian National Oil Corporation
NNPC	Nigerian National Petroleum Corporation
OECD	Organization for Economic Cooperation and Development
OMPADEC	Oil Mineral Producing Areas Development Commission
OTML	Ok Tedi Mining Limited
SCAA	Specialty Coffee Association of America
SOMO	Centre for Research on Multinational Corporations
TBL	Triple bottom line
TNC	Transnational corporation
TRC	Truth and Reconciliation Commission (South Africa)
UDHR	Universal Declaration of Human Rights
UN	United Nations
UNDRD	United Nations Declaration on the Right to Development
UNHCHR	United Nations High Commissioner for Human Rights
USAS	United Students against Sweatshops
WTO	World Trade Organization

1
An Emerging Market for the New Millennium: Transnational Corporations and Human Rights[1]

Scott Pegg

Introduction

Transnational corporations (TNCs) are increasingly subject to high-profile consumer boycotts over their alleged complicity in human rights abuses. Textile manufacturers have, for example, been accused of physically abusing workers, actively assisting government campaigns against labor organizers and forcing workers to toil in 'sweatshop' conditions (see Frynas, Chapter 8 of this book). Resource extraction companies have been accused of providing logistical and financial assistance to repressive state security forces and relying on those forces for protection in countries such as Burma, Colombia, Nigeria and Sudan (Gagnon and Ryle 2001; Larsen 1998; Manby 1999; Pegg 1999). More recently, De Beers, the diamond industry cartel, has come under fire for purchasing diamonds from rebel groups in Angola and Sierra Leone and thus providing the bulk of their financing. De Beers has consequently become one of the latest TNCs to attract the critical scrutiny of non-governmental organizations (NGOs) and suffer the threat of consumer boycotts against its products. The corporate role in tolerating, financing, facilitating and benefiting from human rights abuses is now an issue of considerable media and public interest.

Yet, most of the academic work on transnational corporations ignored the subject of human rights. Edward Graham (1996), for example, wrote a book about designing global regimes to govern TNCs that made no mention whatsoever of human rights. This neglect has been reciprocal: most of the academic work on human rights has tended to overlook the role that TNCs can play in promoting or violating human rights.

The index of one recent edited volume on human rights (Dunne and Wheeler 1999), for example, shows that TNCs are mentioned on only two pages of a 337-page book. There is a major gap between these two literatures that this book attempts to bridge. Its core aim is to investigate, in a variety of ways, both the positive and negative implications of TNCs for human rights.

The idea that corporate behavior should be addressed through a human rights framework is controversial and is rejected by some academics. The next section discusses some of the potential academic critiques of the human rights approach; it presents our view of why we believe that a human rights approach offers an avenue for constructive debate about corporate activities and social responsibility. Readers who are not interested in theoretical debate may want to proceed directly to the section 'Historical background on corporate social responsibility'.

Critique and defense of the human rights approach

Three main types of criticisms seem to be brought forward by academics opposed to making the link between corporate behavior and a human rights framework. First, scholars operating from a narrow realist perspective in international relations theory dismiss the substantive impact and effectiveness of human rights as a force for positive change. Some realists counsel against including any ethical or normative considerations such as human rights in foreign policy decision-making. This is, however, a minority viewpoint amongst realists. As Jack Donnelly (1992, p. 96) points out:

> Few, if any realists are happy with the need to exclude morality from foreign policy ... It is therefore not surprising that most realists hedge the amoral statesmanship that they describe or advocate. At minimum they allow moral considerations a place in international affairs if they do not conflict with considerations of power and interest.

Nothing considered in this volume threatens state survival or prevents leaders from adhering to realist tenets on the balance of power or alliance formation. Indeed, realists will appreciate that our contributors are sensitive throughout the volume to the importance of state power and the limited prospects for advancing a human rights regime to regulate TNCs without the strong support of sovereign states. Our contributors do, however, believe that it is possible to make some, albeit perhaps limited, progress toward minimizing the negative effects of corporate investment through focusing on a human rights framework. After all, as Walter Russell Mead (2001, p. 139) points out, 'even the archrealist Kissinger himself now takes pride in the Helsinki Accords, which realists once dismissed or condemned'.

The second main criticism comes from the other side of the academic spectrum and accuses scholars who focus on human rights questions of being 'conservative', 'in thrall to the status quo' or 'narrowly reformist'. This critique can take a number of different forms. Postmodernists feel aggrieved that the existence of transnational corporations is taken for granted instead of challenged and problematized. Neo-Marxists argue that trying to hold TNCs accountable for their human rights performance is irrelevant because it accepts a capitalist framework for action rather than actively trying to dismantle it.

Robert Cox's famous distinction between 'critical theory' and 'problem-solving theory' provides a relevant departure point for assessing the salience of these criticisms. According to Cox (1986, p. 209):

> Critical theory is theory of history in the sense of being concerned not just with the past but with a continuing process of historical change. Problem-solving theory is nonhistorical or ahistorical, since it, in effect, posits a continuing present ... Problem-solving theories can be represented, in the broader perspective of critical theory, as serving particular national, sectional or class interests, which are comfortable within the given order.

The contributors to this volume do not posit a continuing present. Indeed, in different ways, they are all concerned with identifying positive sources of change that will affect the behavior of TNCs and increase (decrease) their positive (negative) impacts on local host communities, employees, shareholders and stakeholders.

Beyond this, though not written from a critical theory perspective, the contributions in this book are consistent with the spirit of critical theory as Cox defines it. In his words, 'Critical theory is, of course, not unconcerned with the problems of the real world ... Critical theory allows for a normative choice in favor of a social and political order different from the prevailing order, but it limits the range of choice to alternative orders which are feasible transformations of the existing world' (Cox 1986, p. 210). In this sense, the criticism that accepting the reality of TNCs or capitalism as given itself arguably violates critical theory's spirit of engagement with real world problems. As Ken Booth (1997, p. 114) has argued in regard to critical theory and security studies:

> The study of security can benefit from a range of perspectives, but not from those who would refuse to engage with the problems of those, at this minute, who are being starved, oppressed, or shot. It is therefore legitimate to ask what any theory that purports to belong within world politics has to say about Bosnia or nuclear deterrence. Thinking about thinking is important, but, more urgently, so is thinking about doing... Abstract ideas about emancipation will not suffice.

This book engages with the problems of people in countries like Nigeria and Papua New Guinea who are – today – being starved, oppressed, polluted, tortured or shot. It tries to identify policies, agents and sites of change to improve the human condition in the contemporary world. Abstract thinking about emancipation in a corporate-free world will not suffice. Our contributors prefer thinking about doing to just thinking about thinking.

Accepting the reality of corporate capitalism does not condemn us to conservative support for the status quo. In the words of Michael Nicholson (2000, p. 197), this seems 'rather like saying that to research the etiology of AIDS is to imply approval of AIDS'. In diverse ways, the various contributions in this volume share Nicholson's conclusion (2000, p. 197) that 'We can only know what is and what is not possible by looking at what is the case and seeing how it can be rearranged... Hopeful worlds, where hope is not based on hard analysis of what can be done, must be looked at with skepticism.'

The third critique against employing a human rights framework here can be identified under the broad rubric of cultural relativism. Cultural relativist critics argue that human rights are *not* universal. Human rights emanate from a western and liberal perspective and trying to make universal claims for what is essentially a cultural model drawn from European and North American intellectual traditions is a form of neo-colonialism (Mutua 2002).

One version of this argument was famously advanced by political leaders such as Singapore's former Prime Minister Lee Kuan Yew and Malaysia's Prime Minister Mahathir Mohammed who attributed East Asian economic success to so-called 'Asian values' which emphasized order and discipline over individual freedoms. While some of this was obviously the self-serving justification of repressive leaders, there is no denying that different societies place varying emphases on different types of human rights. As Chris Brown (1999, pp. 116–17) points out:

> It clearly is the case that in the post-colonial ... world, different
> countries have different notions of what are the appropriate
> rights – if any – for their inhabitants. In parts of East Asia authori-
> tarian regimes justify restrictions on individual liberty in the interests
> of economic development and, on their account, in accordance with
> local custom. Islamic regimes do not recognize certain rights regarded
> as crucial in Western liberal societies – the right to change one's
> religion being an obvious case in point. It is difficult to see how
> notions of human equality could be consistent with a caste system, or
> with social arrangements that privilege the family rather than the
> individual.

These different visions arguably make it extremely difficult to transfer
western and liberal values outside their given social context. As Chris
Brown (1999, p. 111) explains, 'it is implausible to think that rights
can be extracted from liberal polities, decontextualized and applied as a
package worldwide'. Though he was not himself a cultural relativist, the
late Ernest Gellner (1994, p. 214) also succinctly argued that 'preaching
across cultural boundaries seems to me in most circumstances a fairly
pointless exercise'.

The existence of different cultural value systems pokes a number of
serious holes in what Brown (1999, pp. 122–3) terms the 'sometimes
facile optimism' of western liberals that 'the *real* wishes of the peoples of
Indonesia or China, Saudi Arabia or Iran are represented by those relatively few free spirits who are active in the cause of freedom'. One can
also accept his argument that the failure to acknowledge these different
value systems has perhaps hindered the spread of human rights around
the world. According to Brown (1999, p. 104), 'Along, probably, with the
majority of readers, the present writer would be glad to live in a world in
which liberal, Western freedoms and rights were enjoyed by everyone,
but one of the obstacles to the achievement of such a world is created by
the unwillingness of some human rights activists to admit that the cause
they espouse *is* liberal and Western.'

Acknowledging all of this, however, does not invalidate either the idea
of human rights or our more specific adoption of a human rights framework in this book to evaluate and potentially hold corporations
accountable for their behavior. There is an urgent need to establish some
general criteria to measure business ethics in a globalized world. If
the decisions of every business manager are made on the basis of different ethical rules, firms may have an incentive to justify bad working

practices on the grounds of international differences. Indeed, Donaldson and Dunfee (1999) argue that establishing 'hypernorms' or universal standards of conduct may be essential for the long-term survival and interests of human society as a whole.

Beyond this, their work suggests that certain hypernorms are already universal across all human cultures and that companies should try to uphold them (Donaldson 1989, 1996; Donaldson and Dunfee 1999). One example of those 'core values' is the principle of reciprocity or 'not to do to others what they do not want done to themselves' stated by Confucius and widely accepted in western and non-western societies; another example is the right to good health. While it may sometimes be difficult to interpret these 'core values' in practice, many examples of corporate behavior are clearly unethical. As Donaldson (1996) argues, 'dumping pollutants near people's homes and accepting inadequate standards for handling hazardous materials are two examples of actions that violate core values'. In this regard, it is beyond comprehension that the wanton environmental destruction caused by the Ok Tedi mine (discussed in Chapter 6 of this book) could honor any culture's rights or value system, let alone that of the indigenous peoples of Papua New Guinea. Similarly, the major environmental destruction caused by oil companies in Nigeria (see Chapter 5 of this book) was equally condemned by western environmental campaigners and the local people in Nigeria's oil-producing areas. Acknowledging cultural differences and the western origins of some internationally recognized rights should not prohibit us from speaking out loudly against corporate malfeasance from a human rights perspective.

In moving our analysis forward, this chapter provides some historical background to the relationship between TNCs and human rights through a focus on corporate social responsibility (CSR). It then addresses two fundamental questions concerning business and human rights: when should TNCs be held responsible for human rights, and how should they be held responsible for them? This provides an introductory framework from which other more specific or particular questions can be assessed in subsequent chapters.

Historical background on corporate social responsibility

The contemporary attention given to corporate ethics and human rights issues should not obscure the fact that this is actually an ancient topic. Cicero wrote about immoral and unprincipled business practices as far back as 44 BC. The medieval church also issued pronouncements on the morality of usury and wage labor. More direct antecedents of today's debates include such things as abolitionists launching a boycott campaign against sugar produced by slave labor and nineteenth-century reformers addressing child labor (Ciulla 1991, pp. 67–8; Fabig and Boele 1999, p. 63).

The role of business in supporting repressive regimes was formally addressed at the Nuremberg and Tokyo war crimes trials. The most famous of these trials resulted in the board of directors of the German company I.G. Farben being found guilty of mass murder and slavery due to their direct personal involvement in gross human rights violations (Nattrass 1999, pp. 376–7). Another milestone in the history of business ethics came with the Lockheed bribery scandal in the 1970s. This resulted in the passing of the US Foreign Corrupt Practices Act (FCPA) in 1977 and stimulated tremendous growth in the use of written ethics policies by TNCs (Loomis 1999, p. 153). The first corporate ethics office was established in 1985 by General Dynamics which, at the time, was under investigation for pricing irregularities. The Ethics Officer Association, which started with a dozen members in 1992 now has approximately 650 members.[2] Thus, what sometimes appears to be a new issue actually dates back decades or centuries. What is new, according to Heike Fabig and Richard Boele (1999, p. 63), is that 'today's debates are conducted at the intersection of development, environment and human rights, and are more global in outlook than earlier in this century or even in the 1960s'.

However, the idea that corporations have social responsibilities that extend beyond profit maximization has never been a dominant belief among businessmen or academics. Perhaps the most famous exponent of the idea that corporations do not have responsibilities beyond profit maximization is Milton Friedman. According to Friedman (1962, p. 133), the idea that corporations have any responsibilities beyond maximizing profits for their shareholders represents 'a fundamental misconception of the character and nature of a free economy'. The sole responsibility of business leaders is to generate and maximize profits within the prevailing legal framework. Friedman concludes that 'Few trends could so thoroughly undermine the very foundations of our free society as the acceptance by corporate officials of a social responsibility other than to make as much money for their stockholders as possible' (1962, p. 133). This view still has adherents today. David Henderson (2001) extends Friedman's original insights into a blistering liberal political economy critique of CSR more generally. Henderson argues that CSR is premised on a number of intellectual misconceptions and that it is detrimental to the functioning of a market economy. His conclusion (2001, pp. 147–8) is that

> The potentially damaging effects of CSR...extend to economic systems as a whole, as well as to individual enterprises within them... Welfare may be reduced, not only because businesses are compelled to operate less efficiently, but also because new forms of interventionism arising out of the adoption of CSR, including closer regulation, narrow the domain of competition and economic freedom.

Another recent practical example of this attitude came in the submission from Ann Bernstein, the head of the Center for Development and Enterprise, to the South African Truth and Reconciliation Commission (TRC) hearings on the role of business in supporting apartheid. The entire question of what responsibility South African firms bore for the evils of the apartheid system was, for Bernstein, fundamentally misconceived. In her view,

> Corporations are not institutions established for moral purposes. They are functional institutions created to perform an economic task (production of goods and services and so on). This is their primary purpose. They are not institutions designed to promote some or other form of morality in the world...This does not of course absolve individuals within companies from moral choices, but that is a different matter. (Cited in Nattrass 1999, p. 384)

Marina Ottaway (2001, p. 53), in an essay focusing more specifically on oil companies, makes a similar argument: 'Oil companies may be "organs of society," but they are highly specialized ones, and their strengths lie not in devotion to democracy and human rights but in finding, extracting and distributing oil...taking on the role of imposing change on entire countries does not fit the nature of these organizations.'

While this traditional 'profit maximization' viewpoint remains important, the past decade has seen a noticeable shift toward a concept that is frequently labeled 'corporate social responsibility'. According to John Maresca (2000, pp. 160–1), this new concept of business 'builds on the traditional notion that business is first of all an effort by entrepreneurs to create wealth for themselves and their owners. But today a business can no longer be seen as a creator of wealth solely for its owners.' Rather, business has broader responsibilities that extend beyond its owners and shareholders to include employees, customers, suppliers and host communities. This view is distinct from business philanthropy in that it is based on a sense of responsibility, not generosity. It also, in David

Henderson's (2001, p. 57) phrasing, 'goes well beyond the numerous and varied individual packages of conspicuous good works, special employee benefits, targeted sponsorship exercises and active public relations policies which have long been part of the corporate scene'.

CSR is also distinct from the traditional profit maximization view in its broader accounting of a corporation's impact on society. In this regard, an increasing number of companies now focus on the so-called 'triple bottom line' (Elkington 1997), a concept being promoted by a diverse group of NGOs including Friends of the Earth, the Global Reporting Initiative and Social Accountability International. The triple bottom line concept basically argues that companies should simultaneously be held accountable for their social, environmental and financial performances. Whereas the traditional view assesses companies solely on their financial results, this expanded CSR concept also brings social and environmental results into the equation. This view does not represent standard corporate wisdom, but it is increasingly informing business decision-making at some leading firms. For instance, following the torrent of bad publicity it received in Nigeria, Royal Dutch/Shell explicitly addressed human rights issues in the first of a series of annual reports on the firm's financial, social and environmental responsibilities (Shell International 1998). The triple bottom line concept is also being supported by several important socially-responsible investment and mutual fund companies including Calvert, Domini, Walden Asset Management and Zurich.

There are at least three factors that explain the recent shift toward a broader concept of CSR. First, the rise of conservative political ideology in the 1980s and the discrediting of socialism following the end of the Cold War have led to an increasingly global consensus in favor of capitalism, free markets, privatization and deregulation. These changes have increased the relative autonomy of businesses vis-à-vis sovereign governments. In conjunction with this greater freedom have come calls for businesses to assume greater social responsibilities (Ciulla 1991, pp. 69–72; Maresca 2000, p. 156).

Second, globalization has increasingly transformed the world in the direction of a single economic space. While this process is obviously not complete, many TNCs source, produce, market and/or service an increasing amount of their business overseas. Correspondingly, labor unions adhere to the old maxim to 'follow the work', even if that now means following the work overseas (Mazur 2000). Environmentalists and human rights activists also ensure that corporate misbehavior anywhere in the world is brought to the attention of courts, policy-makers and consumers in important markets.

Third, the rapid development and spread of communications technologies has made it dramatically easier to monitor corporate performance around the world. This has helped expose company practices to
previously unheard of levels of public scrutiny and contributed to what
Debora Spar (1998) has termed the 'spotlight effect'. Companies operate
in an era of higher public expectations which often translate into consumer pressure to improve their environmental, labor and human rights
performances. Until quite recently, most corporations argued that they
could not be held responsible for the abusive labor practices of their
foreign suppliers or subcontractors. Looking specifically at US corporations, Spar (1998, p. 7) argues that:

> As a direct result of heightened human rights activism, sharper media
> scrutiny, and the increased communication facilitated by the
> Internet, US corporations are finding it difficult to sustain their old
> hands-off policy. Under pressure, they are beginning to accept
> responsibility for the labor practices and human rights abuses of their
> foreign subcontractors.

Spar's 'spotlight effect' results when firms realize that the benefits of
lower-cost labor or cheaper components now have to be weighed
against the bad publicity and consumer backlash that their complicity
in human rights abuses could generate.

Arguably, the sustainability of CSR will be determined by its effects on
profits. As David Henderson (2001, p. 128) explains, 'if CSR palpably
fails in financial terms, it cannot last'. To put it another way, the ulti-
mate success or failure of the triple bottom line is likely to be decided by
its effect on the traditional bottom line. Some evidence suggests that
there is no problem here as ethical corporate behavior correlates with
higher profitability. A study by Wiesenberger, a research firm, found that
what it calls 'socially screened funds' had, on average, consistently done
better than other mutual funds, although they tended to be more risky
and marginally more expensive (Carr 1999, p. 115). Companies which
include ethical commitments in their annual reports have also been
found to outperform other companies financially.[3]

The evidence, however, is far from conclusive on this point. To take
one example, the Domini Social Equity Fund, the largest US socially-
screened mutual fund that uses both exclusionary (tobacco and gam-
bling stocks, for example, are excluded) and inclusionary (the fund
seeks to include companies with positive records on such things as
the environment and product safety issues) screens, used to be cited for
consistently outperforming the Standard and Poor's 500 index. More

recent figures, however, indicate that the fund has underperformed the S&P 500 index over one-year, five-year and ten-year periods, and since inception, albeit not by substantial margins.[4] David Henderson (2001, p. 58) also points out that 'embracing CSR would inevitably have consequences that could raise the costs of doing business, could well reduce revenues, and might also cause companies to sponsor low-yielding investments which they would otherwise have turned down'. In and of itself, this does not necessarily mean that CSR will reduce profitability, as it could bring offsetting benefits in terms of increased sales and revenues if companies which adopt it are rewarded by consumers with increased market share. The benefits of CSR may or may not exceed the costs. The evidence to date is inconclusive and it remains quite possible that CSR will have negative overall effects on profitability.

Thus, as John Parkinson (1999, p. 50) points out, 'Even in an era in which companies are highly sensitive to ethical and social issues... the pursuit of profit and responsible behavior are not necessarily co-terminous.' Parkinson argues that while responsible corporate behavior is frequently a prerequisite for long-term profitability, ethical and human rights considerations should be seen as possessing independent weight beyond their effects on the financial bottom line. His conclusion is that managers 'should accept that respect for them will sometimes require companies to make less than the maximum possible profits' (1999, p. 62). The willingness of corporate executives to do this, however, remains open to question. As Lawrence Mitchell explains, even if CSR increases long-term profitability, the emphasis in today's capital markets on short-term profit maximization acts as a strong deterrent against socially responsible corporate behavior. In his words (2001, pp. 236–7), 'the company that tries to rise above the tide risks some period of competitive disadvantage relative to the rest of the fleet. Perhaps it could survive that period. But perhaps not. What manager wants to take that risk?' Most corporate leaders will gladly pursue improvements in their environmental and human rights records if those improvements can be justified in terms of profitability. When push comes to shove, though, and the requirements of the triple bottom line conflict with the exigencies of the traditional bottom line, it is far from self-evident that the expanded CSR concept will win out over the traditional profit maximization view.

When corporations are responsible for human rights

Margaret Jungk (1999, pp. 175–8) argues that there are four essential factors for TNCs to consider in addressing human rights issues. The first three of Jungk's factors essentially relate to the nature of the regime ruling the country where the TNC's operation is located. Her first criterion concerns the *degree* of human rights violations. Are there sporadic, random or isolated cases of human rights violations in the country or are there planned, systematic and continuous violations of human rights? Her second criterion deals with the *nature* of the human rights violations. Are these violations a direct result of government activities or policies or is the government simply unable to secure human rights effectively in its territory? Her third criterion concerns the *type* of rights being breached, specifically whether or not 'fundamental' rights such as the right to life or freedom from torture are being violated.

Jungk's first three government-related criteria are helpful but not fundamental in assessing when corporations should be held accountable for human rights. When states score poorly on these criteria, corporations should vet their investment decisions more carefully and ensure that their operations do not contribute to or benefit from these widespread human rights violations. They should also expect closer scrutiny of their operations from consumers, NGOs and civil society. Corporations that derive strategic business advantages from political instability serving as a barrier to entry to other TNCs (Frynas 1998, pp. 458 and 475) or from their valued role in stable yet corrupt and clientelistic systems (Le Billon 2001, p. 64) are particularly vulnerable here. Similarly, companies that trumpet their investments in community development projects to justify their presence in repressive states should be prepared to have those claims critically audited. However, with the exception of a few cases (perhaps including Angola, Burma and Sudan today, Nigeria under its most recent military dictatorships and apartheid South Africa), the argument that any investment in a particular country is necessarily bad is unlikely to convince most corporate executives, government policy-makers or consumers at large.

Thus, Jungk's fourth criterion is arguably the most important for corporations to consider. She refers to this as the *proximity* criterion and identifies three different possibilities. The first is that the company's operations have 'no connection' to the overall human rights situation in the country. In this case, the company's operations are too small to have any significant impact on either the government or the host communities where it operates. Jungk's second possibility is an 'indirect connection' in which the governing regime is largely supported by revenue generated from the company's operations. Her third possibility is where the company has a 'direct connection' to human rights violations in the sense that 'Human rights violations arise directly in relation to the company's operations or products' (1999, p. 177). Examples here include such things as companies manufacturing equipment used to torture citizens, companies using child or slave labor and companies depending upon military protection to enable their operations to proceed.

The South African Truth and Reconciliation Commission illustrates what can go wrong when the proximity criterion is ignored. In spite of establishing a tripartite framework, somewhat similar to Jungk's proximity scheme, which distinguished three different magnitudes of business involvement with the apartheid regime, the TRC recommended that all businesses in South Africa, whatever their level of involvement with the apartheid regime, should be responsible for restitution. The unfortunate result, according to Nicoli Nattrass (1999, p. 389) was that 'irrespective of whether a firm treated its workers well, protested against apartheid and supported the anti-apartheid movement, the firm is in effect held to be as culpable for apartheid as a racist firm which abused its workers and bankrolled right-wing activities'.

Nattrass is correct that an inability to discriminate between the different levels of corporate responsibility is unlikely to create an environment in which TNCs can legitimately be held accountable for their impact on human rights. With the possible exception of particularly egregious cases (Burma arguably being the best example today), corporations with 'no connection' cannot be held accountable for the fact that human rights violations occur in countries in which they have investments. They can, however, be held accountable for activities in which they have – as in Jungk's scheme – an indirect or direct connection.

Another way of framing this question is to ask whether or not corporations actively play a role in creating, maintaining or exacerbating human rights violations. Beyond the financial support they offer repressive regimes, the argument here is that the centrality of TNCs in creating and exacerbating human rights violations against local populations can be demonstrated in two main ways.

First, corporations can have a *catalytic* effect in bringing local populations into confrontation with military forces. In the Burmese case, the number of troops stationed in the region where the Yadana natural gas pipeline is being constructed increased from five battalions in 1990 to more than fourteen battalions in 1996 (Larsen 1998, p. 6). While TNCs often justify their investments in terms of benefits to the local population, nearly all of the gas produced in the Yadana field is exported to neighboring countries. Revenues accrue directly to the military government and the oil companies themselves. As Jensine Larsen (1998, p. 11) explains, 'virtually no ordinary Burmese citizen or member of an ethnic minority will profit. Instead they will suffer the consequences of a degraded environment and expanded political oppression.' An even more extreme version of this catalytic effect can be seen today in Sudan. As Georgette Gagnon and John Ryle (2001, p. 30) explain:

> In order to extract oil from a contested region, one where the inhabitants are in critical respects considered by the government as a security risk, the oil companies have become part of a counter-insurgency operation. Military operations against rebel forces in Western Upper Nile and military operations designed to clear and secure the oil fields are not distinct from one another. In fact, they are the same. Oil facilities and infrastructure are de facto military facilities, the oil fields are the most heavily militarized locations, oil company property and personnel are viewed as military targets by rebel forces and indigenous rural communities are considered security threats by forces protecting oil company property.

Second, companies can have a *direct* effect on the human rights of local host communities. Garment manufacturers have physically abused and sexually harassed their employees (see Frynas, Chapter 8 of this book). Companies have transported military troops in their helicopters and boats in Burma, Indonesia and Nigeria (Larsen 1998; Ceppi 2000; Pegg 1999). They have also shared their facilities with helicopter gunships in Sudan (Gagnon and Ryle 2001). Furthermore, companies also decide whether or not to make specific requests for military assistance. Oil companies in Nigeria have claimed credit for the peaceful resolution of disputes when they have asked the military authorities not to intervene forcibly. These same companies, however, simultaneously disclaim any responsibility for situations where they have requested military assistance which subsequently resulted in human rights violations with the argument that they are required to do so by domestic law (see Frynas, Chapter 5 of this book for more on the oil industry in Nigeria). Corporations are not powerless actors. They make choices which directly affect the security or insecurity of local populations. Corporate decisions matter and businesses should expect to be held accountable when their decisions result in torture, arbitrary arrest, injuries, deaths and human rights violations for local residents.

Thus, in operationalizing this framework, we can see that foreign oil companies in Nigeria should be held accountable for their 'direct connections' with the Nigerian security forces which have resulted in numerous deaths. Garment industry TNCs could also be held accountable if they directly violated the rights of workers by beating or sexually harassing them in countries such as Indonesia or China. If a company, however, treated its workers well, did not violate their human rights or depend on military protection to guard its facilities, then the company would not have human rights obligations to answer for simply because it produced or marketed its products in Nigeria or China. One can distinguish here between oil companies such as Shell and Chevron – transporting military troops in company boats and helicopters, standing by silently when non-violent protestors are killed and working in an industry that provides more than 90 per cent of Nigeria's export receipts – and a company such as Guinness which manufactures and sells beer in the Nigerian marketplace but has otherwise not done anything to place itself on the world's human rights radar screens.

Such a focus on what proximity the company has to human rights violations eliminates the potential danger of excessively expanding corporate involvement into human rights issues which remain primarily matters of state concern. Most companies, most of the time, are not involved in human rights abuses. Excessively expanding concerns over the corporate impact on human rights to include companies with no direct or indirect connection to human rights violations risks distracting attention from the much smaller number of situations that truly require serious monitoring. Maintaining a narrow focus on proximity also guards against raising unrealistic expectations about what companies can or should do.

Legal liability of TNCs for human rights violations

There are two main ways that corporations can be held accountable for their human rights performance: through legal liability under national or international law, and voluntarily through codes of conduct and self-regulation (see Wawryk, Chapter 3 of this book). There are a number of potential advantages to the legal approach. As the International Council on Human Rights Policy (ICHRP 2002, p. 5) points out:

> Voluntary codes rely entirely on business expediency or a company's sense of charity for their effectiveness. By contrast, legal regimes emphasize principles of accountability and redress, through compensation, restitution and rehabilitation for damage caused. They provide a better basis for consistent and fair judgments (for all parties, including companies).

International legal codes can establish coherent universal standards, something a competing array of private voluntary codes of conduct cannot do. They can also provide a 'level playing field' for all businesses. Finally, there is some evidence that business leaders prefer obligation and clarity to voluntarism and confusion (ICHRP 2002, pp. 6 and 14).

Human rights embody two interrelated foundational claims. First, there is an identifiable subject who has rights. Second, the existence of a subject possessing rights presupposes the existence of a duty-bearer against whom those rights can be claimed or exercised (Dunne and Wheeler 1999, p. 3). While it might seem logical that individuals would hold their human rights against all other individuals and groups, that is not the case. It is states and not individuals, NGOs or TNCs that sign international treaties defining human rights. Thus, as Jack Donnelly (1999, p. 85) points out, 'Human rights, although held equally by all human beings, are held with respect to, and exercised against, the sovereign territorial state ... international human rights treaties establish rights for all individuals. The obligations they create, however, are only for states.'

Nonetheless, there is no logical reason that corporations cannot bear human rights-related obligations. Indeed, to some extent, they already do. Indirectly, states are responsible for preventing human rights abuses by private actors, including companies (ICHRP 2002, p. 7; Muchlinski 2001, p. 32). More directly, the preamble to the Universal Declaration on Human Rights (UDHR) is addressed not only to states but also to 'every individual and every organ of society'. There are two other international procedures that can directly scrutinize corporate respect for human rights standards. These are the International Labor Organization's (ILO) 1977 Tripartite Declaration of Principles Concerning Multinational Enterprises and Social Policy and the Organization for Economic Cooperation and Development's (OECD) 1976 Guidelines for Multinational Enterprises, revised most recently in 2000. Both documents, however, are non-binding and rely on the voluntary cooperation of TNCs. As such, they both remain weak legal instruments (ICHRP 2002, p. 10; Muchlinski 2001, pp. 36–7; Wawryk, Chapter 3 of this book). Moving beyond such weak instruments presents a number of challenges. As Donnelly (1999, p. 95) argues, 'whatever the shortcomings of states in providing for economic and social rights, they pale before those of multinational corporations, which are shadowy, often distant, private entities over which individuals lack even the limited control provided by electoral participation'.

One problem here comes from the question of whether or not corporations as entities can be held responsible for human rights violations. If one accepts the argument originally put forward by H.L.A. Hart that a responsible entity is one capable of making choices and exercising control, then corporations can clearly be seen as responsible entities beyond any role that individuals within them may play as responsible human beings (Addo 1999, p. 17). An additional complication arises here, though, in regard to the question of whether or not parent companies can be held responsible for the behavior of their subsidiaries. The principle that different limited liability companies have separate legal identities is firmly established in English law. This principle holds even when one company owns all the shares of the other company. The end result is that 'the parent company of a wholly owned subsidiary is, on the face of it, no more responsible, legally, for the unlawful behavior of the subsidiary, than would be ... a member of the public for the negligence of a company in which he owns a single share' (Meeran 1999, p. 161).

This doctrine has, however, come under attack in different countries. In Chapter 6, Stuart Kirsch describes the lawsuit against the mining company BHP in Australian courts for the environmental devastation wrought by its subsidiary in Papua New Guinea. In England, there have been a number of cases where English TNCs were sued in English courts by foreigners for the actions of their subsidiaries abroad. Thor Chemicals Holding Ltd was sued in relation to a factory that exposed workers to mercury poisoning in South Africa, while Rio Tinto PLC was successfully sued over health hazards relating to a uranium mine in Namibia. In these cases, the companies responded with *forum non conveniens* motions arguing that the cases should be tried in the countries where the alleged events took place and not in England. As one of the plaintiffs' lawyers has put it, 'The plain truth of the matter is that claimants want to sue in England because they cannot get justice overseas and TNCs want to stay the claims for precisely the same reason ...' (Meeran 1999, p. 170).

Similar developments have also taken place in the United States. There, the Alien Tort Claims Act (ATCA), originally enacted as part of the 1789 Judiciary Act to allow victims of offshore piracy to sue onshore, has been used to sue individuals and corporations in US courts for crimes committed overseas. In 1998, US District Court Judge Richard Paez ruled in the case *Doe v. Unocal*, that Unocal, a US-based oil company, could be sued in US courts for alleged human rights abuses committed by Burmese authorities. Judge Paez argued that the plaintiffs, all Burmese citizens, should be allowed to sue if the company knew or should have known that their joint venture business partner was committing human rights violations on behalf of the joint venture's projects. Unocal challenged this ruling with a motion arguing that the case should be dismissed because there was no evidence that Unocal employees directly violated human rights in Burma. A substantive ruling in favor of Unocal was issued in August 2000 (Muchlinski 2001, pp. 41–2). Upon appeal, the US Ninth Circuit Court of Appeals ruled in September 2002 that Unocal could face trial in the United States for its alleged complicity in aiding and abetting human rights violations committed by Burmese authorities. A similar lawsuit has now also been filed against Unocal in the California state court system as well (Girion 2002).

In April 2000, in the case of *Bowoto v. Chevron*, another US district judge ruled that Chevron (now part of Chevron Texaco), the parent company of Chevron Nigeria Ltd, could be sued over that company's role in transporting Nigerian military troops on two separate occasions to locations where non-violent protestors were subsequently killed and injured. In September 2000, a New York court similarly ruled that *Wiwa v. Royal Dutch Petroleum Company and Shell Transport and Trading Company PLC*, a case brought by relatives of the hanged Nigerian writer Ken Saro-Wiwa alleging Royal Dutch/Shell's complicity in his wrongful death could also move forward. Chevron and Shell each unsuccessfully brought *forum non conveniens* motions arguing that neither of these respective cases should be heard in the United States. In February 2002, the US Supreme Court refused to hear an appeal by Shell against this ruling in the *Wiwa* case, thus upholding the original decision. Substantive rulings on the *Bowoto* and *Wiwa* cases are still pending (Hoppin 2000; Muchlinski 2001, pp. 41–2). Conversely, the US Second Circuit Court of Appeals upheld a ruling dismissing a case brought by indigenous peoples from Ecuador against Texaco (now part of Chevron Texaco) in August 2002 on the *forum non conveniens* grounds that the case should more appropriately be heard in Ecuador.[5]

These court cases have so far taken place in countries with a common law system introduced during English colonial rule, where courts have considerable autonomy to interpret legal rules. But calls have also been made for home country governments to hold corporations legally liable for human rights abuses in foreign jurisdictions. There is some precedent for governments holding their citizens or corporate citizens accountable for their actions overseas. The FCPA, for example, makes it illegal under US law for US business executives to pay bribes to foreign officials in order to secure or retain business. The Australian government pioneered legislation that holds its citizens responsible for child-sex offences even if those offences take place overseas and involve foreign nationals. There is no theoretical reason why home country governments could not regulate the activities of their nationally-based corporations abroad to ensure compliance with relevant human rights

standards. Indeed, in failing to do so, industrialized country governments now 'lag behind northern consumers and investors who are
already expressing their concern' (Woodroffe 1999, p. 137).

There is empirical support for the argument that home country government regulation of TNCs can be effective. In a comprehensive study
of extraterritorial sanctions applied by the US government, Kenneth
Rodman (2001, p. 15) finds that corporations 'were generally more
reluctant to use their global networks to escape home state sanctions
regulations than they have been in relocating to minimize tax liabilities
or shift production to more favorable business climates'. Beyond mere
compliance, Rodman interestingly finds clear evidence that companies
often went beyond the letter of the sanctions law to avoid jeopardizing
their relationship with the US government. As he explains, 'If there was
a strong public, interest group or congressional constituency, corporations were often deterred by the threat of adverse publicity and the com-
plications that might create with customers, shareholders and workers'
(Rodman 2001, p. 127).

Be that as it may, there are a number of practical difficulties here. First,
the elected leaders of many home country governments receive substantial campaign financing from TNCs and would not be likely to enact
any domestic legislation that would seriously hamper corporate interests abroad. Indeed, Rodman (2001, p. 225), perhaps presciently, fore-
casts US Congressional repeal of the ATCA to prevent future *Bowoto,
Doe* or *Wiwa* cases from being brought forward. Of more immediate concern to human rights advocates is the way in which the executive
branch of the US government has recently intervened against the ATCA.
In July 2002, the US State Department issued an opinion on a case
involving Indonesian villagers in Aceh province suing Exxon Mobil over
allegations that soldiers paid by the company to guard its facilities had
tortured, raped and murdered local residents. The State Department's
top legal adviser argued that a verdict against Exxon Mobil could 'risk
a potentially serious adverse impact on significant interests of the US,
including interests directly related to the struggle against international
terrorism'. The State Department also argued that the lawsuit could dis-
courage US foreign direct investment in Indonesia and that this would
hurt Indonesian government revenues and weaken a major US ally.
A similar case against the mining company Rio Tinto was dismissed after
the State Department argued that it could harm US interests in Papua
New Guinea (Alden 2002). Second, there is a clear distinction to be
made between enactment of domestic legislation and enforcement of it.
The FCPA is illustrative here. As Russell Mokhiber and Robert Weissman

(2002) point out, during the entire 25-year history of the FCPA, the US Department of Justice has only prosecuted about 30 cases. In 1988, the FCPA was weakened when Congress amended its provisions to allow facilitation payments by what is sometimes known as the 'grease payment exception'. A 2002 US District Court ruling that interpreted the FCPA extremely narrowly has also further diminished the practical significance of the original legislation. We are thus left with the disjunction that one of the potentially most effective ways to hold corporations legally accountable for human rights violations is also one of the least likely to take place.

In addition to national governments, international organizations may also provide a basis for creating legal obligations for TNCs. Such international avenues could perhaps avoid some of the problems raised above; among others, they may be less prone to influence by TNC financing. A major advantage of using international institutions is that they may represent a greater international consensus on what human rights standards should be. Broad international enforcement could also hold TNCs liable for human rights violations, notwithstanding their place of incorporation or a particular country's willingness to prosecute offenders. Indeed, some international mechanisms already exist for potentially prosecuting TNCs. For instance, the UN Human Rights Committee found that a French tourism project in Tahiti violated the International Covenant on Civil and Political Rights. In that case, *Hopu and Bessert v. France*,[6] a local community from Tahiti successfully objected to a hotel project developed by a private firm in conjunction with a government-owned company, alleging infringements of indigenous lands. Other organizations with established legal mechanisms such as the World Trade Organization (WTO) could also help to enforce human rights standards, as Bill Meyer argues in Chapter 2 of this book.

In addition to international organizations, regional economic integration can also contribute to developing international standards of behavior and enforcement mechanisms for prosecuting human rights violations by TNCs. Bill Meyer (Chapter 2 of this book) envisions the North American Free Trade Agreement (NAFTA) as offering a potential model here. NAFTA included two side agreements, the North American Agreement on Labor Cooperation (NAALC) and the North American Agreement on Environmental Cooperation (NAAEC). The NAALC established National Administrative Offices in each of the three NAFTA countries while the NAAEC established a NAFTA-wide Commission on Environmental Cooperation with headquarters in Montreal. Whatever their other weaknesses, citizens and NGOs may directly bring complaints before any of these bodies. Arguably, though, it is the European Union which offers the best prospects in this context, as it already has well-developed legal mechanisms for addressing human rights violations within Europe. Efforts have been made to extend certain existing legal provisions to cover actions by TNCs, notably through a resolution in the European Parliament entitled 'EU Standards for European Enterprises: Towards a European Code of Conduct'. While the success of the resolution remains uncertain, the proposal demonstrates another potential avenue for creating binding international legal standards for TNCs.

However, there are generic limitations to any legal approach in regulating corporate behavior. First, the development of new laws tends to lag behind the development of new forms of conduct that society might wish to see regulated. In this sense, law is frequently reactive rather than proactive. Second, corporate law has tended to rely heavily on the responsibility or agency of individual corporate officers and not the corporation as a whole (Addo 1999, p. 10). This problem is not insurmountable, but it is a serious obstacle to regulating TNC behavior legally. Third, law can set minimal standards or prohibit certain conduct, but it is much less effective at eliciting positive behavior or promoting higher standards (Parkinson 1999, p. 57). As Michael Addo (1999, p. 13) argues, societal expectations of corporate behavior today 'far exceed what the law expressly requires of them at the moment'. Legal regulations have a valuable role to play in regulating corporate behavior. The limits to the legal approach, however, mean that a gap will necessarily remain between what concerned citizens expect from corporations and what the law explicitly requires of them. Following John Parkinson (1999, p. 57), our argument is that 'it is in plugging this gap that the role of social responsibility is best understood'.

Voluntary approaches and self-regulation of TNC behavior

Voluntary approaches to improving corporate conduct have taken place at both collective and individual levels. Collectively, there has been a proliferation of voluntary approaches in the past few years. The United Nations, for example, has developed the Global Compact which comprises nine basic principles covering human rights, labor standards and the environment which companies are asked to embrace.[7] These principles are drawn from such existing documents as the UDHR, the Declaration of the ILO on fundamental principles and rights and the Rio Declaration from the 1992 UN Conference on Environment and

Development. These nine principles are all framed in vague and general terms and do not require any detailed or auditable commitments. Another recent attempt to encourage corporations collectively to take action has been the Global Sullivan Principles, devised by Reverend Leon Sullivan, the architect of a similar set of principles on doing business in South Africa under apartheid.[8] As with the UN's Global Compact, these principles are framed generally and compliance with them is voluntary. The Council on Economic Priorities has also launched Social Accountability 8000, which is designed to encourage corporate compliance with a certifiable set of labor and human rights standards.[9] These standards are drawn from ILO Conventions, the UDHR and the UN Convention on the Rights of the Child. Corporate compliance with these standards can be audited by certified independent third parties, though compliance ultimately depends on the firms' voluntary acceptance of them.

Collective actions have also taken place within specific industries. Following the Kathie Lee Gifford sweatshop scandal (involving clothing produced in Central America and sold under the name of this American television celebrity), the White House established an Apparel Industry Partnership in August 1996 to secure agreement among manufacturers on acceptable working conditions for all participating companies and their foreign contractors (see Meyer, Chapter 2 of this book). The International Council of Chemical Associations coordinates through its members, the national chemical manufacturers associations, the Responsible Care standards program to improve the environmental, health and safety performance of the chemical industry (see Wawryk, Chapter 3 of this book). Seven oil and mining companies, nine NGOs and the UK and US governments also signed up to the 'Voluntary Principles on Security and Human Rights' in December 2000 (see Winston, Chapter 4 of this book).[10] As Debora Spar points out, the underlying rationale behind these industry-wide approaches is to solve the free-rider problem, where companies who do not raise their labor standards end up having a cost advantage over those who do. As Spar (1998, p. 10) observes, 'If all firms – or at least a good majority of the larger ones – adhere to the same standard, none is individually penalized.'

Numerous individual corporations have also enacted their own codes of conduct governing their employees and business operations. A recent inventory by the OECD, for example, lists 246 individual corporate codes of conduct (Gereffi et al. 2001, p. 57). All of these voluntary initiatives suffer from a number of weaknesses (see Wawryk, Chapter 3 of this book for more on this). First, meaningful self-regulation is likely to be undertaken only by a small number of companies (Woodroffe 1999, p. 132). Second, public commitments may not always translate into changed corporate behavior. One cannot avoid thinking that much of the proliferation of these voluntary initiatives is driven solely by public relations. As Michael Addo (1999, p. 11) puts it:

> On the few occasions when corporations assume responsibilities outside of a legal framework it has either been because of social pressure or in reaction to errors, scandals or incidents involving the corporation concerned. These reactive responses are generally transient and not particularly rigorous in character.

Third, such voluntary efforts depend upon the continued vigilance of concerned citizens, consumers, NGOs and investors or what Margaret Keck and Kathryn Sikkink (1998) have referred to as 'transnational advocacy networks'.

In this regard, though, the picture is not entirely bleak. One of the two areas where Keck and Sikkink (1998, p. 27) find transnational advocacy networks most effective concerns 'issues involving bodily harm to vulnerable individuals, especially when there is a short and clear causal chain (or story) assigning responsibility'. Kenneth Rodman (2001, p. 202) adds that 'NGOs have been most influential vis-à-vis large diversified firms for whom the stake in question represents a small fraction of its overall operations'. Perhaps the best examples here involve Burma. The Amoco (now part of BP), ARCO (now also part of BP), Petro-Canada and Texaco (now part of Chevron Texaco) oil companies all withdrew from Burma, as did non-oil companies like Best Western, Levi Strauss and PepsiCo. For all of these companies, Burma only represented a relatively small proportion of their overall operations.

The extent of such changes should not, however, be exaggerated. The UK firm Premier Oil has, for example, chosen to remain in Burma even after the British government took the unprecedented step in April 2000 of asking the company to withdraw from the country (O'Kane 2000). Talisman, a Canadian oil firm, has chosen to remain in Sudan in spite of damning reports on its involvement in the country's civil war (Gagnon and Ryle 2001), investor divestment campaigns and explicit NGO calls for it to suspend its operations in Sudan. Even after the bad publicity surrounding Shell's links to the Nigerian military, Chevron still transported Nigerian troops on two separate occasions in 1998 and 1999 which subsequently resulted in the deaths of unarmed civilians (Pegg 1999, p. 478). When asked at a shareholders' meeting in May 1999 whether the company would officially demand that the Nigerian military not shoot protestors at Chevron facilities, Chairman and Chief Executive Officer Ken Derr's one word response was 'No' (Manby 1999, p. 298). This same CEO either became a late convert to CSR or plumbed new depths of cynicism six months later when trumpeting Chevron's commitment to the Global Sullivan Principles in November 1999.[11]

On a broader level, the proliferation of voluntary codes of conduct or standard-setting agreements has developed in a process somewhat analogous to what Dorothy Jones (1992) has termed 'the declaratory tradition in international law'. Jones here is referring to the fact that in treaty after treaty, states have, when it comes to human rights, voluntarily 'set down principles to guide their own behavior and to provide standards by which that behavior can be judged' (1992, p. 42). The enforcement mechanisms behind this declaratory tradition have been weak, a fact that the continued persistence of what Ken Booth (1995) has termed 'human wrongs' readily attests to. Like the Global Compact and the Global Sullivan Principles, the principles of this declaratory tradition of international law 'enjoin or call for certain kinds of state behavior but the appeal is almost always to conscience, not to courts' (Jones 1992, p. 58).

The question then becomes, what value do these voluntary initiatives have? Like the declaratory tradition in international law before it, what might be termed the 'corporate declaratory tradition' arguably serves at least two beneficial purposes. First, it provides standards by which corporations can be judged. Importantly, these are not standards imposed upon TNCs by outsiders. Rather, they are standards voluntarily accepted by the firms themselves. Jones's evaluation of the declaratory tradition in international law applies equally to this more recent corporate declaratory tradition: 'through these various declarations, they have sketched a picture of the way that they think the *world* ought to be and, in so doing, have opened themselves to the possibility that they will be taken seriously enough that there will be attempts to hold them to their word' (Jones 1992, pp. 43–4). However vague they are, the fact that companies with known human rights problems in the past, such as Chevron, Shell and Unocal, have signed up to the Global Sullivan Principles at least holds out the hope that they can be held accountable to these standards in the future. This creates the possibility that transnational advocacy networks can 'try to make such statements into opportunities for accountability politics' (Keck and Sikkink 1998, p. 24).[12] Beyond just establishing standards by which TNCs may be judged, Alex Wawryk (Chapter 3 of this book) argues that, in countries where law enforcement mechanisms are weak, self-regulation by TNCs under voluntary codes of conduct may actually be more effective than national or international codes forced on TNCs against their will.

Second, like the declaratory tradition in international law before it, the corporate declaratory tradition is likely to evolve and develop in the coming years. In terms of its historical development, we are presently at a time more or less equivalent to 1950 for the declaratory tradition in international law. At this point, the UN Charter and the UDHR had been adopted. The two International Covenants on Civil and Political Rights and on Economic, Social and Cultural Rights had not yet been promulgated, nor had most of the regional human rights treaties. The Helsinki Final Act was 25 years away and the subsequent development of an increasingly elaborate European regional human rights regime was even further off. If this argument is correct, one might view the present corporate declaratory tradition – with all its flaws in terms of vagueness, abstraction, rhetorical platitudes and a distinct lack of effective enforcement mechanisms – as simply the first step in a long process of necessary historical development. In that sense, these efforts should be nurtured and encouraged whatever their present limitations.[13]

Conclusion

This chapter has introduced some of the issues and debates surrounding TNCs and human rights. By providing a historical background to the concept of corporate social responsibility, it has demonstrated both historical continuities and contemporary novelties surrounding this topic. While a variety of factors have increased the profile of CSR in recent years, its continued hold on the corporate imagination is far from assured. Ultimately, the sustainability of the CSR concept rests on its impact on profits. As Debora Spar (1998, p. 8) argues, in the current climate, 'the advantages of lower-cost labor or lower-cost inputs from more abusive suppliers must be weighed against the crush of negative publicity, the cost of public relations, and the possibility of consumer protests'. It is by no means certain, however, that this calculus will always or even frequently lead corporations to follow the most socially responsible path. Corporations may consciously trade off some bad publicity for the benefits of doing business as usual or they may spend millions changing their public relations image without addressing the underlying problems that tarnished that image in the first place. Even if companies sincerely embrace CSR, changing corporate culture may be a slow process with long lag times between rhetorical acceptance in the board room and tangible results on the ground.

In terms of the types of human rights issues that corporations should be held accountable for, our argument has been that this list should be drawn narrowly. Wholesale condemnations of business involvement in repressive regimes which do not discriminate between degrees or types of complicity in human rights abuses are unlikely to win public support or influence corporate decision-makers. In most cases, human rights issues will remain overwhelmingly the concern of sovereign states, not TNCs. The key question to address in determining whether or not TNCs are actively involved or complicit in human rights violations is their proximity to the issue. When they employ child laborers, sexually harass or physically abuse their workers, import weapons for state security services, transport troops, request military assistance and encourage violence against labor organizers, corporations should be held responsible for those actions regardless of whether they were perpetrated by legally-distinct subsidiaries or 'arm's-length' sub-contractors. Trying to hold them responsible for the human rights situation in a country where their investments provide some marginal benefit to the regime in power is unlikely to succeed and risks distracting attention from more serious cases.

Corporations can be held responsible for human rights by legal regulation and by their voluntary adherence to certain standards of conduct. Both of these methods have their own set of problems and neither alone can provide all the answers. Arguably, there is much scope for greater home-country extraterritorial governance over the actions of their national corporations abroad. Practically, however, this is unlikely to go far. The slow, reactive and minimalist characteristics of most legal regulations mean that there will always be a need for voluntary CSR above and beyond what is expressly required by law. The proven inability of many corporations to adhere to their own codes of conducts and the vague, unenforceable and poorly-defined nature of most collective efforts, such as the Global Compact, illustrate the limitations to a purely voluntary approach. With luck, however, these are early days in the development of the corporate declaratory tradition and some of these problems will be addressed in the coming years.

The remainder of this volume is comprised of eight additional chapters which approach the issue of TNCs and human rights from different conceptual and empirical angles. Chapters 2–4 by Bill Meyer, Alex Wawryk and Mort Winston maintain this chapter's focus on broader theoretical, conceptual and methodological issues. Building upon his own pioneering large-scale quantitative work on the relationship between TNCs and human rights (Meyer 1996) and the responses to it (Smith et al. 1999; Meyer 1999), Bill Meyer begins his chapter by reviewing the academic literature on this subject at both the cross-national and case-study levels. Meyer finds that the existing academic work has produced contradictory or inconclusive findings at both the aggregate and the case-study levels of analysis. Beyond reviewing this literature and offering suggestions for further research, Meyer also evaluates the prospects for constructing a global regime to govern TNCs and human rights. He argues that a focus on the WTO offers the best model for building such a regime.

An international lawyer, Alex Wawryk offers a comparative and comprehensive assessment of how TNCs can be regulated through either legal or voluntary codes of conduct. She specifically investigates the relative merits of four types of codes: public codes of conduct contained in international legal instruments; national codes of conduct promoted by industry associations; private corporate codes of conduct; and codes drafted by NGOs for voluntary corporate adoption.

A philosopher, Mort Winston addresses the ethical and moral dimensions of corporate responsibility for human rights violations in zones of conflict. Corporations with legitimate business interests in exploiting natural resources may find themselves in situations where the revenues derived from those resources support human rights-violating governments or rebel movements. Corporate facilities and equipment have also been used in such situations to commit human rights violations. Winston critically assesses several specific proposals to develop codes of conduct for businesses operating in conflict zones and outlines potential positive roles that corporations can play here.

Chapters 5–9 shift our focus of attention from broader issues to specific case studies where TNCs have positively or negatively affected the human rights of their host communities. George Frynas opens this section with an investigation into one of the most highly publicized cases of corporate involvement in human rights abuses in recent years – the oil industry in Nigeria. Arguably, the hangings of writer Ken Saro-Wiwa and eight other Ogoni leaders in 1995 provided the single defining event that brought this issue to the world's attention. Frynas provides the background to the conflicts surrounding Nigerian oil operations and documents the oil industry's significant adverse effects on human rights in Nigeria.

Stuart Kirsch (Chapter 6) examines the case of the Ok Tedi mine in Papua New Guinea. An anthropologist who has been doing extensive field research on this case for more than a dozen years now, Kirsch focuses his attention on the emerging concept of environmental human rights. In spite of tremendous efforts by the local host communities affected by the mine and their international supporters, the Ok Tedi mine has been a massive environmental disaster. Kirsch concludes his chapter with a series of specific policy recommendations designed to prevent such disasters from occurring again.

Ronie Garcia-Johnson (Chapter 7) examines the rapidly proliferating array of certification schemes designed to promote better working conditions and ensure respect for human rights in the coffee industry. Certification schemes typically have two main components: a set of rules, principles or guidelines and some sort of reporting or monitoring mechanism to ensure that these guidelines actually are followed (Gereffi et al. 2001, p. 57). Within this basic framework, however, an incredible diversity of schemes exists. Garcia-Johnson focuses on the various certification efforts in the coffee industry and critically evaluates their successes, failures and inherent limitations.

In Chapter 8 George Frynas shifts our attention to the labor-intensive garment industry in South and South-East Asia. Methodologically, Frynas's goal here is to investigate the impact of garment industry TNCs on human rights by focusing specifically on labor rights. Examining UN human rights standards and ILO norms, Frynas operationalizes this concept by deriving a list of ten specific labor rights and prohibitions including such things as the right to a safe and healthy working environment, the prohibition against forced or compulsory labor and the right to form and join trade unions. His analysis is based on reports on the garment industry in Asia collated by the Clean Clothes Campaign and the Amsterdam-based Center for Research on Multinational Corporations.

Our volume concludes with Heike Fabig and Richard Boele examining a hopeful model of indigenous community/TNC partnership in the British Columbia forest industry. Logging companies and indigenous peoples have long suffered from mutual suspicion, misunderstandings and conflicts. Fabig and Boele's chapter highlights a novel way out of this seemingly intractable dilemma by focusing on a joint venture agreement between local indigenous communities and TNCs. It concludes by assessing the extent to which this specific example might offer a possible model for transforming indigenous community–corporate relations in other settings.

In both practical and academic terms, the issues surrounding TNCs and human rights are fast proving themselves to be a growth market for the twenty-first century. The different chapters in this volume approach this fascinating topic from a variety of conceptual, methodological and empirical viewpoints. Collectively, they serve to highlight both some of the problems and the promise of greater business involvement in and impact upon human rights.

Notes

1. I would like to thank George Frynas, Becky Johnson, Stuart Kirsch and two anonymous referees for their helpful comments on earlier versions of this chapter. Didem Ekinci and Gizem Sucuoğlu also provided valuable research assistance.
2. 'Doing Well by Doing Good', *The Economist*, 22 April 2000.
3. 'Doing Well by Doing Good', *The Economist*, 22 April 2000.
4. The average annual total return for the Domini Social Equity Fund as of 31 January 2002 was −16.80 per cent for one year, 8.79 per cent for five years, 12.48 per cent for ten years and 12.39 per cent since inception (3 June 1991). The comparable figures for the S&P 500 over the same period were, respectively, −16.15 per cent, 9.03 per cent, 12.98 per cent and 12.82 per cent. Domini Social Equity Fund, semi-annual report, 31 January 2002, available at http://www.domini.com.
5. Project Underground, 'Corporate Convenience and War on Terrorism Mute Voices of Human Rights', *Drillbits and Tailings*, 7(7), 5 September 2002.
6. UN document No. CCPR/C/60/D/549/1993.
7. Available at http://www.unglobalcompact.org.
8. Available at http://www.globalsullivanprinciples.org.
9. Available at http://www.cepaa.org/sa8000_review.htm.
10. Available at http://www.state.gov/g/drl/rls/2931.htm.
11. See http://www.chevron.com/newsvs/pressrel/1999/1999-11-03.html for more on this.
12. For one good example of accountability politics in this regard see Global Witness 1998.
13. See Henderson (2001) for a contrasting argument that (1) these efforts are not positive, (2) they are not in their infancy, and (3) they should not be encouraged.

References

Addo, Michael K. 1999. 'Human Rights and Transnational Corporations – an Introduction', in Michael K. Addo, ed., *Human Rights Standards and the Responsibility of Transnational Corporations*, pp. 3–37. The Hague: Kluwer Law International.

Alden, Edward. 2002. 'US Tries to Halt Rights Lawsuit', *Financial Times*, 6 August 2002.

Booth, Ken. 1995. 'Human Wrongs and International Relations', *International Affairs* 71(1): 103–26.

Booth, Ken. 1997. 'Security and Self: Reflections of a Fallen Realist', in Keith Krause and Michael C. Williams, eds, *Critical Security Studies: Concepts and Cases*, pp. 83–120. Minneapolis: University of Minnesota Press.

Brown, Chris. 1999. 'Universal Human Rights: a Critique', in Tim Dunne and Nicholas J. Wheeler, eds, *Human Rights in Global Politics*, pp. 103–27. Cambridge: Cambridge University Press.

Carr, Edward. 1999. 'Earthly Rewards', in *The World in 2000*, p. 115. London: The Economist.

Ceppi, Jean-Phillippe. 2000. 'Conducting Business in War-Prone Areas', in Gilles Carbonnier and Sarah Fleming, eds, *War, Money and Survival*, pp. 40–3. Geneva: International Committee of the Red Cross.

Ciulla, Joanne B. 1991. 'Why Is Business Talking about Ethics?: Reflections on Foreign Conversations', *California Management Review* 34(1): 67–86.

Cox, Robert W. 1986. 'Social Forces, States and World Orders: Beyond International Relations Theory', in Robert O. Keohane, ed., *Neorealism and Its Critics*, pp. 204–54. New York: Columbia University Press.

Donaldson, Thomas. 1989. *The Ethics of International Business*. Oxford: Oxford University Press.

Donaldson, Thomas. 1996. 'Values in Tension: Ethics Away from Home', *Harvard Business Review* 74(5): 48–57.

Donaldson, Thomas and Thomas W. Dunfee. 1999. *Ties That Bind: a Social Contracts Approach to Business Ethics*. Boston: Harvard Business School Press.

Donnelly, Jack. 1992. 'Twentieth-Century Realism', in Terry Nardin and David R. Mapel, eds, *Traditions of International Ethics*, pp. 85–111. Cambridge: Cambridge University Press.

Donnelly, Jack. 1999. 'The Social Construction of International Human Rights', in Tim Dunne and Nicholas J. Wheeler, eds, *Human Rights in Global Politics*, pp. 71–102. Cambridge: Cambridge University Press.

Dunne, Tim and Nicholas J. Wheeler. 1999. 'Introduction: Human Rights and the Fifty Years' Crisis', in Tim Dunne and Nicholas J. Wheeler, eds, *Human Rights in Global Politics*, pp. 1–28. Cambridge: Cambridge University Press.

Elkington, John. 1997. *Cannibals With Forks: the Triple Bottom Line of 21st Century Business*. Oxford: Capstone Publishing.

Fabig, Heike, and Richard Boele. 1999. 'The Changing Nature of NGO Activity in a Globalising World: Pushing the Corporate Responsibility Agenda', *IDS Bulletin* 30(3): 58–67.

Friedman, Milton. 1962. *Capitalism and Freedom*. Chicago: University of Chicago Press.

Frynas, Jedrzej George. 1998. 'Political Instability and Business: Focus on Shell in Nigeria', *Third World Quarterly* 19(3): 457–87.

Gagnon, Georgette and John Ryle. 2001. 'Report of an Investigation into Oil Development, Conflict and Displacement in Western Upper Nile, Sudan'. Ottawa: Canadian Auto Workers Union, Steelworkers Humanity Fund, The Simons Foundation, United Church of Canada, Division of World Outreach and World Vision Canada.

Gellner, Ernest. 1994. *Conditions of Liberty: Civil Society and Its Rivals*. London: Hamish Hamilton.

Gereffi, Gary, Ronie Garcia-Johnson and Erika Sasser. 2001. 'The NGO–Industrial Complex', *Foreign Policy* (July/August): 56–65.

Girion, Lisa. 2002. 'US Ruling Says Firms Liable for Abuse Abroad', *Los Angeles Times*, 19 September 2002.

Global Witness. 1998. 'A Rough Trade: the Role of Companies and Governments in the Angolan Conflict', London: Global Witness.

Graham, Edward M. 1996. *Global Corporations and National Governments*. Washington, DC: Institute for International Economics.

Henderson, David. 2001. *Misguided Virtue: False Notions of Corporate Social Responsibility*. London: Institute of Economic Affairs.

Hoppin, Jason. 2000. 'Chevron's Nigerian Quagmire: Oil Company Battles Rare Suit in S.F. Over Alleged Human Rights Abuses Abroad', *The Recorder*, 10 April 2000.

ICHRP (International Council on Human Rights Policy). 2002. 'Beyond Voluntarism: Human Rights and the Developing International Legal Obligations of Companies – Summary', Versoix, Switzerland: International Council on Human Rights Policy.

Jones, Dorothy V. 1992. 'The Declaratory Tradition in Modern International Law', in Terry Nardin and David R. Mapel, eds, *Traditions of International Ethics*, pp. 42–61. Cambridge: Cambridge University Press.

Jungk, Margaret. 1999. 'A Practical Guide to Addressing Human Rights Concerns for Companies Operating Abroad', in Michael K. Addo, ed., *Human Rights Standards and the Responsibility of Transnational Corporations*, pp. 171–86. The Hague: Kluwer Law International.

Keck, Margaret E. and Kathryn Sikkink. 1998. *Activists Beyond Borders: Advocacy Networks in International Politics*. Ithaca: Cornell University Press.

Larsen, Jensine. 1998. 'Crude Investment: the Case of the Yadana Pipeline in Burma', *Bulletin of Concerned Asian Scholars* 30(3): 3–13.

Le Billon, Phillipe. 2001. 'Angola's Political Economy of War: the Role of Oil and Diamonds, 1975–2000', *African Affairs* 100(398): 55–80.

Loomis, Worth. 1999. 'The Responsibility of Parent Corporations for the Human Rights Violations of Their Subsidiaries', in Michael K. Addo, ed., *Human Rights Standards and the Responsibility of Transnational Corporations*, pp. 145–59. The Hague: Kluwer Law International.

Manby, Bronwen. 1999. 'The Role and Responsibility of Oil Multinationals in Nigeria', *Journal of International Affairs* 53(1): 281–301.

Maresca, John J. 2000. 'A New Concept of Business', *The Washington Quarterly* 23(2): 155–63.

Mazur, Jay. 2000. 'Labor's New Internationalism', *Foreign Affairs* 79(1): 79–93.

Mead, Walter Russell. 2001. *Special Providence: American Foreign Policy and How It Changed the World*. New York: Alfred A. Knopf.

Meeran, Richard. 1999. 'The Unveiling of Transnational Corporations: a Direct Approach', in Michael K. Addo, ed., *Human Rights Standards and the Responsibility of Transnational Corporations*, pp. 161–70. The Hague: Kluwer Law International.

Meyer, William H. 1996. 'Human Rights and MNCs: Theory Versus Quantitative Analysis', *Human Rights Quarterly* 18(2): 368–97.

Meyer, William H. 1999. 'Confirming, Infirming, and "Falsifying" Theories of Human Rights: Reflections on Smith, Bolyard, and Ippolito through the Lens of Lakatos', *Human Rights Quarterly* 21(1): 220–8.

Mitchell, Lawrence E. 2001. *Corporate Irresponsibility: America's Newest Export*. New Haven: Yale University Press.

Mokhiber, Russell and Robert Weissman. 2002. 'No Kidding: Anti-Bribery Law Takes a Hit', Focus on the Corporation electronic column, available at http://lists.essential.org/pipermail/corp-focus/2002/000114.html.

Muchlinski, Peter T. 2001. 'Human Rights and Multinationals: Is There a Problem?', *International Affairs* 77(1): 31–47.

Mutua, Makau. 2002. *Human Rights: a Political and Cultural Critique*. Philadelphia: University of Pennsylvania Press.

Nattrass, Nicoli. 1999. 'The Truth and Reconciliation Commission on Business and Apartheid: a Critical Evaluation', *African Affairs* 98(392): 373–91.

Nicholson, Michael. 2000. 'What's the Use of IR?', *Review of International Studies* 26(2): 183–98.

O'Kane, Maggie. 2000. 'UK Firm Linked to Burma Slavery', *Guardian*, 27 July 2000.

Ottaway, Marina. 2001. 'Reluctant Missionaries', *Foreign Policy* (July/August): 44–54.

Parkinson, John. 1999. 'The Socially Responsible Company', in Michael K. Addo, ed., *Human Rights Standards and the Responsibility of Transnational Corporations*, pp. 49–62. The Hague: Kluwer Law International.

Pegg, Scott. 1999. 'The Cost of Doing Business: Transnational Corporations and Violence in Nigeria', *Security Dialogue* 30(4): 473–84.

Rodman, Kenneth A. 2001. *Sanctions Beyond Borders: Multinational Corporations and U.S. Economic Statecraft*. Lanham, Maryland: Rowman and Littlefield.

Shell International Ltd. 1998. *Profits and Principles – Does There Have To Be a Choice?* London: Shell International Ltd.

Smith, Jackie, Melissa Bolyard and Anna Ippolito. 1999. 'Human Rights and the Global Economy: a Response to Meyer', *Human Rights Quarterly* 21(1): 207–19.

Spar, Debora L. 1998. 'The Spotlight and the Bottom Line: How Multinationals Export Human Rights', *Foreign Affairs* 77(2): 7–12.

Woodroffe, Jessica. 1999. 'Regulating Multinational Corporations in a World of Nation States', in Michael K. Addo, ed., *Human Rights Standards and the Responsibility of Transnational Corporations*, pp. 131–42. The Hague: Kluwer Law International.

2
Activism and Research on TNCs and Human Rights: Building a New International Normative Regime
William H. Meyer

Introduction

The impact of transnational corporations (TNCs) on human rights was once a largely neglected subject. Early attention to human rights after the Second World War was focused almost exclusively on the actions of nation states. That was perhaps as it should be, given the fact that governments are both the worst violators of human rights, and the institutions that are charged by international law with the primary responsibilities for protecting them. More recently, human rights violations by TNCs have received increased attention. There has been a spate of new studies that seek to research the connections between transnationals and human rights. New political activism has also sought to identify and reduce violations of human rights by TNC production facilities (for example, sweatshops).

This chapter reviews recent developments in the areas of research and activism pertaining to TNCs and human rights. My purpose is to recap these trends with an eye toward the next steps needed to establish a new international regime that could effectively improve respect for, and observance of, human rights by TNCs. Suggestions for political action and research on transnationals will follow my review of what has been done to date.

Research

Research on the impact of TNCs on human rights presents us with a classic 'levels of analysis' problem. Universal human rights, like other topics (war, trade and so on) in international relations (IR), can and should be studied at several different analytical levels. The level at which one focuses any particular study depends largely on the types of questions one most wants to answer. Do we want to uncover specific violations of rights that have been committed by particular TNCs? Are we interested in the overall global trend that characterizes the impact of TNCs on rights across nations? Do we want to understand how the TNC-to-human-rights connection fits into larger theories of IR (for example, theories of international political economy or globalization)? These are all important questions, but each requires its own particular methodology in order to provide sufficient answers and each requires research at different levels (or in different dimensions) of analysis. The research to date has tried, at different times, to address all of these questions. My review of this literature divides these works into cross-national studies versus case studies.

My own research into TNCs and human rights began at the cross-national level (Meyer 1996). As a first step, I used aggregate data on corporate investment and various measures of human rights to establish the global trends between TNCs on the one hand, and levels of human rights in Third World states on the other. My conclusion was that, on balance, the overall impact of TNCs on rights was positive. These results were first reported in *Human Rights Quarterly* (*HRQ*) in 1996, and subsequently appeared in chapter 3 of my book (Meyer 1998). Based on the best available data from the US Commerce Department, the net impact of TNCs on human rights appeared to be beneficial. In other words, I found consistent, positive correlations between increased TNC investment and better levels of human rights.

Smith et al. (1999) have done an excellent follow-up to my cross-national study. Smith and her team read my 1996 *HRQ* article with skepticism and decided to replicate my work using part of my data set along with other data that I had not employed. Using World Bank data on investment, and comparing that information to the same measures of rights that I had used, Smith's group was able to demonstrate a consistent and negative correlation between TNCs and human rights (Smith et al. 1999). Their publication in *HRQ* gave me a chance to respond. I was forced to give some thought to the deeper question of what it means to 'test' IR theories (for example, TNCs are bad vs. TNCs are good) by comparing the predictions of each theory to empirical, statistical analyses.

I was not willing to 'recant' my own study. In my response to Smith et al. I stand by the conclusions of my cross-national research. However,

I have no reason to challenge the validity or reliability of Smith's study either. Rather, my most recent thoughts in this regard led me to make some rudimentary observations about theory-testing and theory-building in IR (Meyer 1999). I will not recreate that argument here. Suffice it to say that, in my opinion, both the view that TNCs are beneficial, and the view that TNCs endanger basic rights, are weakened by empirical studies that have shot holes in each theory. My research calls into question the anti-TNC view. Smith's results tend to undermine the validity of the pro-TNC view.

Empirical results at the case-study level are equally mixed. The cases I analyzed indicate patterns of abuse in India and northern Mexico. One of my case studies was the 1984 Union Carbide disaster in Bhopal (India), which had inspired me to research TNCs in the first place. Union Carbide was responsible for over 7,000 deaths and 65,000 injuries in India. To this day, people continue to suffer from the long-term effects of the 1984 disaster. In the *maquiladora* zone of northern Mexico, environmental destruction and union-busting have been standard operating procedures for many TNCs (Meyer 1998, chapter 5). Similarly, George Frynas (Chapter 5 of this book) documents complicity in human rights abuses by global energy companies in Nigeria. TNCs have contributed to severe environmental and social damage in the Niger Delta, which – combined with TNC disregard and refusals to pay for the cleanup – has led to widespread popular protests. In response to protests, increasing numbers of government soldiers have been deployed to protect oil production. Frynas (Chapter 5 of this book) suggests that TNCs share responsibility for the human rights atrocities committed by the Nigerian army. Shell has not only admitted to paying some of the security forces that committed human rights violations, but oil companies have also been guilty of complicity by providing equipment and logistical support to the Nigerian military for attacking anti-oil protesters (see also Manby 1999).

In contrast to the horror stories coming out of India and Nigeria, case studies by Spar (1998), Knight (1995) and Imle (1999) point to positive steps taken by some of the highest profile TNCs. Gap, Reebok and Starbucks have taken limited steps to reduce child labor and sweatshop working conditions (Spar 1998, pp. 9–11). Some US TNCs have recently exported cleaner, greener technology to their plants in Mexico (Knight 1995, pp. 32–3). In marked contrast to natural resources extraction in Nigeria, Heike Fabig and Richard Boele (Chapter 9 of this book) point to positive human rights effects of natural resources extraction by a TNC in the Canadian context. While not as common perhaps as the reports of abuse, these examples show that at least some of the TNCs in the

Third World and elsewhere are seriously attempting to improve working and environmental conditions.

In sum, cross-national research and case studies have produced evidence that can be invoked (in part) by both TNC defenders and TNC detractors. This means that more investigation is needed in order better to specify the conditions under which TNCs are most likely to violate rights, and the conditions under which TNCs are more likely to improve rights. While each side of this debate has taken some knocks, neither the pro-TNC view nor the anti-TNC view has been 'falsified' as of yet (Meyer 1999). My suggestions for the best new directions for future research will follow a brief discussion of recent political activism in the area of TNCs and human rights.

The politics of compliance monitoring and full disclosure

Activists and NGOs have worked hard in recent years to bring human rights violations by TNCs to our attention. These same actors have also taken the lead in developing new strategies for improving rights compliance by transnationals. While a comprehensive review of these efforts is beyond the scope of this chapter, I want to focus on two strategies in particular. Compliance monitoring must become the indispensable link between setting standards for TNCs and uncovering the daily violations of these same standards. A second approach, the full disclosure campaign, has scored at least one recent success. I suggest here that compliance monitoring and full disclosure are necessary (but not sufficient) elements of the emerging international regime for TNCs and rights.

Compliance monitoring can trace its origins to the media scandals that brought attention to sweatshops in 1996. Before the 1990s, there was little talk about regularized monitoring of TNC production facilities as a way to protect human rights. The recent steps toward creating an inspection regime for transnationals and rights grew out of the Apparel Industry Partnership (AIP). The AIP was created in 1996 by a coalition of private corporations, human rights NGOs, labor groups, and the Clinton administration.

President Clinton first developed policies on rights and TNCs due to his interests in trade with China. Renewing China's most-favored nation (MFN) trading status in 1994 brought much criticism of Clinton from human rights groups. In response, the Clinton administration released their 'Model Business Principles' in 1995. The Model Business Principles were a suggested (voluntary) code of conduct for US TNCs to follow (in China and other parts of the Third World). When celebrities like

Kathy Lee Gifford and Michael Jordan came under criticism in 1996 for sweatshops that produced goods bearing their names, Ms Gifford and President Clinton formed an alliance to signal their good intentions. The AIP was the result of Clinton and Kathy Lee Gifford's much publicized efforts.

The AIP released an expanded code of conduct and promised to find ways to enforce the code (see Meyer 1998, chapter 6 for more on this). The primary 'enforcement' mechanism became compliance monitoring. The AIP discussed 'external' and 'independent' monitoring by outside human rights organizations (independent of the manufacturers). However, to date, almost all monitoring of TNC production facilities in the Third World has been done by 'monitors' who work for the corporations. This raises questions about a conflict of interests, and brings into question the legitimacy of the monitors' work (see below). The AIP code and self-monitoring by TNCs could be little more than a good public relations ploy by the businesses. They may give us no more than 'kinder, gentler sweatshops'.

At roughly the same time as the formation of the AIP, many NGOs developed their own model codes of conduct. One of the best came from the Coalition for Justice in the *Maquiladoras* (CJM), a Texas-based non-profit group that focuses on TNCs in northern Mexico. CJM's code, like many others, has provisions for worker health, safety, and fair employment practices. Unlike most others, the CJM code sets additional requirements for TNCs to protect the environment. The CJM also sets standards for community impact by transnationals in its code. In all respects, the CJM code creates more detailed (and tougher) standards for TNCs than does the AIP code (Meyer 1998, chapter 6). Amnesty International (AI) also published a useful (and expanded) code of conduct for TNCs in 1996.

Under pressure from non-governmental organizations and public opinion, TNCs have come to institute their own codes of conduct. Even the notorious Nike corporation has its own code (as do many TNCs) that dates back to 1992. But are these codes ever enforced? In the case of Nike's own code, the answer is clearly no. Nike's subcontractors in China, Indonesia and Vietnam have consistently violated its own code of conduct, despite Nike founder Philip Knight's claims to the contrary (Meyer 1998, chapter 6).

Two years of negotiations within the AIP created some limited progress on compliance monitoring. In 1998, the AIP announced the charter for a new organization: the Fair Labor Association (FLA). At the same time, the AIP released a new anti-sweatshop code. The FLA, like the AIP, requires factory monitoring by its members.[1] The FLA goes further, however, and requires that 'a significant number' of factories submit to *external* monitoring (National Consumers League 1998). The AIP suggested, but never required, external monitoring. The FLA itself is a new association that is jointly controlled by companies, labor unions, and human rights groups. The association will select the groups to do the external monitoring, and make summaries of the monitors' audits available to the public.

The key to all of this, obviously, is effective independent and external monitoring. Activists, particularly college students, have kept the heat on the AIP and the FLA. Shortly after the FLA charter was announced, student activists met in Washington DC to protest the limited and insufficient nature of the FLA. Groups like the United Students Against Sweatshops (USAS) charge that the FLA is just a 'smokescreen' because it does not go far enough in regard to full disclosure of information relating to factory inspections (Wickham 1999). The FLA charter requires only the publication of inspection summaries. USAS wants much more (see below).

One of the speakers at the DC rally against the FLA was Chie Abad, a former worker at one of Gap's sweatshops in Saipan. Abad said she was fired from this Gap subcontractor because of her efforts to organize a union. Saipan is the largest island of the Northern Marianas chain. These Pacific islands are under US sovereignty as part of a UN trust territory. Abad spoke at the 1999 DC rally, and then made a follow-up presentation at the University of Delaware. She worked for four years in Saipan for the Sako corporation, a Korean-owned facility that produces clothing for Gap, working her way up to assistant supervisor at the plant before being fired in October of 1998. Abad now travels around the country speaking out against sweatshops. Global Exchange, a San Francisco-based non-profit organization that fights against corporate abuses of workers, funds her current efforts. Global Exchange has also worked hard to document abuses of human rights by TNCs operating in the Third World.

Abad's testimony is especially telling. She provides evidence suggesting that compliance monitoring, when left to the TNCs themselves, has not worked to improve sweatshop working conditions. Abad is a Filipino. She had to pay a labor recruiter $2000 to secure her job in Saipan. Others have paid as much as $5000–10,000 for the same initial recruitment fees.[2] Most of the workers in Saipan are brought in from China, Thailand, the Philippines and Bangladesh. Like the labor force in most Third World sweatshops, 90 per cent of Sako's employees in Saipan are women. Living and working conditions in Saipan are deplorable. Workers put in 14-hour days, seven days a week. They are not paid overtime. They must live in slum-like company-owned camps that are ringed with barbed wire and patrolled by armed guards. They must pay Sako $100 for their room and $120 for their food each month, which eliminates most of their take-home pay.

Workers in Saipan sweatshops make about $3 per hour, while a living wage on the island would require over $5 per hour. Workers for Sako who became pregnant were either forced to have abortions or fired. When Abad organized a vote of Sako's workers in 1997 to form a union, the company threatened to cancel its contracts and move the plant to Russia. The subsequent vote was narrowly defeated, coming within 1 per cent of the votes needed to establish a new union. Abad was fired the following year, mainly, she believes, due to her efforts to keep the unionizing movement alive.

Sako in Saipan turns out clothing for Gap and Banana Republic. Gap is a member of the AIP. As such, Gap posted its corporate policies on fair labor conditions in the Sako plant. However, according to Abad, these posted policies have never been followed. Abad also tells of the Gap-employed factory 'monitors' who have an office only five minutes away from the Sako facility. Abad was present when these monitors inspected Sako. The monitors have seen first-hand the lack of safety equipment (no safety glasses or gloves), the blocked fire exits, and the general sweatshop working conditions that Sako employees are subjected to. However, according to Abad, none of these conditions changed after the monitors' visits.

Abad's story indicates how woefully inadequate the existing compliance monitoring system is. Even if the monitoring could be made stronger under the new FLA system (an optimistic prospect at best), much more than compliance monitoring would be required to establish an effective international regime for TNCs and human rights. In regard to Saipan, the US government has both political and moral responsibility to intervene in a more direct way to protect worker rights. As a trust territory, Saipan is under US federal jurisdiction.

The islands of the Northern Marianas were given local control over their own wages and borders more than twenty-five years ago in order to boost the local economy and to keep out immigrant labor. What resulted, however, was an open door to TNCs and a flood of foreign labor such that the unemployment rate of the indigenous labor force is now at 15 per cent (Sobek 1999). President Clinton once suggested a federal takeover of Saipan's labor controls. Dozens of bills were placed before Congress to this effect, but those efforts were thwarted in large part because TNCs operating in Saipan were consistently opposed. These businesses have relied on powerful friends on Capitol Hill to scuttle new legislation (including Dick Armey and Tom DeLay, both House Republicans from Texas).

Lawsuits are another avenue for bringing the TNCs to heel. Abad herself is party to class-action suits brought against TNCs in Saipan, alleging physical abuse, forced abortions and rat-infested quarters for workers there. Retailers and their subcontractors are being held accountable under the federal Racketeer Influenced and Corrupt Organizational Act. Two suits were filed in 1999 in Los Angeles and in Saipan. A third lawsuit has been filed by Global Exchange and the UNITE textile union in San Francisco. Among the eighteen firms named in these suits are Gap, Gymboree, Tommy Hilfiger, J. Crew, Lane Bryant, the Limited, Marshal Fields, Oshkosh, and Wal-Mart.[3] Abad noted that some of the defendants have recently settled out of court for roughly $3 million (including Gymboree and J. Crew) while court cases against the others are still pending.

In addition to compliance monitoring and class-action suits, the full disclosure movement led by USAS also holds some promise. The full disclosure movement was born at Duke University when students organized to pressure their administration to ensure that clothing licensed by Duke was not produced in sweatshops. The heart of the full disclosure approach is to require that all TNCs producing licensed collegiate wear reveal the names and locations of all of their production facilities. Full disclosure is a necessary complement to the compliance monitoring approach. How can we have full monitoring of TNC sweatshops unless independent monitoring agencies know where *all* of those facilities are located? The USAS campaign has quickly spread to over 150 campuses nationwide, and at least fifteen major schools have promised their student bodies full disclosure of vendor locations relating to the production of clothes bearing college logos (Wickham 1999).

There is resistance by TNCs to full disclosure, but also some recent willingness, by at least one high-profile sneaker manufacturer, to meet, in part, the demands for disclosure. TNC reluctance is 'justified' by the transnationals due to the highly competitive nature of this market. Most TNCs argue that they cannot risk full disclosure, because this information could then be used by their competitors to locate production facilities and steal corporate secrets. However, the public and media pressure that may force TNCs to acquiesce in the long run is also great, due to the lucrative nature of this market. Manufacturers produce over $2.5 billion worth of goods each year, bearing the names of hundreds of colleges. Desires to protect this important source of income can be used to force TNCs toward disclosure. Nike became the first when, in October 1999, the company announced the names and locations of 41 overseas factories. Nike's action puts pressure on other apparel makers to follow suit, especially because some universities have threatened to drop their licensees unless they make similar disclosures. Nike's announcement must be viewed with guarded optimism, however, because the company was willing to identify only 41 out of its total of 545 factories worldwide (Greenhouse 1999).

The limited steps taken thus far toward independent compliance monitoring and full disclosure are important victories, when viewed in historical perspective. As recently as ten years ago, even these limited steps would have been impossible to imagine, or too much to hope for. Compared to what would be needed by way of a permanent and institutionalized process for ensuring human rights compliance by TNCs, however, the progress to date is barely a beginning. In order to understand the scope of the many elements that would be required for an effective international regime governing TNCs and human rights, I want to turn now to the larger topic of international normative regimes.

A regime for TNCs and human rights: a role for the WTO?

Trying to induce TNCs to respect human rights, and trying to find a way to punish those TNCs that do not, amounts to nothing less than building a new normative regime in international politics. This is no small task, and it will necessarily take a long time to build an effective regime. Fortunately, we know how this can be done, at least in general terms, because we have seen it done before. The building of international normative regimes has received a great deal of attention from scholars of human rights. I speak, of course, of the regime that has been built, and is still being expanded, to ensure protection by governments of universal human rights. While the effectiveness of this post-war intergovernmental regime has been relatively limited, there have been undeniable successes. As Donnelly (1998, p. 144) reminds us in the context of his discussion of genocide in Bosnia, 'A link between human rights and international peace and security has always been a central part of United Nations doctrine. In the post-cold war era, it has become a part of UN practice.' While it is easy (and necessary) to criticize the UN (and other international actors) for not doing more (and for not acting more quickly) to stop genocide in Bosnia (and in Rwanda, and in Kosovo, and so on), it is important to understand that UN actions in Bosnia were significant. We should not underestimate the important strides that have been taken during the post-Second World War era to force recalcitrant governments to respect basic rights and fundamental freedoms.

As Donnelly and others have also pointed out, building international normative regimes must proceed through some basic and necessary steps. The process begins with the setting of standards, progresses to monitoring and documentation of abuses, then achieves the goal of making those abuses illegal under international law, and culminates in the creation of effective institutionalization of ways to punish offenders (Donnelly 1998, chapter 1). By briefly comparing the progression of the human rights/nation-state regime to the progress in creating a similar regime for human rights/TNCs, we can get a better understanding of how to give the latter some potent sanctions. Table 2.1 compares and contrasts the existing nation-state regime to the nascent TNC regime across four key dimensions.

Table 2.1 shows four necessary phases for building any effective international normative regime: standard setting, monitoring and documentation, law, and enforcement. While the politics of regime building

Table 2.1   Building international normative regimes

Regime	Standard setting	Monitoring and exposing abuses	Binding law	Enforcement
Human rights and nation states	UDHR (1948)	Amnesty International (AI) US Department of State Human Rights Watch UN Commission on Human Rights	International Covenant on Civil and Political Rights International Covenant on Economic, Social, and Cultural Rights Regional Conventions Specialized Conventions	Human Rights Courts Special Tribunals International Criminal Court
Human rights and TNCs	Codes of conduct (AI, AIP, CJM, etc.) ILO Declaration on Labor Rights (1998)	Global Exchange USAS	World Trade Organization (WTO) for labor rights and standards on the environment	WTO Dispute Mechanism

requires attention to all four dimensions throughout the process, it is also the case that the creation of a regime generally works from left to right through these areas as the regime becomes increasingly institutionalized. Many of us are already familiar with the process of creating the international human rights regime for governments. Post-war standard setting began with the Universal Declaration of Human Rights (1948). Monitoring and documentation of human rights abuses has a long history and is done by many actors, four of which are highlighted on Table 2.1 (Amnesty International, the US Department of State, Human Rights Watch and the UN Commission on Human Rights). Binding international law for nation states is codified in the two UN Covenants on human rights (one for civil and political rights and the other for economic, social and cultural rights), in the various regional documents (for example, the European Convention on Human Rights) and in the many specialized international conventions (for example, those concerning torture, women's rights and so on). Enforcement (notably the weakest element of the regime) is made possible via regional courts (especially the European Court of Human Rights), specialized tribunals (for example, those created for Yugoslavia and Rwanda), and, in the future, via the new International Criminal Court.

Creating an effective human rights regime for TNCs is still very much a work in progress, but the outlines of this regime are clearly visible. Standard setting has already been partially accomplished by the many corporate codes of conduct that have been promulgated in the 1990s (by NGOS, by TNCs, and by governments agencies). We can also find standards for labor rights in the longstanding work of the International Labor Organization (ILO). In 1998, the ILO issued a declaration establishing core labor standards as universal principals of human rights. Monitoring and documentation of human rights abuses by TNCs is also well underway, coming from many of the same NGOs that have developed codes of conduct (for example AI, the Coalition for Justice in the *Maquiladoras*), from Global Exchange, and, indirectly, through the full-disclosure activism.

The hardest job in creating an effective regime for TNCs remains to be done. That will be the interconnected tasks of establishing binding international laws and investing an international agency with real enforcement powers. In regard to first generation rights to security of the person (for example, freedom from physical abuse and torture), it may be best to rely on domestic jurisdiction by local courts. Physical abuse of workers and murder of labor organizers (to take two of the most egregious examples) are already illegal under the laws of all nations. Our task in that regard is to pressure local governments to enforce these laws.

Foreign aid can also be used to help developing nations increase their capacity to enforce their own laws. TNCs could then potentially be held accountable for violating security of the person. When it comes to labor standards (second generation rights) and environmental standards (third generation rights), however, international legal standards and international enforcement become top priorities. Because of the global reach of TNCs, without international law and international enforcement of labor rights and environmental standards effective protection of these areas is virtually impossible.

My suggestion for law and enforcement of labor and environmental rights is that we must move beyond institutions created expressly for human rights and into the realm of the international trading regime. I see the World Trade Organization (WTO) as the best hope in this regard. The primary advantage of working through the WTO is that it has binding authority to enforce its own standards on member governments. The WTO has the authority and ability to impose mandatory sanctions. It is perhaps the only global organization (other than the Security Council) with this power. Of course, the members of the WTO are governments, not TNCs. Hence the WTO has the power only to sanction governments, not the TNCs themselves. Therefore, even within the WTO, the impact on TNCs is only indirect. But this is an unavoidable restraint. Unless and until TNCs become direct parties to international law (that is, they have 'legal standing' before international human rights tribunals, and treaties create specific obligations for corporations), a normative regime for TNCs must 'get at' corporate violations of rights indirectly through the governments that do have power over TNCs within their borders. We also have a model to follow in this regard. That is the process under the North American Free Trade Agreement (NAFTA) to protect and enforce labor and environmental standards.

The treaties that created NAFTA include the North American Agreement on Labor Cooperation (NAALC) and the North American Agreement on Environmental Cooperation (NAAEC). The NAALC set up National Administrative Offices (NAOs) within the US, Canada and Mexico. The NAAEC created the Commission on Environmental Cooperation (CEC), headquartered in Montreal. The NAOs and the CEC exist, respectively, to investigate labor abuses and environmental destruction.

Labor unions and other NGOs can file complaints with the NAOs. The NAOs are then required to hold each government responsible for enforcing its own labor standards. Eight of the nine suits filed between 1995 and 1999 were with regard to violating the right to unionize. Petitioners are free to bring their complaints before the NAO of any of the three states. Under the terms of the NAALC, NAOs can impose sanctions for violations of labor laws, for use of child labor, for failing to meet health and safety standards, or for violating minimum wage requirements (see Meyer 1998, chapter 5 for a more detailed discussion).

Similarly, individuals and NGOs can file complaints before the CEC. The CEC is made up of cabinet-level officials from each government. The final step in resolving environmental disputes among NAFTA nations allows the CEC to levy fines against a government for failure to enforce its environmental laws (Meyer 1998, chapter 5).

The NAOs and the CEC create no labor standards or environmental regulations of their own. They enforce the pre-existing standards of the member nations. While the NAFTA process for protecting labor and environmental rights can be criticized for several weaknesses, my point here is simply that NAFTA has institutionalized an international process for enforcing second and third generation human rights (for example, labor rights, environmental rights). The process needs to be strengthened and expanded in important ways, but it also represents something to build on for those parties interested in protecting worker rights and the environment. Furthermore, proposals have already been advanced that can take this model to a global level via the WTO.

The WTO, once a relatively obscure part of international politics, became front-page news due to its 1999 meetings in Seattle. An interesting coalition of labor groups, environmental organizations, consumer advocates, and Third World lobbies banded together to expose what they see as the pernicious impacts of the WTO. Critics deride the WTO as an anti-democratic club for 'fat cats' and corporate interests that allegedly undermines public health and safety, threatens accountable policy-making, and endangers the economic interests of developing nations.[4] Rather than entering into the merits of these charges, I want to discuss the WTO's potential for having a positive impact on labor and environmental rights.

Even before protesters took to the streets in Seattle, the US and EU positions on necessary reforms in the WTO spoke to some of their concerns. President Clinton claimed that he wanted to 'put a human face' on the global economy. He proposed a new round of global trade talks (the Millennium Round). The ministerial meeting in Seattle was the first step in that process. As part of the new round, the US proposed creation of a working group on trade and labor standards. Working groups lay the groundwork and draft resolutions for the plenary sessions of the WTO to consider. Clinton also proposed giving the ILO observer status at the WTO, and increasing coordination between WTO and ILO activities.

Similar reforms would be made to bring environmental concerns into the ambit of WTO authority. The US is already conducting a review of the environmental consequences of the new round. The WTO has an Environment and Trade Committee that could function much like the new working group on labor, drafting new regulations that would enforce and improve existing environmental protections within member governments (similar to NAFTA's CEC). The US is pushing for elimination of all tariffs on environmental technologies (for example, greener industrial equipment) as a way to facilitate trade in these goods, especially exports to the developing world. The US also demands that member governments be given the right to retain environmental standards that are higher than those required by existing international agreements.

US policy also favors increased 'transparency' within the WTO. As stated by Clinton's Trade Representative, Charlene Barshefsky, transparency would include rapid release of documents, enhancing the input of NGOs, allowing NGOs and other interested parties to file *amicus curiae* briefs at WTO dispute panels and opening dispute settlement proceedings to public observers (Barshefsky 1999). Dispute panels are the heart of the WTO sanctioning process. They hand down authoritative decisions regarding trade disputes between WTO members. WTO dispute panels have the power to impose mandatory economic sanctions on non-compliant members. Dispute panels have already heard over 50 cases since the establishment of the WTO in 1995.

These dispute panels are the targets of the WTO's critics' primary concerns. In part as a response to the unrest in Seattle, Clinton restated and emphasized his administration's prior offer to open up the dispute panels to NGO participation. Labor and environmental groups would be given a seat at the hearings and allowed to voice their concerns. Only WTO member governments, however, would have a vote in the final decisions on whether or not to impose sanctions.

Many groups came to Seattle to pressure the WTO to open its proceedings to non-governmental labor, environmental and Third World interests. Global Exchange, Global Trade Watch and Third World Network were among the most outspoken. Global Exchange criticized the WTO's preference for making decisions behind closed doors. Global Trade Watch feared that critics of the WTO will be either co-opted, or excluded from the decision-making process. Third World Network cautioned that more liberalization of trade by the WTO would lead to political instability and economic hardships in developing nations. While these criticisms are important, and especially relevant to the WTO's track record to date, there is also much more common ground between the protestors and the positions of the OECD governments than either side seems to realize. Looking ahead to the needed reforms within the WTO, both the short term and the long term can bring important changes that would improve human rights in many areas.

Over the short term, the WTO should move quickly to set up a working group on labor rights, to bring NGOs and other interested groups to the negotiating table, and to increase transparency by opening all WTO hearings and documents to the public. All of these things could be done almost immediately. Over the mid-term (3–5 years), and within the context of the trade round launched in November 2001 in Doha, Qatar, the WTO must draft an agreement on global labor standards (perhaps using the ILO 1998 declaration as a guide). At the same time, a similar agreement needs to be established for environmental standards. Over the long term, the WTO needs to establish a grievance process for violations of labor rights and environmental destruction similar to the NAFTA mechanisms in these areas. These new WTO dispute panels for labor and the environment (like NAFTA's NAOs and CEC) must also be open to individual and NGO petitions.

None of these reforms will come easily. It is important to note that the strongest political opposition to new WTO authority over labor and environmental standards comes from Third World governments. In many cases, these are the same Third World countries in which most TNCs prefer to set up their sweatshops. They are also the same countries favored by TNCs because of their lax (or non-existent) enforcement of environmental protections. It is also worth restating that nothing proposed here would bring legal or economic sanctions directly against the TNCs themselves. The economic penalties would have to be imposed on national governments, with the hope that this would induce those governments to tighten their reins on transnational corporations. It is also important to stress the fact that all of these reforms are necessary but not sufficient conditions for creating an effective new regime to govern TNCs and human rights.

Clinton's foreign policy took the position that, in the future, all new trade agreements must contain enforceable standards for labor rights and environmental protection. The US was generally supported in this position by EU and the other NAFTA countries. By moving human rights activism and human rights research into these relatively new areas, we can get on the right side of globalization. We can put the new institutions of globalization (such as the WTO) to work to protect the rights of workers, while improving the conditions of their environment and their communities. As is often heard in the battle cries of the new activism on rights and the WTO: 'No globalization without representation.' One might equally say: 'No globalization without human rights.'

More recently, President George W. Bush has expressed reservations regarding the Clinton preference for mixing labor and environmental issues into free trade pacts. Clinton added the side agreements on labor rights and environmental protection to the NAFTA free trade agreement. The Clinton administration also negotiated a subsequent bilateral trade agreement with Jordan that was the first pact to include labor and environmental provisions within the main text. The US Trade Representative (USTR) in the Bush administration, Robert Zoellick, has criticized the Clinton approach of using trade sanctions to enforce international labor and environmental standards. President Bush and USTR Zoellick both support continuation of NAFTA and expansion of the Free Trade Area for the Americas (FTAA), as did Clinton. However, both Bush and Zoellick want to renegotiate the labor and environmental elements of the Jordan trade agreement before they ask for Senate ratification of the pact. The new White House does not want to set a precedent for necessarily incorporating labor and environmental standards into future trade agreements. This is a clear reversal of the policy followed by the Clinton administration in the wake of the 1999 'battle in Seattle' (and protests at other WTO conferences).

To conclude, I would like to return to matters involving scholarly research on human rights and TNCs. While activists push their governments to include labor rights and environmental protection in all new trade agreements, those of us doing the analytic work on rights and TNCs need to make further progress that will reinforce and support these political actions.

The next steps for research

As noted above, the empirical research on the connections between TNCs and human rights has produced results that are, at best, mixed. There is evidence at both the cross-national level and from the many case studies to indicate that some TNCs do some good and that some TNCs do much harm. Studies using aggregate data from many countries have delineated both a positive correlation between TNCs and human rights, and a negative correlation between transnationals and rights. My overall assessment of these conflicting results argues that neither the pro-TNC view nor the anti-TNC view has yet been falsified by the existing research (Meyer 1999). These facts lead to further questions and a logical next step for research in this area. Under what conditions are TNCs most likely to have a beneficial impact on rights? Conversely, under what conditions are transnationals most likely to have a negative impact on human rights? Mort Winston has made a suggestion about the first place to look.

Winston (1999, pp. 828–9) suggests we begin by constructing a 'new grand theory' of human rights and TNCs:

> It would begin by pointing out that in the twentieth century, and especially following the Second World War, countries that tried to exercise their economic sovereignty by pursuing policies that were viewed as inimical to the interests of global capitalism became the targets of US-led attempts to destabilize and overthrow their governments... while those that accepted foreign investment as beneficial or inevitable were largely left alone or enlisted as allies. Better protection of human rights and gradual democratization were allowed to grow within the context of a free market economy... However, in the countries that chose to pursue a socialist course... war and economic boycott led to the immiseration of their populations while internal authoritarianism produced repression and violation of first generation rights.
>
> Put another way, human rights violations are positively correlated with resistance to liberal economic policies: globalization has been good for human rights as long as there was no resistance to it. Resistance was immediately punished by capital flight, economic boycotts and sanctions, and attempts at political destabilization, which whether they succeeded or failed led to greater political repression and violations of civil and political rights. The situation has been like that of the 'Borg' in Star Trek movies where everything is fine as long as you agree to be assimilated.

I find Winston's suggestion of the 'Borg thesis' intriguing for a number of reasons. We must set aside a critique of Winston's analysis that points out that he seems implicitly to ascribe the existence of 'internal authoritarianism' in 'socialist' nations (for example, Cuba and North Korea) to 'US-led' efforts against these same nations. Can we really blame the US for the repression inside North Korea? I doubt it. But the 'Borg thesis' does give us one new variable that may be related to the contextual impact of TNCs on rights: the extent to which a nation does or does not agree to be 'assimilated' into the global liberal economic system. Winston's claim is that we should find a positive correlation between resistance to assimilation and increasing levels of human rights viola-tions. Presumably, one could distinguish between different levels of willing assimilation to capitalism across Third World nations, and then enter this measure into an expanded analysis of transnationals and human rights.

I also agree with Winston's (1999, p. 829) assessment when he goes on to say that:

> The current belief that 'globalization is inevitable' is really an acknowledgement that 'socialism is dead.' This means, in effect, that the only paths towards democratization and human rights that are now available are ones that also embrace market liberalization ... So the question now becomes: How will it be possible to most effectively promote and protect human rights within the context of economic globalization?

Above I suggested that a partial answer to Winston's question is for the politics of TNCs and rights to focus our attention over the short term on establishing enforceable standards for labor rights and environmental protection under the aegis of the WTO. In regard to research, we may want to try to measure and assess the impact of the 'Borg thesis'. But I also think future research needs to go into more contextual detail at a lower level of analysis.

Winston's 'Borg thesis' directs our attention to the international level (degree of willingness to assimilate to capitalism across nations). Future research on human rights and TNCs must also identify those aspects within nations that can help us to understand the differential impact of transnationals on rights. One place to look may be at the nature of those economic enterprises themselves. For example, is it the case that TNCs involved in light manufacturing (for example, textile 'sweatshops') are more likely to abuse the rights of their workers than are TNCs that are involved in heavy manufacturing (steel plants, and so on), or those in resource extraction (mining, and so on)? Or is the reverse true?

What we need most right now (in terms of the research agenda) is some creative thinking that can identify and investigate characteristics of TNC production at several levels of analysis, and then tie these contextual variables directly to the conditions under which TNCs are more likely to violate (or to respect) human rights. Research of this sort would be of great utility to the activists and diplomats who are working hard to build an international politico-ethical regime that will force TNCs to respect and to promote human rights.

Notes

1. Private sector members of the FLA include Liz Claiborne, L.L. Bean, Nike, Patagonia, Phillips Van Heusen, Reebok, and Tweeds. Non-profit members are the International Labor Rights Fund, the Lawyers Committee for Human Rights, and the National Consumers League. The Interfaith Center for Corporate Responsibility and UNITE (the Union of Needletrades, Industrial and Textile Employees) are two members of AIP that refused to sign up to the FLA agreement because they feel the FLA does not go far enough to improve wages or to ensure independent monitoring (see Manning, 1998).
2. All following references to Abad's testimony were taken from her public talk at the University of Delaware on 11 November 1999.
3. 'Lawsuits Describe Sweatshops in Saipan', *Wilmington News Journal*, Wilmington, Del., 14 January 1999, p. A3.
4. It is beyond the scope of this chapter to assess the validity of the many criticisms of the WTO. In my opinion, some of these charges are valid, and others are way off base.

References

Barshefsky, Charlene. 1999. 'Toward Seattle: the Next Round and America's Stake in the Trading System', Public address to the Council on Foreign Relations, New York City, 19 October. Available at www.usia.gov/topical/econ/wto99/pp1019.htm.

Donnelly, Jack. 1998. *International Human Rights*. Boulder: Westview Press.

Greenhouse, Steven. 1999. 'Nike Identifies Plants Abroad Making Goods for Universities', *New York Times*, 8 October 1999.

Imle, John F., Jr. 1999. 'Transnationals and the New World of Energy Development', *Journal of International Affairs* 53(1): 263–80.

Knight, C. Foster. 1995. 'NAFTA Promises Payoff in Environmental Benefits', *Forum for Applied Research and Public Policy*, Summer.

Manby, Bronwen. 1999. 'The Role and Responsibility of Oil Transnationals in Nigeria', *Journal of International Affairs* 53(1): 281–301.

Manning, Jeff. 1998. 'Sweatshop Pact Advances', *The Oregonian*, 4 November.

Meyer, William H. 1996. 'Human Rights and MNCs: Theory vs. Quantitative Analysis', *Human Rights Quarterly* 18(2): 368–97.

Meyer, William H. 1998. *Human Rights and International Political Economy in Third World Nations: MNCs, Foreign Aid and Repression*. Westport, Connecticut: Praeger.

Meyer, William H. 1999. 'Confirming, Infirming and "Falsifying" Theories of Human Rights: Reflections on Smith, Bolyard and Ippolito through the Lens of Lakatos', *Human Rights Quarterly* 21(1): 220–8.

National Consumers League. 1998. 'Preliminary Agreement: Charter Document for the Fair Labor Association, Prepared by the Apparel Industry Partnership', 2 November.

Smith, Jackie, Melissa Bolyard and Anna Ippolitio. 1999. 'Human Rights and the Global Economy: a Response to Meyer', *Human Rights Quarterly* 21(1): 207–19.

Sobek, Stephen. 1999. 'Coalition Uses Web to Reveal Lawmakers' Stance on Sweatshops', Gannett News Service (online), 27 July. At www.gannettonline.com.

Spar, Deborah L. 1998. 'The Spotlight and the Bottom Line: How Multinationals Export Human Rights', *Foreign Affairs* 77(1): 7–12.

Wickham, Kathleen. 1999. 'Students Call for End to Sweatshop Conditions', Gannett News Service (online), 12 July. At www.gannettonline.com.

Winston, Morton. 1999. 'Review of *Human Rights and International Political Economy in Third World Nations* by William H. Meyer', *Human Rights Quarterly* 21(3): 828–9.

3
Regulating Transnational Corporations through Corporate Codes of Conduct

Alex Wawryk

As a result of the failure of transnational corporations (TNCs) to observe minimum standards of human rights in their operations, a number of different legal means for regulating the behavior of TNCs have been suggested and debated over the years. As the title implies, this chapter is concerned specifically with the regulation of TNCs through the adoption and enforcement of a code of conduct. A code of conduct is a written policy or statement of principles intended to serve as the basis for a commitment to a particular conduct (Dubin 1999, p. 42). To be effective as a means of regulation, a code of conduct should not only set out the principles to guide behavior but must also establish mechanisms for implementation, monitoring and enforcement and review of the code.

In this chapter, I examine four types of codes of conduct, discussing the issues involved in the formulation of each type of code, and the strengths and weaknesses of these types of code as a means for regulating the behavior of TNCs. These codes are: public codes of conduct contained in instruments of international law; private, internal codes of conduct drafted by individual corporations in order to guide the conduct of employees and other actors associated with a company's operations; national codes of conduct promoted by an industry association for adoption by its members; and non-government, non-industry codes of conduct drafted by non-government organizations for voluntary adoption by corporations.

Public international codes of conduct

A public international code of conduct aimed at regulating TNCs is a set of rules, establishing standards for the behavior of TNCs, contained in an instrument of international law. Examples include the OECD Guidelines for Multinational Enterprises and the ILO's Tripartite Declaration of Principles Concerning Multinational Enterprises and Social Policy.[1]

There has recently been an increased interest in the international community in controlling the effects on human rights of TNCs through public international codes of conduct (United Nations 2000; European Parliament 1999). However, gaining the consensus of the economically, culturally and politically disparate states of the international community on the four primary aspects of an international code – the purpose(s) of the code, the actors to be regulated, the content of the code, and the legal nature of the code – is a cumbersome, time-consuming process that requires a great deal of political skill and compromise. It is not only the disparate interests of the international community that make an agreement hard to achieve, but the complexity and interdependence of these four elements.

Issues to be addressed in formulating a public code of conduct

A number of different purposes may underlie a public code of conduct concerning TNCs and their observance of human rights. For example, the international community may wish to establish a new means of regulating TNCs by drafting a legally binding code of conduct that directly regulates the behavior of TNCs and establishes a new enforcement and monitoring mechanism. Alternatively, the international community may wish to draft a voluntary code to guide the behavior of TNCs according to a set of uniform principles. A third aim may be to improve compliance with human rights standards by increasing the effectiveness of national laws, that is, to aim to improve government regulation of TNCs at the national level.

As regards the actors to be governed by a code of conduct, there are two candidates for regulation: states and TNCs. State governments are responsible for negotiating the coverage, provisions and legal force of a code and are responsible for its enforcement. The question arises as to whether, and to what extent, a code aimed at regulating the behavior of TNCs should place obligations on governments. When negotiating the content of a code, governments are often extremely reluctant to accept any provisions that place limits upon their sovereignty. Obligations that could be placed upon states may include an undertaking to publish the code; enact legislation ensuring that TNCs report on their application of, and compliance with the code, for example in their annual reports;

make the code applicable to domestic companies; and make compliance with the code a term of any contracts with foreign companies (Feld 1980; Cohen 1996; Conservation International 1997).

Although it might be expected that an international code would place obligations directly on TNCs, this would be difficult, if not impossible, in the case of a legally binding code. Traditionally, states have been the only subjects of international law, that is, the only entities with international legal personality, including the capacity to possess duties and claim rights under international law.[2] States are extremely reluctant to recognize the full international legal personality of corporations, particularly if this empowers TNCs to participate in the treaty-making process on equal terms with states and claim rights under international law. Further, it must be determined which TNCs are to receive international legal personality, and finally, there are legal difficulties associated with enforcing the international obligations placed directly upon corporations (Dubin 1999; Voon 1999).

While some existing public international codes contain provisions that are directly addressed to TNCs,[3] the obligations placed upon the corporations are voluntary, reflecting the difficulties associated with making corporations subjects of binding international law.

As far as content is concerned, a range of matters could be included in the code. For example, the proposed draft United Nations Human Rights Code of Conduct for Companies addresses the following issues very broadly: general obligations; war crimes, crimes against humanity and other crimes; non-discrimination and freedom from harassment and abuse; slavery, forced labor and child labor; respect for national sovereignty and right of self-determination; healthy and safe working environment; fair and equal remuneration; hours of work; freedom of association and the right to collective bargaining; consumer protection; and environmental protection and human rights (United Nations 2000).

Alternatively, a code of conduct may address one particular area of human rights but in more detail. An example may be a code of conduct for private sector mining and energy companies operating on the traditional lands of indigenous peoples. The advantage of such a code is that it can be tailored to meet specific human rights issues arising from a particular industry.

In terms of gaining state agreement to the content of a binding international code of conduct, a code may fail if it is too comprehensive. Codes such as the UN Restrictive Businesses Code,[4] 'with limited, overseeable structures and without pretence to regulate all kinds of conduct have been successful', whereas very comprehensive codes, such as the

UN Code of Conduct for Transnational Corporations,[5] have been too ambitious to succeed (Fikentscher 1982, p. 602).

As regards the legal nature of the code, a public code of conduct for companies may be voluntary, mandatory, or a 'zebra' or 'hybrid' code where some provisions are mandatory and other provisions are voluntary. There are three categories of international legal instruments that could be used to incorporate a code of conduct: an international convention or treaty; a declaration of principles, adopted at an international conference; and a resolution of an international organization, such as the United Nations General Assembly. Of these options, only treaties are legally binding.

Two major advantages of a code of conduct set forth in a treaty are that a treaty can create a legal basis for international administration and enforcement of the code, and a treaty formally binds the parties to give effect to the code through good faith implementation and enforcement. However, there are a number of practical problems associated with a binding code. One is the unwillingness of states to bind themselves formally to provisions that they perceive will limit their sovereignty. Second, it can take years for the disparate states of the international community to reach consensus on the provisions of a binding code, if at all.[6]

Given these limitations, a voluntary code has certain advantages over a binding code (Fatouros 1981). Governments are often more willing to accept the provisions of a voluntary code precisely because it does not bind them to action, leaving more flexibility in interpretation and implementation. Furthermore, proponents of voluntary codes have argued that a code based on moral suasion, and supported by TNCs through self-interest and a sense of civic responsibility, is the only desirable code of conduct (Fatouros 1981, p. 951). Opponents of voluntary codes argue that in the absence of any follow-up mechanism implemented by governments, it is unlikely that TNCs would comply with an international code of conduct drafted by states, finding it profitable to continue to act in a manner that is inconsistent with the code's provisions (Ocran 1986).

But the effectiveness of a code of conduct does not depend on the legal form alone: 'the actual legal effect of a legal instrument depends upon a complex interaction of factors, especially legal form, substantive content, language and formulation, and the institutional and procedural machinery used for implementation' (Fatouros 1981, p. 949). In the case of a mandatory code, considerable freedom of action may be left to TNCs and governments, depending upon the language of the code, its machinery for implementation, and the willingness of governments to adopt the code. Conversely, voluntary codes can establish norms of conduct that will be observed as much as if they were mandatory.[7] A code that is fully supported by states, even if it is not legally binding, may be more effective than a code contained in a treaty that is undermined by reservations.

States are more likely to accept as binding a general code that contains broad statements of principle to guide behavior, rather than a specific code containing detailed obligations regarding the practices of TNCs that are to be regulated. The more detailed the obligations, the less likely it is that the range of states will accept the provisions. Thus, in practice, it may be more effective to have a general, voluntary public code, supplemented by more detailed, internal codes of conduct adopted by individual TNCs to regulate the conduct of their employees.

Whether mandatory or voluntary, all codes require an implementation mechanism to be effective. The implementation of a public international code may be undertaken at the national and/or international level. The issue of most sensitivity at the international level is the establishment and selection of an international body to undertake the major implementation functions. These functions include:

- administrative, technical, and monitoring responsibilities, of which reporting by governments and/or corporations on progress in implementing the code is the most significant activity;
- dispute settlement procedures, which may be formal (judicial, arbitration) or informal;
- complaints procedures;
- in the case of a mandatory code, provisions for enforcement, including sanctions and penalties for breach of the code; and
- mechanisms for review and future revision of the code.

The establishment of an implementation mechanism is a complex process that depends on the purpose of the code, the actors regulated, the obligations contained within the code and the legal nature of the code. For example, sanctions will generally not be appropriate for a voluntary code. In the case of a mandatory code, the sanctions will depend on whether the code regulates states or corporations and the precise obligations levied on these actors. And, of course, the implementation mechanism that is proposed may then affect the willingness of states to support the code and the obligations contained therein. If a code with stringent sanctions is proposed, then states may not support a binding code and/or there may be many reservations to a code, undermining its effectiveness.

Strengths and limitations of a public international code of conduct

A public international code of conduct regulating the behavior of TNCs has a number of advantages. First, if such a code becomes part of the body of public international law, then states are required to observe its provisions. Even a voluntary code contained in a non-binding instrument of international law acts as a moral force, particularly one that is generally and universally accepted; and has the chance to develop into customary international law.

Second, a public international code of conduct provides a consistent expected standard of behavior for TNCs across all countries, that is, a 'level playing field'. This is an advantage because the increased cost associated with integrating human rights concerns into company procedures may place one TNC at a competitive disadvantage compared with another TNC that does not integrate human rights considerations into their operations, thereby acting as a deterrent to adoption of the code and/or affecting the decision to invest in certain countries (Baker 1993, p. 417; Cassel 1996). A public international code accepted by the international community also provides a 'legitimizing force' for TNCs that wish to improve compliance with human rights but will conflict with host government policies when they do so, for example, in the case of government requirements to use the military to protect TNC production facilities from demonstrations.

Third, a public international code of conduct that contains one international monitoring or implementation mechanism allows reports on compliance with the code to be compared far more easily than a large number of disparate national or private internal codes of conduct.

In terms of the limitations of a public code there are also a number of disadvantages. First, it may take years to negotiate and gain consensus on a code of conduct contained in an instrument of international law, if agreement can be reached at all.[8] The system is characterized by long delays in negotiations and weak substantive obligations arising from the need to compromise to obtain agreement among the many states of the international community. In contrast, a private industry or internal code can be adopted quickly and the principles can be drafted to address the most urgent and relevant human rights issues confronting particular TNCs.

Second, the international legal system requires enormous resources to negotiate codes and – where an international body is established to oversee the implementation of the code – to undertake the administrative, technical, and monitoring responsibilities, and operate the dispute settlement procedures, complaints procedures and review procedures. Many United Nations bodies, which rely on funding by state governments, are vastly underfunded, which negatively affects their ability to monitor and enforce international laws. This is likely to be the case for an international body established to oversee the implementation of a code regulating TNCs.

Third, many developing countries lack the resources and institutional capacity to fulfil the commitments required of them under the international implementation mechanism, such as meeting their obligations to report periodically to the international body charged with oversight of the code. This has been a problem with reporting obligations under current international instruments of human rights law, where many developing countries have fallen behind in their reporting obligations.

The effective implementation of a code depends on the willingness and ability of national governments successfully to enforce it. In many developing countries, even if the will to enforce a treaty through national legislation is present, the legal institutional capacity to monitor and enforce the code through the national legal system is absent. Without adequate national enforcement, a code adopted by the United Nations that is imposed on corporations without their consent and participation may simply fail to change corporate behavior.

Private internal corporate codes of conduct

A private internal corporate code of conduct is a 'written statement of ethics, law, or policy (or some combination thereof), delineating the obligations of one or more classes of corporate employees' (Pitt and Groskaufmanis 1990, p. 1559). Private internal codes of conduct are popular with TNCs in the textiles, clothing and footwear industries, including Gap, Levi Strauss, Nike and Reebok, as a means of addressing labor rights in developing countries (see Frynas, Chapter 8 of this book for more on this). A range of other corporations have adopted private internal codes, including Body Shop, BP, Nokia, PepsiCo, Petro-Canada, Rio Tinto, Royal Dutch/Shell, Statoil, Volkswagen and Xerox.

Issues to be addressed in formulating a private internal code of conduct

While the genuine desire to act as a 'good corporate citizen' is one reason for the adoption of an internal code of conduct, in the majority of corporations the code must also offer the prospect of increased long-term profitability of the corporation if it to be accepted by the shareholders.[9]

Thus, internal corporate codes of conduct usually give priority to the long-term interests of the shareholders from the outset, as members of the board and senior management that do not give priority to profits are liable to be removed by the shareholders (Baker 1993, p. 423).

Internal codes apply to the employees of the company adopting the code. The key issue beyond this is whether the code will be applied to a TNC's contractors and subcontractors. The internal codes adopted by the major US clothing and footwear TNCs such as Levi Strauss, Reebok and Nike apply to their subcontractors in the countries in which they do business, and it is generally agreed in the field of labor rights that companies must take responsibility for their contractors and subcontractors (Krug 1998, p. 670). Similarly, some transnational oil companies are taking responsibility for the observance of their internal code of conduct by the companies' contractors and subcontractors. For example, Occidental imposes the same standards on its contractors and consultants in Ecuador working in the field as it does on itself. Each infringement of the company's guidelines on environmental control, industrial safety and community relations involves a fine of up to $10,000 (Williams 1997b, p. 48).

As regards the content of a private internal code of conduct, a range of matters may be considered for inclusion. It can contain mainly broad statements of principles, such as a statement of the company's position on human rights issues, and/or more detailed provisions or guidelines regulating the behavior of company employees, which may not be appropriate or acceptable in a public international code of conduct.

The development and adoption of an internal corporate code of conduct is voluntary and the provisions are not legally binding. However, an internal code can be a useful tool for protecting human rights as long as it incorporates an effective implementation mechanism. A number of authors (Baker 1993; Bloomfield 1999; Compa and Hinchliffe-Darricarrère 1995; Krug 1998; Pitt and Groskaufmanis 1990; Toftoy 1998) have discussed the implementation mechanisms that a private internal code must contain to be effective and the deficiencies of these mechanisms in practice. The features that should be addressed in a code are:

- ongoing training and awareness procedures for employees, contractors and subcontractors;
- internal monitoring procedures, including the ongoing auditing and reporting on human rights conditions by company officials, and surprise visits to production facilities by senior management;
- independent, third-party monitoring of the company's compliance with the code (including contractors and subcontractors), either by

independent examiners, or through the external verification of the results of in-house monitoring conducted by company officials;

- a complaints mechanism by which employees and local people can invoke the code without fear of reprisal;
- sanctions for non-compliance, for example, termination of employment for non-compliance by employees, and for contractors or sub-contractors, cancellation of contracts and/or monetary penalties;
- machinery for disseminating and collecting information on implementation of, and compliance with, the code; and
- institutional arrangements to modify the code or formulate more detailed rules.

Strengths and limitations of private internal codes of conduct

Internal private codes offer a number of advantages. First, in countries where law enforcement mechanisms are weak, self-regulation by corporations under their own voluntary codes, which are drafted to suit the particular needs of the corporation, may actually be more effective than national or international codes forced upon corporations (Cueto 1997, p. 608). In such countries, a private code of conduct that is voluntarily adopted because of a genuine acknowledgment of corporate social accountability and/or an explicit recognition that such a code will increase the long-term profitability of corporations, is more likely to be implemented by companies, and thereby has a greater potential for success in 'promoting integrity among international corporate executives' (Baker 1993, p. 414). On the other hand, a code that is simply adopted as a public relations exercise, and is not diligently enforced and monitored, will fail to change corporate culture and be no more than a 'paper tiger'.

Second, private internal codes avoid the time-consuming process of negotiation involved in drafting an instrument of international law. Unlike treaties, internal codes can be tailored to the individual needs of corporations and countries, and to the needs of the customers. Internal codes offer flexibility, lower cost implementation and are quicker to draft and implement than international codes.

Third, a company with a track record of adhering to an internal code of conduct will gain a good reputation for managing environmental and human rights issues, thereby increasing government and public confidence in the company. This may lead to the company receiving preferential contracts and other benefits such as reduced inspections by regulatory agencies, lower license and permit fees and expedited environmental approvals. On the other hand, a company that signs a voluntary industry code of conduct and fails to live up to it could attract more criticism and attain a poorer reputation than if it had not become a signatory in the first place.

Well-drafted private codes of conduct that are consistent with international law can act as instruments of 'moral persuasion, strengthened by the authority of international organisations and the support of public opinion' (Cueto 1997, p. 608). Private codes may enhance and support national legislation, and can be used by national courts to interpret ambiguities in binding laws, particularly in the environmental sphere. Furthermore, private codes provide standards against which NGOs can measure company performance. There is evidence that, with human rights and environmental groups scrutinizing company operations, private codes have actually improved corporate behavior (Gereffi et al. 2001).

The most common criticisms of voluntary private internal codes of conduct relate to the weakness of enforcement provisions and compliance monitoring mechanisms. Usually, the enforcement, compliance and monitoring provisions are the weakest elements of internal codes of conduct, being either inadequate or simply non-existent. While independent, third-party monitors provide the best method for ensuring the independence and reliability of monitoring results, many corporations have resisted independent oversight in the case of labor codes of conduct and in the implementation of environmental management systems. Companies usually prefer a system of self-compliance, or a system of monitoring conducted by consultants retained by the company or company personnel (Dubin 1999, p. 63; Porges 1997, p. 3).

The mechanics of third-party monitoring itself raises difficulties. External monitoring can be carried out by privately retained consulting groups, but these groups may be susceptible to influence by the corporation and suspicions may be cast upon the independence and reliability of the results. External monitoring can be done by a coalition of human rights and other NGOs, or intergovernmental organizations, but a major problem with these options, aside from the question of funding, is one of practicality: one group trying to monitor a number of different codes for different companies, including compliance by different contractors and subcontractors, raises enormous logistical difficulties (Toftoy 1998, p. 928).[10]

Other criticisms of implementation mechanisms are that the rules can be easily circumvented by employees; enforcement provisions usually outline rules of procedures for settling disputes but lack concrete rules for enforcing specific forms of behavior; most corporate codes are characterized by a lack of definite sanctions for non-compliance;

and compliance programs are undermined by financial pressures and organizational dynamics – with the result that private codes are often nothing more than public relations ploys with little practical effect (Baker 1993; Hepple 1999; Pitt and Groskaufmanis 1990).

In the field of labor rights, the ILO has expressed further concerns about the proliferation of diverse private codes and their relationship to the role of the ILO and the Tripartite Declaration of Principles Concerning Multinational Enterprises and Social Policy. The ILO has found that issues that excite public opinion and sympathy, such as the use of child labor, are often addressed in private corporate codes whereas other rights, such as freedom of association, the right to bargain collectively, and the promotion of employment and training, are not. This has led to the perception that private codes are arbitrary, focus on standards with emotional appeal, and undermine the universality of the ILO standards. On the other hand, it has been argued that these codes make it possible to go beyond the ILO machinery and aid in the interpretation and application of at least some standards (Hagen 1998, pp. 273–6).

Furthermore, the effective implementation of private codes by some corporations does not mean that exploitative practices have been eliminated in all enterprises. The application of codes by TNCs such as Levi Strauss and their contractors and suppliers may benefit their workers, but not mitigate the plight of workers in domestic industries where there are no codes. There is thus a danger that the workforce in developing countries could be dichotomized between those who work for TNCs and obtain the benefit from higher standards, and those who do not (Hagen 1998, p. 276). Similarly, there may be a difference within the same country between the standards observed by TNCs that implement private codes and TNCs that do not. For example, the US Workplace Code of Conduct developed by the Apparel Industry Partnership (see Meyer, Chapter 2 of this book for more on this), which applies to the overseas operations of American TNCs but not those of other countries, may lead to different conditions for workers according to whether they are employed by American or non-American TNCs.[11]

There are also real doubts about the usefulness of a private code adopted by TNCs operating in conflict zones, particularly TNCs engaged in subsurface resource exploitation, where government use of the military to secure concession areas and/or production facilities leads to human rights abuses, as has been the case in Burma, Colombia, Ecuador, Nigeria and Sudan (see Winston, Chapter 4 of this book for more on this). Despite its best efforts, the commercial presence of a TNC may perpetuate these abuses (Gagnon and Ryle 2001).

A TNC, once it has adopted a private code to which it is genuinely committed, may be deterred from investing in a country where compliance with its own code is likely to result in conflicts with the host government, but where compromise exposes the TNC to negative publicity in its home country. Unfortunately, in this situation a TNC without a similar concern for human rights, that does not have a private code and is unlikely to be exposed to negative publicity in its home country, may take the opportunity to invest in the country, thereby perpetuating the abuse of human rights under even worse conditions.

Finally, a TNC that incurs the costs of developing and implementing an internal code of conduct may, in the short term, put itself at a competitive disadvantage in some parts of the world, where other corporations not subject to a code will not incur the costs involved in developing and enforcing a code of conduct. However, the short-term disadvantage may be outweighed in the long run by benefits such as a better reputation, leading to increased public confidence in the corporation and preferential contracts with governments.

Industry association codes of conduct

An industry association code of conduct refers to the self-regulation by an industry association of its member corporations through a statement of principles that is aimed at providing standards or rules for corporate behavior. Such a code is voluntary because it is initiated, monitored and enforced by the industry association. An industry association code differs from a voluntary agreement between industry and government, which is a written contract bilaterally negotiated between governments and companies.

A legally non-binding industry code may be 'mandatory' in the sense that membership in the association is conditional upon adoption of the code. Examples of this type of code include the international chemical industry's Responsible Care® code, which regulates environmental, health and safety issues in the chemical industry; and the American Petroleum Institute's (API) Environmental Stewardship Program, which, as part of the by-laws of the API, is mandatory for API members (API 2001). Alternatively, an industry association may not require its members to adopt the code as condition of membership of the association, for example, the international mining industry's *Mining and Environment Guidelines*.[12]

Responsible Care®, which is the most sophisticated self-regulatory environmental, health and safety code in existence, demonstrates the strengths and limitations of industry association codes as an alternative to legislation. The Canadian Chemical Producers Association initiated the program in 1985, partly as a reaction to serious chemical accidents such as the Union Carbide disaster in Bhopal in 1985, and partly because of wider concerns about the costs of such accidents and the health and environmental effects of chemical production in general (Gunningham 1998a, p. 159).

The purpose of Responsible Care® is continuously to improve the environmental, health and safety performance of the chemical industry. The International Council of Chemical Associations (ICCA) coordinates and promotes worldwide adherence to Responsible Care® through its members, the national chemical manufacturers associations. Each national association accepted as an ICCA member must report annually on its progress in the scheme. Eight fundamental, standardized features, which have been expanded into 34 'milestones', form the basis for reporting to the ICCA. The progress of each national association against each milestone is rated according to four implementation status levels (ICCA 2000).

By April 2002, Responsible Care® had been adopted by 46 national chemical associations. Although the scheme is in varying stages of development and implementation around the world, the program of the American Chemical Council (ACC) in the US (formerly the Chemical Manufacturers Association) demonstrates the essential features of the program at the national level.

At the heart of Responsible Care® as adopted by the ACC is a set of Guiding Principles and six Codes of Management Practice.[13] The six Codes of Management Practice are community awareness and emergency response, distribution, pollution prevention, process safety, employee health and safety, and product stewardship. It is a condition of membership in the ACC that companies subscribe to the set of Guiding Principles, through the signature of the Chief Executive Officer, and incorporate the six Codes of Management Practice into their operations.[14] These Codes of Practice incorporate and go well beyond existing legal requirements.

National progress in implementing Responsible Care® is measured internally through member self-evaluation and externally through a voluntary management systems verification (MSV®) process. Progress in implementing the scheme is assessed using independently verifiable performance measures for the six Codes of Practice. Some companies make available the results of the self-evaluation audits through their internet sites, and the ACC reports on company progress in implementing the scheme on its website.

The external MSV® process is managed for the ACC by the independent consulting firm Verrico Associates. An MSV® team is usually made up of a facilitator, volunteer verifiers from other ACC member companies, and community participants. The team visits a company's corporate headquarters and one or two plant sites to conduct interviews with a cross-section of employees (ACC 2000). As of January 2002, 110 companies in the US had participated in the management systems verification process, including industry leaders like DuPont (March 1995), Ashland Chemical (February 1997), Dow Chemical (March 1999) and Shell Chemical (October–December 2000) (ACC 2002). The ACC is currently developing an accredited, third-party audit process by which member companies can gain certification of their compliance with ISO 14001 standards for environmental management systems consistent with Responsible Care® certification.

A key feature of Responsible Care® is public participation, which is achieved through the ACC national Public Advisory Panel, which was replaced in 2002 by a Chemical Advisory Panel (ACC 2001). The Public Advisory Panel is composed of 15 (unpaid) environmental, health and safety 'thought leaders', including academics, environmental consultants and activists, who provide independent advice to the industry on the development and implementation of Responsible Care®. Panel meetings often include tours of chemical industry sites and discussion with representatives of local communities (CMA 1999).

Strengths and limitations of industry association codes of conduct

First, an industry association code, as a private rather than a public code, has a number of the same advantages as a voluntary internal code of conduct, including the following: it is quicker and easier to draft and implement industry association codes than public international codes of conduct; and a company with a good reputation for adhering to an industry code of conduct will obtain commercial benefits resulting from increased government and public confidence in the company and the industry.

Second, the avoidance of 'command and control' regulation is perceived by industry to be a major benefit. An industry code of conduct can be drafted to suit the particular needs and structures of different industries, offering increased flexibility and low cost and innovative methods for improved performance in the area of regulation. Responsible Care® has detailed codes that are tailored to the needs of the chemical industry. It offers companies the benefit of flexibility and lower costs, and provides the opportunity for firms to be innovative in improving health, safety and environmental performance (Gunningham 1995; Trainor 1997; Wells 1997). The program has already delivered emissions reductions and other improvements in environmental performance (Gunningham 1998a, p. 171).

Third, voluntary industry codes of conduct may provide a tool for ensuring compliance with existing laws through the 'creation of an atmosphere in which an economically viable environmental ethic can be inculcated within the management of business and industry' (Ong 1997, p. 103). Responsible Care® has contributed to the development of an 'industry morality' where environmental protection is seen as a legitimate aspiration of companies, and there is considerable scope for peer group pressure to act as an agent for change. The structure of the chemical industry, which is characterized by strategic alliances, product swapping and technology sharing, has allowed the national chemical manufacturers' associations to exert pressure for environmental improvement (Gunningham 1998a, pp. 162–4).

Fourth, an industry code of conduct such as Responsible Care® may improve dialogue and relations between the public, interested groups and the industry, through forums such as the National Advisory Panels. Public participation in an industry code of conduct offers the opportunity to empower the community, improve public relations, and ensure that the self-regulation of the industry is honest and transparent. Responsible Care® seems to have improved dialogue with local communities, although it has not resulted in ongoing dialogue with environmental groups, who are concerned that they will be accused of being co-opted by industry (Gunningham 1998a, pp. 171–2).

Fifth, an industry association code offers the advantage of avoiding the diffusion of a number of individual private internal codes of conduct, and the resulting difficulties this creates in terms of monitoring compliance with the code. With one organization responsible for monitoring compliance, uniformity in reporting indicators and formats can be achieved across different corporations, and, if monitoring is done externally, the results may be seen as more trustworthy. The requirement that the national chemical manufacturers' associations report annually to the ICCA according to standardized performance measures has led to uniformity in reporting, thereby providing a basis for comparing the performance of different companies across countries, and identifying recalcitrant firms and exposing them to adverse publicity.

Sixth, industry codes of practice can also make a positive contribution in developing countries by supplementing existing environmental and human rights legislation and law enforcement mechanisms where these are weak or inadequate (Cueto 1997; Wälde 1992). Assuming the code is effectively implemented, an industry code of conduct provides an additional opportunity to improve corporate compliance with human rights by requiring companies, not governments, to adopt and enforce their own standards of behavior and avoid violations of rights. In this respect, an industry code that is adopted jointly by a number of corporations operating overseas offers an advantage over private internal codes, by allowing signatory corporations to act in numbers under a united front. A coalition of firms can send much stronger signals to governments that they intend to uphold human rights than individual firms acting alone (De George 1997, p. 1201).

Finally, an industry association code also offers the opportunity to provide a level playing field for TNCs by removing the competitive disadvantage that may be faced in the short term by a single company whose costs are increased by implementing a private internal code of conduct.

In terms of the limitations of an industry code, the lack of credible and effective enforcement and monitoring procedures is a major drawback of industry codes of conduct. Internal industry monitoring schemes are open to manipulation by corporations and the public often perceives the results as unreliable. Indeed, the problems associated with relying on internal monitoring under Responsible Care® led to the introduction of the external MSV procedures by the ICCA in 1996. However, these procedures are still relatively new. In 1999, external verification of compliance and performance had begun and results have been made public in 20 countries (ICCA 2000, p. 5).

The independence and reliability of external monitoring undertaken by an industry body that is concerned with advocacy on behalf of the industry, and is committed to defending the sectoral interests of the industry, is also questionable. As with private codes, the external monitoring and verification by accredited, independent organizations is a crucial aspect of a viable self-regulatory scheme, but again, third-party monitors and auditors are liable to capture by the industry (Gunningham 1998b, p. 27).

Furthermore, where internal or external monitoring reveals non-compliance with the code, there are no effective sanctions available to industry associations to punish the recalcitrant firm. Under Responsible Care®, the industry association can terminate membership by the company, but in practice the likelihood of expulsion is extremely low, as most associations prefer not to wield the stick on a voluntary scheme.

Also, as most companies can profitably exist outside the association, apart from public exposure and negative publicity, this sanction lacks credibility.

There are thus serious doubts as to whether an industry association responsible for public relations and advocacy on behalf of its members can effectively and credibly implement a scheme for environmental and human rights protection.

Another limitation of a voluntary industry scheme is the possibility of 'free-riding', where some firms do not make the necessary expenditures under the scheme, preferring instead to save costs while benefiting from the improved public image of the industry. Firms that do adopt the code may be placed at a short-term competitive disadvantage. Furthermore, free-riders that continue to operate in a manner against the spirit of the code may, through negative publicity, undermine the benefits of an improved public image and enhanced industry credibility, and thereby deter other companies from joining the scheme. This is a problem in the chemical industry, where the smaller chemical enterprises who do not have the capacity and resources to make the same long-term investments as the large TNCs, and who are not sensitive to adverse publicity as they do not have high public profiles, face the incentive to free-ride (Gunningham 1998a, pp. 164–5).

Finally, as with a private internal code, any industry standards adopted by only some national associations may lead to a dichotomy between people who receive the benefits of a code and those who do not.

Non-government organization codes of conduct

A fourth type of code of conduct is one drafted by non-government organizations for adoption by corporations. Corporate adoption of this type of 'NGO code of conduct' is completely voluntary, although, once adopted, companies will be subject to some type of compliance monitoring. A number of NGO codes of conduct are currently in existence.[15] These are largely concerned with environmental protection and human rights.

An example of an NGO code in the environmental sphere is the CERES Principles for corporate environmental conduct. The Coalition for Environmentally Responsible Economies (CERES) was formed by social investors, environmental groups, religious organizations, public pensions trustees and public interest groups in the United States shortly after the Exxon Valdez incident in 1989. On 7 September 1989, CERES published a set of 10 voluntary principles for corporate environmental conduct, initially called the Valdez Principles, but renamed the CERES Principles in June 1992. The CERES Principles are designed to provide investors with information about corporations' environmental responsibility, enabling those investors to influence corporate conduct regarding the environment through the allocation of investment capital (Pink 1990, p. 188; Smith 1993, p. 308).

Adoption of the CERES Principles is completely voluntary. The principles call on corporations to adopt an active role in protecting the environment, rather than complying with minimum legal requirements set by governments. By adopting the principles, corporations 'publicly affirm' their belief that they 'have a responsibility for the environment, and must conduct all aspects of their business as responsible stewards of the environment by operating in a manner that protects the Earth' (CERES 1992). Signatories to the principles make commitments in the areas of protection of the biosphere; sustainable use of natural resources; reduction and disposal of wastes; energy conservation; risk reduction; safe products and services; environmental restoration; informing the public; management commitment; and audits and reports.

CERES monitors compliance with the principles. Signatory corporations undertake to conduct an annual self-evaluation of progress in implementing the principles; support the timely creation of generally accepted environmental audit procedures; and annually complete the CERES Report, which is made available to the public. The CERES Report is standardized, with each signatory corporation answering the same set of questions in the same format. These questions collect information on the corporations' adherence to the principles in order to assess emergency response and public disclosure policies, relationships with suppliers, energy use and environmental auditing programs (Smith 1993, p. 313). This is a relatively unique situation, as many corporations are unwilling to subject their environmental policies to independent oversight by NGOs such as CERES.

As of April 2002, 60 corporations from a range of industries had signed the CERES Principles, including The Body Shop International PLC, Coca-Cola, Energy Management Inc, Ford Motor Company, General Motors Corporation, ITT Industries, Nike, Polaroid Corporation and the Timberland Company (CERES 2002).

Strengths and limitations of NGO codes of conduct

As NGO codes of conducts are private codes, they exhibit some of the same strengths as private internal codes. For example, NGO codes are relatively quick and easy to draft; may be an effective means of changing corporate behavior in countries where law enforcement mechanisms are weak; offer a mechanism for NGOs to measure company performance; and may enhance and support the provisions of national legislation, or may fill gaps in the law. For example, the CERES Principles go beyond requirements of environmental legislation by requiring corporations to adopt an active role in protecting the environment, not merely complying with minimum legal requirements. As another example, the Sullivan Principles, which established a code of conduct for United States corporations operating in South Africa, promoted policies of equality towards black people in South Africa where the legal regime of apartheid entrenched discrimination.

As with industry codes, NGO codes offer some advantages over private internal codes of conduct. An NGO code will avoid the diffusion of a number of individual codes, and the difficulties this creates in terms of the non-uniformity of standards; the exclusion of basic, less 'emotive' rights from the content of the private codes; a lack of comparability of performance indicators across corporations; and the difficulties of monitoring a large number of corporations with different codes. Also, an NGO code that is adopted jointly by a number of corporations offers the benefit of acting in numbers under a united front.

The major limitation of NGO codes of conduct is the significant difficulty in practice of getting corporations to accept these codes. With the exception of the Sullivan Principles, where the principles provided a degree of legitimacy to the continued operations of TNCs in South Africa in the face of public calls for withdrawal from the country, broad codes of conduct sponsored by NGOs have not attracted widespread support.[16]

There are a number of reasons why this is so. First, companies incur greater costs complying with NGO codes of conduct than adopting their own private internal codes of conduct. For example, the CERES Principles demands compliance activities such as changing board members, disclosing information and submitting to public audits that are relatively costly. Second, corporations generally resist the independent monitoring of company compliance by NGOs, which is a general feature of these codes, partly because managers resist more stringent monitoring. Third, some corporations resist a 'one size fits all' approach, preferring to opt for the flexibility of a private internal code.

Fourth, environmental codes such as the CERES Principles are designed to solve and avert a set of environmental problems created by corporations. Some companies may be averse to signing an NGO code if it means implicitly acknowledging that they contribute to negative environmental conditions, or if it can be seen as an admission of fault. A related deterrent is the fear that external audit and disclosure provisions will expose corporations to the risk of increased litigation and heavier legal liability than that created by law. To counter this concern, the CERES Principles were amended in 1992 to include a disclaimer that they are 'not intended to create new legal liabilities, expand existing rights or obligations, waive legal defences, or otherwise affect the legal position of any signatory company, and are not intended to be used against a signatory in any legal proceeding for any purpose' (Zondorak 1991, p. 485).

While companies may resist signing NGO codes in favor of industry codes that may incorporate weaker substantive obligations, including those relating to monitoring and enforcement, the very existence of NGO codes allows consumers and NGOs to place pressure on industries to improve their standards. This has been the case in the American forestry industry, where the timber supply corporations initially resisted the NGO code of the Forest Stewardship Council (FSC) in favor of a less stringent industry code, the Sustainable Forest Initiative. However, NGO campaigns against the huge retail giants resulted in these stores adopting preferential contracts with timber suppliers who complied with the FSC code, thereby forcing the forestry industry to embrace the tougher FSC standards (Gereffi et al. 2001, pp. 60–1).

It has also been argued that companies can act ethically and in accordance with human rights without incurring the costs of signing an NGO code. The expenditures incurred in adopting an NGO code of conduct may be resisted by companies that are not satisfied with the provisions of an NGO code, and who may prefer to adopt their own internal code. Companies that act ethically but do not subscribe to an NGO code may be unfairly seen to be unethical by the public.

NGO codes also suffer the shortcomings of other private codes, such as ineffective monitoring and enforcement procedures, including the vulnerability to capture of independent monitors and auditors; the dichotomization of the workforce in emerging economies between those who are covered by the code and those who are not; and the adoption of these codes by companies not out of a genuine concern for human rights, but as a public relations ploy or 'camouflage', in order to have an excuse for operating in and profiting from operations in regimes associated with fundamental human rights abuses. For example, signatories to the Sullivan Principles were criticized for adopting the principles as a means of providing legitimacy for their operations in South Africa and, by their presence, helping to prop up the apartheid regime (Compa and Hinchliffe-Darricarrère 1995, p. 674).

Conclusion

The great advantage of a public international code of conduct is that a code can be made legally binding on states, requiring all states which endorsed that treaty to implement the provisions of the convention. By placing obligations on states, a public international code can recognize the role and responsibilities of governments in regulating TNCs. Such a code can also achieve uniformity in standards across the globe. However, it is likely to be extremely difficult to achieve consensus on a public international code: a system of international enforcement and monitoring would require enormous additional funding from states, and the lack of adequate institutional capacity in many developing countries will undermine the application of international standards once they have been translated into national legislation.

A number of common themes run through the analysis of private codes, whether these are internal company codes, industry association codes or NGO codes of conduct. The relative flexibility, relatively low cost of implementation, speed of drafting and adoption of private codes means that these codes can actually 'get off the ground'. Industry and NGO codes offer the further advantage over private codes of providing a level playing field for TNCs in an industry. However, private codes generally suffer from a major shortcoming, namely the woefully inadequate nature of monitoring and enforcement systems, which render these codes ineffectual. In this respect, the role of human rights and environmental NGOs as 'watchdogs' is absolutely crucial if private codes are to change corporate behavior.

More generally, it must be remembered that while this chapter is concerned with regulating TNCs, the activities of other large corporations operating solely within state borders also have a significant impact on the enjoyment of human rights. Whatever type of code is proposed for regulating TNCs, such a code should also contain principles that can be applied and extended to all corporations if human rights are to be properly observed.

Notes

1. Organization for Economic Cooperation and Development, *Guidelines for Multinational Enterprises*, annexed to the OECD *Declaration on Investment and Multinational Enterprises*, OECD Doc C(76)99 (1976), 15 *ILM* 967 (1976); International Labor Organization, *Tripartite Declaration of Principles Concerning Multinational Enterprises and Social Policy*, ILO Doc GN 204/4/2 (1978), 17 *ILM* 423 (1978); (2nd edn 1991), International Labor Organization, http://www.ilo.org.

2. There are now exceptions to this rule, for example, individuals have standing under the First Optional Protocol of the International Covenant on Civil and Political Rights to make complaints to the Human Rights Committee about alleged breaches of the Covenant. However, difficulties remain with making TNCs subjects of international law.
3. For example, the OECD Guidelines for Multinational Enterprises and the ILO's Tripartite Declaration of Principles Concerning Multinational Enterprises and Social Policy.
4. United Nations Conference on Restrictive Business Practices, *The Set of Multilaterally Agreed Equitable Principles and Rules for the Control of Restrictive Business Practices*, UN Doc TD/RBP/CONF/10 (1980), 19 *ILM* 813 (1980), adopted by the UN General Assembly, GA Res 63, 35 UN GAOR, Supp (No. 48) 123, UN Doc A/35/48 (1980).
5. Proposed Text of the Draft Code of Conduct on Transnational Corporations, UN ECOSOC, 2nd Sess., Annex, at pmbl, UN Doc E/1990/94 (1990).
6. In the field of indigenous rights, it took 10 years (1985–1994) for the UN draft Declaration on the Rights of Indigenous Peoples to be presented to the Commission on Human Rights; and the Commission's Working Group, which began discussion on the draft Declaration in 1995, had yet to begin discussion on the majority of provisions as of the start of the year 2002.
7. A code contained in a non-binding instrument of international law may be effectively observed for a number of reasons: there is a moral and political obligation on the part of states to observe the provisions of non-binding instruments of international law; a voluntary code may be used by national courts to interpret other explicitly binding agreements; implementation mechanisms may insert a degree of compulsion into the code; public pressure and the cost of bad publicity may force TNCs to comply with the code; and the negotiations themselves may have an effect on the behavior of corporations, even if a formal code is never attained (Baade 1979, pp. 40–9; Ocran 1986, p. 132; Rubin 1995, pp. 285–6; Sanders 1982, p. 244; United Nations Secretariat 1976, pp. 34–5).
8. For example, negotiations for the failed UN Code of Conduct for Transnational Corporations revealed deep divisions between developed and developing countries that could not be resolved. In the end, after years of negotiations, the code never came into being.
9. There are a number of reasons why a private code may lead to increased long-term profits. An effective internal code of conduct may improve the corporation's public image, thereby increasing public trust and confidence in the corporation; strengthen the mutual trust between a TNC and the host government, increasing goodwill and leading to preferential relations with host governments; improve political stability, and reduce risk, conflict and delays attending controversial development projects; dissuade governments from enacting more costly, inflexible legislation; and decrease the potential for legal action in the future (Baker 1993; Hepple 1999; Pitt and Groskaufmanis 1990; Bray 1999; Wasserstrom and Reider 1998; Williams 1997a).
10. The textile industry demonstrates these problems. Monitoring compliance with a diverse range of codes in the textile industry, where locations are widely scattered and/or where there is a large number of 'business partners', is costly and difficult. The existence of many codes leads to problems

of reliability, consistency and comprehensiveness across monitoring programs, and the possibility of fraud. Independent monitoring by a number of NGOs may lead to inconsistent interpretations and reports, while the provision of adequate funding remains a problem. Suggestions that one body, such as the ILO, monitors compliance presents enormous logistical difficulties, as the independent agency attempts to assess compliance with divergent codes by many different contractors (Hagen 1998, pp. 273–6; see also Frynas, Chapter 8 of this book).

11. Although the AIP Workplace Code is an NGO code for the clothing and apparel industry, the analogy holds true as the code is a type of private (but uniform) code internally adopted by TNCs.
12. *Mining and Environment Guidelines*, adopted at the International Round-table on Mining and the Environment, Berlin, 25–28 June 1991.
13. The Guiding Principles and Codes of Management Practice for the ACC are available from the ACC internet site http://www.americanchemistry.com.
14. In 1998, commitment to the Guiding Principles was a condition of membership in 12 national associations. In 1998, in 22 countries, over 80 per cent of corporate members of the national association had signed the Guiding Principles (ICCA 1998, Table 1).
15. Examples of NGO codes of conduct are: Amnesty International's Human Rights Guidelines for Companies; the MacBride Principles, which were designed to influence the activities of US companies operating in Northern Ireland; the Slepak Principles, which established a code of conduct in the field of human rights for American TNCs operating in the former Soviet Union; the Miller Principles, which sought to establish a code of conduct for TNCs operating in China and Tibet; and the 'Maquiladora Standards of Conduct', which were developed in response to concerns about pollution, unsafe working conditions and poverty-level wages in the *maquiladora* zone along the US–Mexico border.
16. By April 1998, 49 companies had reached agreement in some fashion to implement the MacBride Principles – 'to the extent they lawfully can do so' – of which 12 companies have since ended their ties with Northern Ireland, leaving 37 companies with agreements out of approximately 100 eligible companies (Perez-Lopez 1993, p. 40; McCrudden 1999, p. 194).

References

ACC. 2002. 'Management Systems Verification Participants List Through 1/2002', http://www.americanchemistry.com/.
ACC. 2001. *Responsible Care® News*, September 2001, http://www.americanchemistry.com.
ACC. 2000. 'Responsible Care® MSV – ISO 14001 Matrix', http://www.americanchemistry.com/.
API. 2001. *Environmental Stewardship Program Pledge for CAREFUL Operations*, http://api-ec.api.org/environ/.
Baade, Hans. 1979. 'The Legal Effects of Codes of Conduct for Multinational Enterprises', *German Yearbook of International Law* 22: 11–52.

Baker, Mark. 1993. 'Private Codes of Conduct: Should the Fox Guard the Henhouse?', *University of Miami Inter-American Law Review* 24(3): 399–433.

Bloomfield, Heidi. 1999. ' "Sweating" the International Garment Industry: a Critique of the Presidential Task Force's Workplace Codes of Conduct and Monitoring System', *Hastings International and Comparative Law Review* 22: 567–95.

Bray, John. 1999. 'Petroleum and Human Rights: the New Frontiers of Debate', *Oil and Gas Journal* (1 November): 65–9.

Cassel, Douglas. 1996. 'Corporate Initiatives: a Second Human Rights Revolution?', *Fordham International Law Journal* 19: 1963–84.

CERES. 1992. *Guide to the CERES Principles 2*, 'Introduction', reprinted in J. Andy Smith III. 1993. 'The CERES Principles: a Voluntary Code for Corporate Environmental Responsibility', *Yale Journal of International Law* 18: 307–17.

CERES. 2002. 'Endorsing Companies,' http://www.ceres.org/about/endorsing_companies.htm.

CMA (US). 1999. 'Public Advisory Panel Elements of Responsible Care', http://www.cmahq.com/responsiblecare.nsf/.

Cohen, Madeline. 1996. 'A New Menu for the Hard-Rock Cafe: International Mining Ventures and Environmental Cooperation in Developing Countries', *Stanford Environmental Law Journal* 15: 130–86.

Compa, Lance and Tashia Hinchliffe-Darricarrère. 1995. 'Enforcing Labour Rights through Corporate Codes of Conduct', *Columbia Journal of Transnational Law* 33: 663–89.

Conservation International. 1997. *Reinventing the Well: Approaches to Minimising the Environmental and Social Impact of Oil Development in the Tropics*. Washington: Conservation International.

Cueto, Santiago. 1997. 'Oil's Not Well in Latin America: Curing the Shortcomings of the Current International Environmental Law Regime in Dealing With Industrial Oil Pollution in Latin America through Codes of Conduct', *Florida Journal of International Law* 11(3): 585–611.

De George, Richard. 1997. ' "Sullivan-Type" Principles for U.S. Multinationals in Emerging Economies', *University of Pennsylvania Journal of International Economic Law* 18(4): 1193–210.

Dubin, Laurence. 1999. 'The Direct Application of Human Rights Standards to, and by, Transnational Corporations', *Review of the International Commission of Jurists* 61: 35–66.

European Parliament. 1999. *Resolution on European Union Standards for European Enterprises Operating in Developing Countries*, adopted 14 January 1999, *OJC* (Official Journal of the European Communities) 104 at 180.

Fatouros, A. 1981. 'On the Implementation of International Codes of Conduct: an Analysis of Future Experience', *American University Law Review* 30: 941–72.

Feld, W. 1980. *Multinational Corporations and U.N. Politics: the Quest for Codes of Conduct*. New York: Pergamon Press.

Fikentscher, Wolfgang. 1982. 'United Nations Codes of Conduct: New Paths in International Law', *American Journal of Comparative Law* 30: 577–604.

Gagnon, Georgette and John Ryle. 2001. 'Report of an Investigation into Oil Development, Conflict and Displacement in Western Upper Nile, Sudan'. Ottawa: Canadian Auto Workers Union, Steelworkers Humanity Fund, The

Simons Foundation, United Church of Canada, Division of World Outreach and World Vision Canada.

Gereffi, Gary, Ronie Garcia-Johnson and Erika Sasser. 2001. 'The NGO-Industrial Complex', *Foreign Policy* 125: 56–65.

Gunningham, Neil. 1995. 'Environment, Self-Regulation, and the Chemical Industry: Assessing Responsible Care', *Law and Policy* 17(1): 57–109.

Gunningham, Neil. 1998a. 'The Chemical Industry', in Neil Gunningham and Peter Grabosky, eds, *Smart Regulation: Designing Environmental Policy*. New York: Oxford University Press.

Gunningham, Neil. 1998b. 'Environmental Management Systems and Community Participation: Rethinking Chemical Industry Regulation', *University of California Los Angeles Journal of Environmental Law and Policy* 16(2): 319–98. Reprinted on-line by the Gale Group, at http://www.searchbank.com/searchbank/adelaide, 1–73.

Hagen, Katherine. 1998. 'Issues Involving Codes of Conduct from an ILO Perspective', *American Society of International Law Proceedings* 92: 267–77.

Hepple, Bob. 1999. 'A Race to the Top? International Investment Guidelines and Corporate Codes of Conduct', *Comparative Labor Law and Policy Journal* 20: 347–61.

ICCA. 1998. *Responsible Care® Status Report*, http://www.icca-chem.org/rcreport98/.

ICCA. 2000. *Responsible Care® Status Report*, http://www.icca-chem.org/rcreport/.

Krug, Nicole. 1998. 'Exploiting Child Labor: Corporate Responsibility and the Role of Corporate Codes of Conduct', *New York Law School Journal of Human Rights* 14: 651–76.

McCrudden, Christopher. 1999. 'Human Rights Codes for Transnational Corporations: What Can the Sullivan and MacBride Principles Tell Us?', *Oxford Journal of Legal Studies* 19: 167–201.

Ocran, T. 1986. 'Interregional Codes of Conduct for Transnational Corporations', *Connecticut Journal of International Law* 2: 121–48.

Ong, David. 1997. 'International Legal Developments in Environmental Protection: Implications for the Oil Industry', *Australasian Journal of Natural Resources Law and Policy* 4(1): 55–106.

Perez-Lopez, Jorge. 1993. 'Promoting International Respect for Worker Rights through Business Codes of Conduct', *Fordham International Law Journal* 17(1): 1–47.

Pink, Daniel. 1990. 'The Valdez Principles: Is What's Good for America Good for General Motors?', *Yale Law and Policy Review* 8: 180–95.

Pitt, Harvey and Karl Groskaufmanis. 1990. 'Minimizing Corporate Civil and Criminal Liability: a Second Look at Corporate Codes of Conduct', *Georgetown Law Journal* 78: 1559–654.

Porges, Jennifer. 1997. 'Codes of Conduct', *Asian Labour Update* 26: 1–5.

Rubin, Seymour. 1995. 'Transnational Corporations and International Codes of Conduct: a Study of the Relationship between International Legal Cooperation and Economic Development'. *American University Journal of International Law and Policy* 10(4): 1275–89 (reprint with Introduction); originally published. 1981. *American University Law Review* 30: 903–21.

Sanders, Peter. 1982. 'Implementing International Codes of Conduct for Multinational Enterprises', *American Journal of Comparative Law* 30: 241–54.

Smith, J. Andy III. 1993. 'The CERES Principles: a Voluntary Code for Corporate Environmental Responsibility', *Yale Journal of International Law* 18: 307–17.

Toftoy, Ryan. 1998. 'Now Playing: Corporate Codes of Conduct in the Global Theater. Is Nike Just Doing It?', *Arizona Journal of International and Comparative Law* 15(3): 905–29.

Trainor, Karen. 1997. 'Taking the Myth Out of Environmental Management Systems', *1997 Australian Mining and Petroleum Law Association Yearbook* 555–63.

United Nations. 2000. UN Sub-Commission on the Promotion and Protection of Human Rights, 'Proposed Draft Human Rights Code of Conduct for Companies', Working paper prepared by David Weissbrodt. E/CN.4/Sub.2/2000/WG.2/WP.1/Add.1 (25 May).

United Nations Secretariat. 1976. *Transnational Corporations: Issues Involved in the Formulation of a Code of Conduct*, UN Doc E/C.10/17, 20 July 1976. New York, United Nations.

Voon, Tania. 1999. 'Multinational Enterprises and State Sovereignty under International Law', *Adelaide Law Review* 21(2): 219–52.

Wälde, Thomas. 1992. 'Environmental Policies towards Mining in Developing Countries', *Journal of Energy and Natural Resources Law* 10(4): 327–57.

Wasserstrom, Robert and Susan Reider. 1998. 'Petroleum Companies Crossing New Threshold in Community Relations', *Oil and Gas Journal*, 14 December, 24–7.

Wells, Dick. 1997. 'Corporate Environmental Management Systems', *1997 Australian Mining and Petroleum Law Association Yearbook* 530–63.

Williams, Bob. 1997a. 'Foreign Petroleum Firms Developing New Paradigm for Operating in Rain Forest Region', *Oil and Gas Journal*, 21 April, 37–42.

Williams, Bob. 1997b. 'Oxy's Strategy on Environment, Community Issues Key to Success of Project in Ecuador's Rain Forest', *Oil and Gas Journal*, 21 April, 45–9.

Zondorak, Valerie. 1991. 'A New Face in Corporate Environmental Responsibility: the Valdez Principles', *Boston College Environmental Affairs Law Review* 18: 457–99.

4

Corporate Responsibility for Preventing Human Rights Abuses in Conflict Areas

Morton Winston

The majority of the violent conflicts during the past fifty years have been intra-state civil wars or armed rebellions, and in a significant number of cases such conflicts have been driven at least in part by revenues derived from natural resources such as oil or minerals. In countries such as Angola, Burma, Colombia, Indonesia, Nigeria and Sudan, governments or armed rebel groups have financed wars by revenues derived from gas and oil exploitation, and by black market diamonds and other minerals in the Democratic Republic of the Congo and Sierra Leone. When such conflicts erupt, corporations with legitimate business interests in the country often find that their reputations have been damaged through their association with the human rights abuses that accompany such conflicts. Company equipment and facilities have been used on some occasions by security forces to commit human rights violations, and revenues derived from their business operations have supported corrupt authoritarian regimes that systematically violate the human rights of their own citizens. The role of corporations, particularly transnational corporations (TNCs) in the oil and gas and mining industries, in relation to the causes of civil conflict, and their possible role in preventing and managing such conflicts, have recently become subjects of intense interest and controversy.

The present chapter seeks to address several questions within this larger debate, specifically: can business investment, particularly when it is directed towards the exploitation of buried natural resources, be regarded as a neutral, apolitical act that has no relationship to the causes of civil conflict and human rights abuses? Should TNCs embrace corporate social responsibility? Should businesses engage or disengage from

conflict zones, and what considerations should influence such decisions? When companies decide to remain engaged in countries experiencing civil conflict or serious patterns of human rights abuses, can they
play a constructive role in helping to prevent and resolve conflict?
If so, what should their role be? The discussion will move from an
analysis of the problem towards some possible constructive solutions to it,
emphasizing particularly some promising recent initiatives that involve
multi-stakeholder partnerships between TNCs, governments, and non-
governmental organizations (NGOs) representing civil society.

The exploitation of mineral wealth as a cause of violent conflict

Unlike light manufacturing industries, such as apparel, toys, and electronics, resource-based extractive industries have little choice about
where to go, but they do have a choice about *whether* to go, and about
the *manner* in which their business ventures are conducted. In the past,
many extractive industry companies have hoped that they could survive
and prosper despite the presence of social conflicts that their activities
help to create and fuel. But the world has changed. The social contract
between business and society is in the process of being renegotiated and
demands from civil society groups, from consumers, from some governments, and from intergovernmental organizations, have raised the
expectations about the role of companies, and have called into question
their very license to continue to operate in countries beset by violent
internal conflict. There is an active and broad-based social movement that
is demanding greater social and environmental responsibility on the part
of TNCs. This movement has been asking that corporations acknowledge
their social responsibilities to protect the environment and preserve
endangered species and ecosystems, to protect and promote human
rights, to contribute to sustainable development and social equity, and
to contribute to the maintenance of peace.

While many company managers in the extractive industries will say that
they are concerned about human rights and peace, they often follow such
attestations by claiming that their companies cannot do anything in such
situations because they are required to maintain 'political neutrality'
and may not interfere with the domestic politics of their host countries.
They often add that, by developing the oil and other mineral wealth of
these countries, their companies are contributing to economic growth that
will inevitably lead to a general improvement of life for everyone in the
community, and that is where their company's social responsibility ends.

Unfortunately, this rosy picture is contradicted by facts. The development of mineral resources in poor countries is one of the root causes of violent civil conflict and of the human rights abuses that frequently accompany it, a finding supported by various recent academic studies. Based on their econometric analysis, Collier and Hoeffler (1998, 2000) found that natural resource exports had the largest single influence on the risk of an outbreak of civil war, as these exports provided easily lootable resources which relied little on human cooperation. Case studies further demonstrate how, in some instances, firms may directly benefit from a conflict. Using the example of Angola, Frynas and Wood (2001) demonstrated how certain foreign oil firms gained competitive advantages vis-à-vis their commercial rivals by being associated with private security interests or by mediating financial deals for arms purchases. As specific firms may aggravate or even benefit from conflicts, their actions can hardly be regarded as politically neutral.

Geoffrey Chandler (2000), who was the head of Amnesty International's UK Business Group from 1991–2001, had this to say about the standard political neutrality and economic development arguments:

> The latter has to be seen against the background of a world of increasing international inequality and is demonstrably untrue in a number of countries where there has been no attempt to ensure equity in the distribution of oil wealth. One of the most detailed studies of the local impact of oil production in the context of conflict, by the UK Inter-Agency Group in Colombia in early 1999, reported that the development of oil in Casanare had brought no significant improvement to the lives of the poor who have 'suffered disproportionately from the increase in political violence and from environmental problems'. Political neutrality, other than in the sense of abstaining from interference with government or party politics, is not within a company's capability. The company's very presence is a factor in the situation. As a corporate citizen, silence and inactivity in the context of oppression and human rights violations will be taken as complicity with a regime which is economically supported by its activities. (p. 14)

To the extent that legitimate businesses are seen as profiting from conflict, corruption and human rights abuses, or are seen as providing the resources needed in order for these conflicts to continue, they will inevitably attract criticism from those elements of global civil society that see this kind of behavior as a violation of the terms of the emerging social contract between business and society. But this is only half right: in fact, the intervention of the TNC may well have been one of the major *causes* of the emergence of civil conflict.

Imagine for a moment that you are a member of an elite group living in a desperately poor and underdeveloped country, and you are suddenly told that the discovery of hidden oil, gas or other mineral deposits within your territory or off your shores is potentially worth billions of dollars. Naturally, you would want to exploit this once-in-a-lifetime opportunity. You might also want to make sure that your family gets a share of future revenues. The prospect of exploitation of oil and gas and mineral deposits has a well-known 'resource curse' effect (for a good review, see Ross 1999). Buried oil, gas or mineral wealth acts as a 'honey pot' that attracts corruption and stimulates conflicts among local elites seeking to line their own pockets at the expense of the welfare of the community. From the point of view of the managers of TNCs, the trick is to get a license to operate in this country by outbidding one's competitors. But in order to do this, one needs to do business with whatever government happens to be in power, whether or not it is democratically elected, corrupt, or respects human rights. As an outside party, if you demand that the government reform itself, you may lose the deal to your more unscrupulous competitors. So you make a deal knowing that the people you are dealing with may not be legitimate or may not have the best interests of their nations at heart. Other groups within the society soon begin to realize that they are being cut out of the deal. Competing elites jockey for power and to gain access to the revenues from natural resources. Secessionist movements may spring up seeking to wrest control over the resource-rich territory. Popular protests and civil conflicts will often follow and will tend to be accompanied by government repression and human rights violations. These abuses will stimulate some to take up arms and resist what they see as unjust oppression, which will in turn produce more repression, and a self-perpetuating cycle of violence will begin.

In an internal paper for the United Nations Department of Political Affairs, Yilma Makonnen (2000, pp. 4–5), makes the following observations:

> Despite monumental achievements in almost every area of human endeavor during the last decades, the prospect for greater international peace and security has regrettably been eroded by widespread violent conflict in many parts of the world... close examination of present-day intra-state violent conflict reveals that the underlying motive for these conflicts and the players involved, have changed. With the emergence of national and international non-state actors as

central and prominent players, it is becoming increasingly evident that many of the recent violent conflicts are *provoked by the desire to capture or control strategic resources*. National government elites, warlords, transnational corporations, financial institutions and international crime syndicates, such as drug traffickers, money-launderers, arms dealers and mercenaries, have become the new actors in violent intra-state conflicts. These changes have contributed to the increased complexity of the nature of violent conflict and presented the international community with the enormous challenge of confronting the issue of responsibility and of seeking appropriate solutions. (Emphasis added)

Companies can no longer afford to be silent witnesses to civil conflict and human rights abuses, because they often play a role in producing them. By offering the opportunity to transform poor countries into rich ones, TNCs engender conflict and corruption. This is the root reason why commercial activity of this kind cannot be viewed as apolitical. Since TNCs in the extractive industries can no longer pretend that their activities are politically neutral and typically lead to greater prosperity for all, they can also no longer avoid the ethical corollary that because they have a causal role in the genesis of social conflict, they also have a moral responsibility to help prevent it.

The corporate social responsibility movement

As Pegg noted in Chapter 1 of this book, the past decades have witnessed a broadening of the concept of corporate social responsibility (CSR). This was accompanied by the promotion of the 'triple bottom line' (TBL) approach by companies and NGOs (see Pegg, Chapter 1). However, while some TNCs have now 'turned the corner' on CSR, and have taken steps to acknowledge the responsibilities of 'corporate citizenship' (as I have argued elsewhere; Winston 2002), for the most part they have done so only after they have been publicly shamed for their silence or complicity. Shell was severely rebuked for its silence over the execution of Ken Saro-Wiwa in Nigeria and for its assent to the Abacha government's use of its Mobile Police to violently repress Ogoni and Ijaw demonstrators (see Frynas, Chapter 5 of this book). Under intense pressure from civil society groups, Shell amended its business principles in 1997 to include a commitment to uphold the principles of the Universal Declaration of Human Rights. BP was publicly embarrassed by revelations of its involvement with Colombian paramilitary forces in connection with its Casanare oil operations, and followed Shell in 1998 by adopting a human rights policy. According to a survey undertaken by the Communications Group (1997) on the attitudes of 250 major European companies, businesses are increasingly confronted by pressure groups on corporate responsibility issues, and most feel that pressure group activity is significantly affecting the conditions under which their company operates, often via government regulation brought about by NGO campaigns.

But while Shell, BP and several other extractive companies have now amended their corporate business philosophies to include an explicit commitment to the values and principles of the Universal Declaration of Human Rights, many other large companies have been publicly shamed for their involvement in human rights abuses but have resisted taking this step. Public pressure forced Amoco and ARCO (which are now both part of BP), Petro-Canada and Texaco (now part of Chevron Texaco) to withdraw from Burma in 1998, but TotalFinaElf and Unocal have stayed despite heavy criticism over their role in supporting the military government of Burma, specifically in connection with the construction of the Yadana gas pipeline (Larsen 1998). Talisman Energy of Calgary has been hammered in the Canadian media for its role in providing revenues to the government of Sudan that support its brutal war against rebel forces in the southern part of the country, but Talisman's CEO Jim Buckee continues to argue that they need to stay there, and the Canadian government has refused to impose sanctions that would force them to leave (Gagnon and Ryle 2001). In 2001, Chevron (now part of Chevron Texaco) came under criticism because of a $25 million payment to Chad, which was part of the deal enabling the construction of the Chad–Cameroon Pipeline to go forward, when President Debi turned round and immediately spent $4 million of the signing bonus to buy weapons. While Shell and Elf previously withdrew from Chad because of ethical and political concerns, the US majors Chevron Texaco and ExxonMobil continue to operate there despite criticism (for a briefing, see Guyer 2002). Indeed, at the present time not a single US-based transnational oil company has said publicly that its corporate ethos extends to its responsibility to protect human rights and to promote peace.[1]

By hunkering down and adopting a wait and see attitude, the US-based oil majors perhaps hope that these new demands will go away. Companies that have accepted the TBL approach reside mainly in the UK and Western Europe, creating something of a 'transatlantic divide'. The resistance to CSR on the part of many US corporations is based on several factors. First, there is a general pattern of American exceptionalism, the wariness many Americans have about entangling themselves in international agreements that can limit one's sovereignty, independence and freedom of action. Compared to other developed western nations, the US government has failed to adhere to a large number of international treaties and conventions on human rights and on other issues; the recent decision by the Bush Administration to withdraw the US signature to the Rome Convention of the International Criminal Court being only the latest in a rather long list of examples. The exceptionalist pattern of the US government sets a poor example for US-based TNCs whose managers likewise tend to be wary of international law, and in fact, are among the most powerful groups that consistently lobby the US government to remain detached from international agreements, except in the arena of trade and investment, where such agreements are often designed to protect their own interests. Exceptionalists believe that because America is the current global hegemon – the sole remaining 'Superpower' – the country does not need to play by the same rules that bind everyone else. This attitude springs from what Senator J. William Fulbright called 'the arrogance of power', and it is one of the reasons why America is so resented in many parts of the world.

Second, there is the greater litigiousness of American society, which leads to the fear on the part of many US-based TNCs that making public commitments with respect to their policies concerning human rights will make them legally liable for any failure to honor them. This kind of thinking is part of the general evasion of social accountability that infests many US corporations, as evidenced, for instance, by the collapse of Enron. If one of the largest US-based energy companies cannot even be trusted to be transparent and minimally honest to its own employees with respect to its financial accounts, what hope is there that it will be accountable for its social and environmental performance? The third factor is simply that many US-based TNCs are stuck within the old paradigm – the view that the only social responsibility of corporations is to make money for their shareholders, an idea supported by some influential US social scientists (see, for example, Friedman 1962). In addition, US oil majors were under little pressure from successive US administrations to change their behavior.

The emerging consensus within global civil society around the values of environmental quality and human rights, equitable development, and peace, and the social expectations they generate has evolved faster than the corporate response. As a result there is a gap between social expectations and corporate performance that is dangerous not only to the reputations of individual companies, but to the very legitimacy and long-term sustainability of the global economy. The expectations that society has for business have widened and will not contract, and global media communications and an active global civil society will leave transnational companies that fail to act responsibly with no place to hide. The ethics of corporate social responsibility and accountability constitute a feature of globalization that is not going to go away: it is only going to get stronger as more examples of corporate abuse come to light. Those companies that can move most quickly to close the gap between social expectations and corporate performance will be the ones that will advance and prosper in the global economy of the future. This is the essence of the 'business case' for corporate social responsibility.

Managing human rights risks

For those TNCs that have turned the CSR corner, the question is no longer '*Why* should we be socially responsible?' but '*How* should we be socially responsible?' This is where things really become interesting and challenging, for it is often difficult to translate words into action. One of the most basic challenges for TNCs in the extractive industries that are trying to practice CSR is whether or not to invest in countries with repressive governments. Businesses generally believe that investment and constructive engagement is a better way to influence governments to become more open and democratic and to respect human rights than withdrawal and isolation. Many NGOs take the opposite view and argue that some human rights abusing governments can only be influenced to change by means of intense economic and political pressure, and that investment in energy and mining enterprises runs the risk of aggravating an already bad situation while providing the government with revenues that can be used for repression. Which of these views is right? The best answer is probably that it depends on the specific characteristics of each case, the specific geopolitical context, and the specific role that the company is willing to play in such situations. In some cases, it may clearly be wiser for a given company to stay out of a given country at a given time. It is far less costly to avoid a bad investment than to have to bail out of it later, and the dilemma of engagement or withdrawal is much more difficult to solve when one already has large sunk costs. In the end, these kinds of decisions rest on managerial judgments based on risk–reward analyses. All too often, however, corporate managers have not sufficiently factored in the human rights risks involved in investing in countries with repressive governments. This is despite the fact that there may be good business reasons to protect corporate reputations.

Amnesty International and the Prince of Wales International Business Leaders Forum (2002) recently released a report on the risks that companies face when they operate in zones of conflict or in countries with poor human rights records. This is the most comprehensive examination of these issues to date, and provides information about human rights risks affecting major transnationals in several industry sectors: extractive, food and beverage, pharmaceutical and chemical, infrastructure and utilities, heavy manufacturing and defense, and IT hardware and telecommunications, based upon data obtained from Amnesty country reports over the past several years.[2] The categories of human rights abuses that are covered include torture, disappearance, extrajudicial execution, hostage-taking, harassment of human rights defenders, denial of freedom of assembly and association, forced labor, bonded labor, child labor, forcible relocation, arbitrary arrest and detention, discrimination against women, and denial of freedom of expression. The risk map focusing on the extractive sector highlights three major kinds of human rights risks that extractive industries often have to face: (1) relationships with abusive security forces, exemplified by BP in Colombia and Talisman in Sudan; (2) failure to respect land rights and rights to participation in decision-making of indigenous peoples, exemplified by Occidental Petroleum and the U'wa people in Northeast Colombia, and Freeport-McMoRan and the Amungme people of Papua, Indonesia; (3) forced labor abuses, for instance, associated with Unocal in Burma; and (4) complicity in third-party abuses, as exemplified by the lawsuit against Shell in regard to the company's role in the execution of Ken Saro-Wiwa by the military government of General Sani Abacha in Nigeria in 1995.[3]

The risk maps provide correlations between the presence of extractive industry majors in countries that have been experiencing these and other serious human rights abuses. While not intended to be comprehensive, the countries highlighted include Algeria, Angola, Australia, Brazil, China, Colombia, Democratic Republic of the Congo, India, Indonesia, Iran, Kazakstan, Malaysia, Mexico, Myanmar (Burma), Nigeria, the Philippines, Russia, Saudi Arabia, Sudan, Turkey and the US. The companies that are exposed to various categories of human rights risks in these and other countries include Alcoa, Anglo American, BG, BHP Billliton, BP, ChevronTexaco, ENI, ExxonMobil, Norsk Hydro, Repsol, Rio Tinto, Schlumberger, Shell and TotalFinaElf, among others. The desire to exploit natural resources by legitimate business interests often involves them in human rights abuses, particularly when they are located in countries experiencing civil conflict, or which have oppressive and corrupt governments. Significant costs are associated with acts of sabotage, lost production, extortion, kidnapping, security provision, higher insurance costs, and risk to reputation. In many cases, corruption accompanies the exploitation of mineral and oil wealth in these countries as corrupt government officials skim off much of the revenues generated; while the local communities most affected are left with environmental damage, loss of sustainable livelihoods, and government repression. While these risk maps are useful in highlighting broad patterns of human rights risks, they focus on cases in which companies are already invested in countries that are known to have poor human rights records, and as such, do not provide much guidance as to whether or not a particular company should invest in a particular country, nor what the company should do when it finds itself deeply invested in a country that is descending into civil conflict.

The discussion of specific cases and specific roles for the private sector actors in countries experiencing civil conflict was significantly advanced by the publication of *The Business of Peace: the Private Sector as a Partner in Conflict Prevention and Resolution* (Nelson 2000). This manual, which was jointly published by the Prince of Wales International Business Leaders Forum, International Alert and the Council on Economic Priorities, provides a detailed roadmap for companies that are convinced that they can no longer afford to ignore the causes and costs of destructive social conflicts, and which have taken creative and constructive steps, in partnership with NGOs, governments, and intergovernmental organizations such as the UN, in finding solutions to conflict in various parts of the world. It provides a detailed analysis of management issues, roles and dilemmas, as well as discussion of several actual cases in which companies have stepped up to the plate on issues of this kind, and how they have done it. The report makes it clear that no one expects that business leaders will substitute for diplomats and NGO activists – but it argues persuasively and in depth that business leaders can function as partners in conflict resolution and peacemaking along with these other actors.

The report is far too long and detailed to be accurately summarized in this chapter, but I would like briefly to highlight some of the main conclusions and recommendations that it makes with respect to corporate engagement in conflict prevention and conflict resolution. First, the report argues that, 'In today's global economy [companies] have a growing commercial rationale for playing this role, in order to avoid the direct and indirect business costs of conflict and to reap the business benefits of peace. They also have a moral imperative and a leadership responsibility, given the increasingly central position of the private sector as decision-makers and influencers at the national and international levels' (p. 11). Second, in terms of their engagement strategies, the report argues that businesses must 'move beyond strategies of compliance and risk minimization, although these are necessary "starting-points". Their goal should be to pursue strategies of pro-active, systematic value-creation, aimed at creating positive value for as many stakeholder groups as possible, including, but not exclusively, shareholders.' Companies can create value for society in three main areas of corporate activity or influence: their core business operations, their social investment and philanthropic programs, and through their engagement in public policy dialogue, advocacy and institution building. Third, companies can engage with each other in collective actions that may be too risky or inappropriate for single corporations to conduct, and they can engage in cross-sector partnerships between business, government and civil society organizations that 'will be absolutely crucial in building peace and preventing and resolving conflict' (p. 12). Finally, companies can provide leadership at the local, national and international levels that will help to shape 'the values, rules, and norms of the society and the way its citizens accept, interpret, and implement these'.

The report provides specific guidance as to how companies can employ each of these types of engagement strategies in countries that are conflict prone, currently experiencing conflict, or in a post-conflict reconstruction phase. Among the various specific suggestions the report makes are that companies can help strengthen local economies by lobbying governments for more equitable distributions of the economic benefits that their business operations generate; they can use their influence to increase the amount of money spent on building the human capital of the society, for instance, on education and training and on the provision of health, public health, and nutrition services; they can help to address persistent problems of poverty and economic marginalization of minorities and under-represented groups; they can encourage good governance practices and greater transparency in government; and they can support the passage of human rights and environmental treaties and laws that create public goods for the local, national and global society. In addition to social investment and policy dialogue, companies can engage with other sectors in multi-track diplomatic efforts designed to prevent or resolve conflicts, and support economic transitions from wartime to peacetime economies.

But the report takes pains to stress that, 'In the vast majority of conflict situations the business community has neither the skills, nor the resources or mandate to act alone. One of the most important actions that the private sector can take in such situations is to explore the potential for working together with other sectors, both government and civil society' (p. 120). The report also notes that, 'Anecdotal evidence, supported by a small but growing body of empirical research, suggests that such partnerships can provide added value to both their participants and society-at-large', but that many of these sorts of partnerships 'face substantial practical and strategic challenges ... [including] ... bridging diversity in terms of the participants' different objectives, operating processes and time-scales, to issues such as addressing power imbalances, assessing the value-added of such partnerships and responding to concerns about representation and legitimacy' (p. 120). The bottom line for progressive companies that are trying to practice a socially responsible approach is not that they must *withdraw* from involving themselves in social issues, but rather that they need to *engage* with those governments, NGOs and intergovernmental organizations that are working to bring about peace and social justice, and cooperate with these other actors in devising solutions to social problems.

Rethinking the role of TNCs in resolving conflicts

Not everyone agrees that transnational oil companies are the appropriate agents to bring about the reform of corrupt authoritarian governments, greater protection of human rights and the resolution of internal conflicts. Marina Ottaway (2001) compares the current push to use business enterprises as vehicles for social improvement to the Charter Companies of the seventeenth century, such as the Dutch East India Company, but she questions whether it is desirable or wise for private corporations to play the role of political and moral reformers:

> First, they are not the right organizations for furthering moral causes. Oil companies may be 'organs of society', but they are highly specialized ones, and their strengths lie not in devotion to democracy and human rights but in finding, extracting, and distributing oil ... Second, the concept of oil-company executives lecturing developing-country officials on human rights and democratic governance is jarring because it evokes an image from a past that should not be restored: charter-company officials who saw themselves as agents of civilizations in distant countries 'not ruled by Christian kings' (as they were described during that era). All that's missing are the pith helmets ... Finally, trying to put oil companies in the role of

reformers creates a process where nobody wants to take responsibility. The so-called partnership between NGOs, developed countries, and transnational corporations is beginning to look like a game in which each actor tries to pass the hot potato of reforming reluctant governments to somebody else. Neither the U.S. government, the World Bank, nor the human rights NGOs could convince the military regime in Nigeria to mend its ways in the past and cannot force change in Myanmar or Sudan today. So they saddle the oil companies with the task. (Ottaway 2001, p. 53)

Ottaway's misgivings about casting transnational oil companies as merchants of morality in the developing world deserve careful examination. Certainly NGOs like Amnesty International would not wish to see oil companies begin mounting campaigns for the protection of human rights in the public media. It is already problematic when governments employ the rhetoric of human rights in their public diplomacy, since most governments employ human rights selectively as a political tool to be used against their political adversaries, while under-representing the poor human rights records of their allies, and, of course, denying that their own governments are guilty of human rights abuses. Companies can be expected to adopt a similar selective public posture in order to enhance their public reputations with respect to their competitors, while continuing to make deals behind closed doors that may lead to human rights or environmental abuses. Besides, as Ottaway suggests, there is no reason to believe that human rights or environmental campaigning is something that oil and mining transnationals are any good at. Without the necessary expertise, and a serious commitment to political impartiality and objectivity that is the hallmark of the best human rights and environmental advocacy NGOs, companies that venture into the field of advocacy politics are likely to make a mess of it, and their efforts risk degrading the discourse of human rights like their 'greenwashing' undermines the environmental movement. The image of oil executives lecturing officials of developing country governments about the need to protect human rights and environmental quality does indeed have an unsavory taste to it, particularly when the messengers represent companies whose own records are less than stellar and where the issues that are being raised have little direct bearing on the company's business interests and operations in the country. Oil company executive diplomacy should not be used as a substitute for traditional kinds of intergovernmental dialogue conducted by trained professional diplomats. Neither is it appropriate in most cases for oil companies to attempt to provide social services and public goods that the local governments should be providing. In some countries, transnationals build roads, schools and health clinics, and provide other kinds of services, for instance, micro-credit lending agencies, designed to benefit the local communities in the vicinities of their operations. But is this the proper role for corporations? It usurps the responsibility of government, and has the appearance of returning us to the era of charter companies of the past. On the other hand, should companies simply pass the buck on such issues back to ineffective governments that are either unwilling or unable to provide these kinds of services themselves?

Questions of this kind are arising because the roles of governments, corporations and civil society organizations are changing within an emerging multi-stakeholder system of global governance. Services that were once viewed as the responsibility of governments are being privatized under the influence of neoliberal economic philosophies; some NGOs are taking up the role of protecting worker's rights that was formerly seen as the exclusive province of trade unions and their motives for doing so are being questioned; and TNCs are being urged to 'be part of the solution' to urgent social problems of conflict resolution, human rights protection and protecting environmental quality. As the terms of the social contract are being renegotiated the roles usually associated with these different categories of political and economic actors are becoming blurred and confused. In this transition period what is needed is an honest effort by all parties to clarify the boundaries and to define the respective roles and responsibilities of government, businesses and civil society in this emerging system of global governance. There needs to be a new division of moral labor, but one in which the respective roles and responsibilities of businesses, governments and civil society organizations are clearly distinguished and defined. Failing this there will continue to be role confusion and diffusion of responsibility, and the drive to give economic globalization a human face will end in failure.

There are, however, some positive examples of initiatives in which businesses, government officials and NGOs have worked together to negotiate and create solutions to social problems, particularly in the field of conflict prevention and resolution. By examining several of these initiatives it is possible to discern some models of how multi-stakeholder partnerships can provide useful solutions to social and environmental problems. The United Nations Global Compact has sponsored a series of dialogues involving TNCs, government representatives and NGOs that aims to provide useful case studies which illustrate how these emerging partnerships can work. The first of these dialogues took place in April 2001 and the second a year later.[4] There were four working groups, dealing with revenue sharing, transparency, conflict impact assessment and risk management, and multi-stakeholder partnerships. The report on multi-stakeholder partnerships included discussions of several cases. As an illustration, I will briefly summarize one of these, the US–UK Voluntary Principles on Security and Human Rights.

On 20 December 2000, the governments of the US and the UK announced that agreement had been reached on a set of voluntary principles designed to prevent human rights abuses by security forces such as those in Nigeria in the mid-1990s. The principles deal with the use by companies of private security forces to protect their property and employees, and with their relationship with government security forces operating in the regions where they have facilities. Among these guidelines are ones that state that companies will not employ security forces that have been known to commit human rights abuses, that they will attempt to employ private security personnel drawn from the local population, and that all reported instances of human rights abuse will be recorded and investigated. The eight companies that endorsed or welcomed these principles were the oil companies, BP, Chevron, Conoco, Shell and Texaco, and the mining companies, Freeport-McMoRan, Copper & Gold Inc. and Rio Tinto. The NGOs which officially welcomed the commitments were Amnesty International, Business for Social Responsibility, Council on Economic Priorities, Fund for Peace, Human Rights Watch, International Alert, the International Federation of Chemical, Energy, Mine and General Workers' Unions, Lawyers Committee for Human Rights, and the Prince of Wales Business Leaders Forum. These companies and NGOs were members of the contact group that negotiated these principles, but the initiative was launched and managed by the Bureau of Democracy, Human Rights and Labor of the US Department of State, and the British Foreign Office. This is an example of an instance in which the three sectors cooperated in developing a constructive response to the problem of preventing human rights abuses in conflict situations.

However, none of the parties to this effort were completely satisfied with the results. A spokesperson for Amnesty International was reported as saying that while the principles were, 'encouraging steps in the right direction ... we are concerned that these are voluntary in nature and we will continue to push for a regulatory framework and independently verifiable monitoring. We are hopeful that companies will engage with this process' (Wright 2000). Harold Koh, then the US Assistant Secretary of State for human rights, admitted that the principles were only a starting point, 'At this stage, these principles are a voluntary agreement between two governments and a number of leading companies and NGOs (non-governmental organizations) and a labor union. Nevertheless, we hope and expect they'll be seen as the emerging global standard for strengthening human rights safeguards in the energy sector around the world.' I happen to know from my personal involvement in this initiative that the deal almost did not come off: several of the companies and several of the NGOs involved were reluctant fully to support these voluntary principles, and the announcement was delayed for several weeks while behind-the-scenes negotiations continued on compromise language.[5] Nevertheless, in the end an agreement was reached.

Since the announcement in late 2000, work has continued on this initiative, despite the change in administration in the US. Several more European companies have now endorsed and adopted these guidelines, and the terms of reference have been expanded to include countries other than Nigeria, in particular, Cameroon, Chad, Colombia, Equatorial Guinea and Indonesia. The current Assistant Secretary of State for Democracy, Human Rights, and Labor, Lorne Craner, has committed his bureau to continue to develop these principles and is encouraging other US TNCs to join in adopting them. In a recent speech (Craner 2001), he outlined several roles that governments can play in promoting corporate social responsibility. I quote his remarks in part:

> We have an important role in supporting and facilitating public–private efforts to promote corporate responsibility. This does not mean dictating what should be done. Rather it means bringing seemingly disparate groups together for serious efforts to address mutually recognized problems... Facilitating a dialogue implies, however, a certain degree of openness. Civil society, including business, academics, NGOs and unions, must be willing to work together. Some of the problems facing businesses today have no easy answer nor do they have a one sided answer. Solutions crafted by all the interested stakeholders are often the most informed, credible, and enduring.

Multi-stakeholder dialogues are often difficult and time-consuming processes, but when they succeed they produce outcomes that have social legitimacy as well as practical relevance. In addition to openness and a willingness to face mutual problems, the success of these initiatives depends a great deal on the willingness of all interested parties to compromise. The way forward for socially responsible corporations lies in their willingness to participate in such multi-stakeholder dialogues, and to work with civil society organizations and governments in negotiating solutions to specific problems.

Bringing global corporations onto the 'third side'

Negotiation is something that business executives understand, but is sometimes a challenge for NGOs which are not as used to working in partnerships, striking deals and making concessions in order to achieve compromises acceptable to all parties. William Ury (1999, p. 17), who wrote about using negotiation skills to resolve political conflicts, argued that every conflict involves not two but three sides. The 'third side' to every conflict consists of actors, from either inside or outside the community at risk, who have in common that they are *people* who use 'a certain kind of *power* – the power of peers – from a certain *perspective* – of common ground – supporting a certain *process* – of dialogue and nonviolence – and aiming for a certain *product* – a "triple win" '. Both of the main parties to the conflict get something they want, and the larger society – national, regional and global – gets a peaceful and secure environment in which to conduct business and pursue development. The key skills that third-siders bring to the table are *negotiation skills*. In fact, Ury thinks that we are in the midst of a 'Negotiation Revolution' in which organizations of all types are being transformed from 'top-down' command and control pyramidal structures, to networked self-organizing systems in which everyone ends up negotiating everything. This transformation, he argues, is bringing humankind back to our original *modus vivendi*, the one we followed for millions of years as so-called primitive hunter-gathers before the agricultural revolution some 10,000 years ago. In an information-based economy where knowledge is the principal source of wealth and power, we are all reverting to a hunter-gather lifestyle in which we 'hunt and gather' information, rather than nuts and berries, for our livelihoods. As a result, Ury (1999, p. 109) says, 'many of the social conditions that helped our nomadic hunter-gather ancestors learn to coexist appear to be reemerging today. The Knowledge Revolution offers us the most promising opportunity in ten thousand years to create a co-culture of coexistence, cooperation, and constructive conflict'. In terms of Ury's analysis, one can reframe the message of the corporate social responsibility movement as saying to global corporations, in effect – 'Join us on the third-side.' Contrary to Ottaway's suggestion, there is reason to believe that doing so is not only in the long-term interest of businesses, but that negotiation is also something that business executives are good at.

But in order for these types of negotiations to succeed, both NGOs and TNCs will need to overcome stereotypes about one another. NGO activists are traditionally suspicious of the motives of business and are used to working in a confrontational, campaigning mode that tends to undermine social cohesion and damages the trust needed for multi-stakeholder partnerships to succeed. The business community tends to view NGOs as 'trouble-makers' and as unreliable partners. Both corporations and NGOs have reputations to protect, and both feel uncomfortable getting too close to the other side. Over the past several years, through the efforts of various companies and NGOs who have been willing to take the risk of engaging in dialogue with one another, steps have been taken to break down these stereotypes and some measure of trust is being established. Further progress can be made if companies become more transparent in reporting what they are doing in the field of social and environmental responsibility, and not just in glossy brochures and expensive public relations campaigns, but through verifiable third-party social audits of their activities against generally accepted performance indicators and performance benchmarks. The Global Reporting Initiative, Social Accountability's SA8000 workplace standards, and the UN Global Compact, are steps in this direction, but more companies need to get involved in these initiatives and report their activities in the field in a more credible and transparent fashion.

At the same time more NGOs need to understand the potential benefits of engagement with the private sector, and to develop new skills and new forms of activism that move them away from the 'naming and shaming' tactics that they have mainly used in the past. Amnesty International has been one of the leading human rights NGOs taking this path. To quote Sir Geoffrey Chandler again on AI's decision to adopt the corporate engagement strategy, 'A fundamental decision was whether to spend scarce resources in looking for company violations, or to influence fundamental company principles and practice which could be applicable to the entirety of their operations. We chose the latter ... [although] we did not abandon public protest, which remains an important weapon in the wings. But protest is a means to an end, not an end in itself. Protest is relatively easy, engagement difficult' (cited in Nelson 2000, p. 136). Protest politics and moral stigmatization by NGOs and some media organizations have been the main drivers of the corporate social responsibility movement to date. But as more business executives come to understand the benefits of CSR and recognize that their power and position in society gives them certain moral responsibilities, it is possible, perhaps even likely, that more companies will integrate CSR into their business strategies, come over to the third side, and so become part of the solution to preventing civil conflict and human rights abuses, rather than remaining silent witnesses.

Notes

1. On 20 November 2001 Amnesty International USA filed a shareholder resolution with ExxonMobil Corporation, the world's largest oil and gas company, asking that it adopt a 'comprehensive and verifiable human rights policy, which shall include an explicit commitment to support and uphold the principles and values contained in the Universal Declaration of Human Rights'. A number of large pension funds and investment firms joined Amnesty in filing this resolution. The company has recently indicated that it intended to advise its shareholders to vote against this resolution. Nevertheless, at the ExxonMobil Annual Shareholder meeting in Dallas, Texas on 29 May 2002, 6.8 per cent of shareholders voted for this resolution, more than enough to bring the measure back for another two years. For more information on this shareholder campaign see the Shareholder Action Network, http://www.shareholderaction.org site, and the Amnesty International USA site: http://www.aiusa.org/.
2. The companies included in the study were restricted to those in the FTSE 100 UK, the top 100 members of the FTSE Eurotop 300 ex-UK, and the top 100 members of the FTSE All-World North American index as of June 2001. The report does not address other sectors such as footwear and apparel, logging, agriculture, tourism or finance.
3. On 5 March 2002 a US Federal Court ruled that a civil lawsuit charging transnational oil giant Shell with complicity in human rights violations will go forward. The ruling in *Wiwa v. Royal Dutch Petroleum Company and Shell Transport and Trading Company, PLC* by Judge Kimba Wood held that Royal Dutch/Shell could be held liable in the US for cooperating in the persecution and execution of environmental activists in Nigeria. The court refused to dismiss the lawsuit brought by surviving relatives of Ken Saro-Wiwa and John Kpuinen, which alleges that Shell played a role in the execution of the two men as well as other violations. The court also refused to dismiss similar claims against Brian Anderson, the former head of Shell's Nigerian subsidiary, and claims by an additional plaintiff, who remains anonymous for her safety, alleging that she was beaten and shot while peacefully protesting the bulldozing of her land by Shell. Information available online: http://www.earthrights.org/shell/.
4. Available online: http://www.unglobalcompact.org/.
5. Bennett Freeman, who was the principal convener of this initiative for the US Department of State, also discusses this case. See United Nations Global Compact (2002).

References

Amnesty International UK and the Prince of Wales International Business Leaders Forum. 2002. 'Business and Human Rights: a Geography of Corporate Risk'. London: Amnesty International. Available online at http://www.humanrightsrisk.org.

Chandler, Geoffrey. 2000. 'The Responsibilities of Oil Companies', in Eide Asbjørn, Helge Ole Bergesen and Pia Rudolfson Goyer, eds, *Human Rights and the Oil Industry*. Antwerper: Intersentia.

Collier, P. and A.E. Hoeffler. 1998. 'On the Economic Causes of Civil War', *Oxford Economic Papers* 50: 563–73.

Collier, P. and A.E. Hoeffler. 2000. 'Greed and Grievance in Civil War', Policy Research Working Paper 2355. Washington, DC: World Bank.

Communications Group. 1997. 'Putting the Pressure on: the Rise of Pressure Activism in Europe: a Survey of the Attitudes of Major Companies across Europe towards Pressure Groups and Activists', The Communications Group plc, London.

Craner, Lorne W. 2001. 'Privatizing Human Rights: the Roles of Government, Civil Society and Corporations'. Remarks to the Business for Social Responsibility Conference. Seattle, Washington, November 8.

Friedman, Milton. 1962. *Capitalism and Freedom*. Chicago: University of Chicago Press.

Frynas, Jedrzej George and Geoffrey Wood. 2001. 'Oil and War in Angola', *Review of African Political Economy* 28(90): 587–606.

Gagnon, Georgette and John Ryle. 2001. 'Report of an Investigation into Oil Development, Conflict and Displacement in Western Upper Nile, Sudan'. Ottawa: Canadian Auto Workers Union, Steelworkers Humanity Fund, The Simons Foundation, United Church of Canada, Division of World Outreach and World Vision Canada.

Guyer, Jane I. 2002. 'Briefing: the Chad–Cameroon Petroleum and Pipeline Development Project', *African Affairs* 101(402): 109–15.

Larsen, Jensine. 1998. 'Crude Investment: the Case of the Yadana Pipeline in Burma', *Bulletin of Concerned Asian Scholars* 30(3): 3–13.

Makonnen, Yilma. 2000. 'Natural Resource Based Violent Intra-State Conflict: Towards the Development of Social Responsibility Guidelines for Non-State Actors in Conflict Prevention and Peace-Building'. New York: United Nations Department of Political Affairs.

Nelson, Jane. 2000. *The Business of Peace: the Private Sector as a Partner in Conflict Prevention and Resolution*. London: The Prince of Wales International Business Leaders Forum, International Alert, and Council on Economic Priorities.

Ottaway, Marina. 2001. 'Reluctant Missionaries', *Foreign Policy* (July/August): 44–54.

Ross, Michael L. 1999. 'The Political Economy of the Resource Curse', *World Politics* 51(2): 297–322.

United Nations Global Compact. 2002. 'Policy Dialogue on Business in Zones of Conflict: Case Studies of Multistakeholder Partnership'. New York: United Nations.

Ury, William. 1999. *Getting to Peace: Transforming Conflict at Home, at Work, and in the World*. New York: Viking Press.

Winston, Morton. 2002. 'NGO Strategies for Promoting Corporate Social Responsibility', *Ethics and International Affairs* 16(1): 71–87.

Wright, Jonathan. 2000. 'Oil, Mining Firms Adopt Human Rights Principles'. London: Reuters.

5
The Oil Industry in Nigeria: Conflict between Oil Companies and Local People

Jedrzej George Frynas

The Nigerian oil industry received extensive international media coverage following the execution of Ken Saro-Wiwa in 1995. As leader of the Movement for the Survival of the Ogoni People (MOSOP), Saro-Wiwa denounced the Nigerian government and the transnational oil corporations – especially Royal Dutch/Shell – for having caused considerable environmental and social damage to the Ogoni people, while providing few benefits in return. While the intensity of Ogoni campaigns decreased after Saro-Wiwa's execution, other ethnic and political groups across the Niger Delta – especially the Ijaw ethnic group – mounted major protests directed against oil operations.

A frequent response of the government to anti-oil protests was the use of repressive security measures. International human rights organizations such as Human Rights Watch provided detailed evidence of extra-judicial killings, rapes, arrests and floggings of anti-oil protesters.[1] Activists from human rights and environmental organizations advocating the rights of the oil-producing communities also faced regular harassment from the authorities. This included arbitrary arrests, intimidation and beatings (Human Rights Watch 1999a, pp. 131–3). In dealing with anti-oil protests, the Nigerian authorities used regular units of the police and the army as well as the navy. The authorities also created special units of the security forces, consisting of the police and the military, to deal with anti-oil protests, such as the Rivers State Internal Security Task Force in 1994 (Human Rights Watch 1995, p. 14).

That the Nigerian state committed severe human rights abuses against anti-oil protesters is well documented. It is less obvious to what extent oil companies were directly or indirectly responsible for human rights abuses. Various pressure groups maintained that Shell (the biggest oil producer in Nigeria) and the other foreign oil companies were directly or indirectly involved in human rights violations, but the companies themselves deny any such complicity.[2] Shell's Deputy Managing Director in Nigeria – Egbert Imomoh – reportedly said at a hearing of a human rights panel in February 2001 that 'We completely reject all accusations of the abuse of human rights.'[3] This chapter attempts to assess the human rights impact of oil operations by focusing on conflicts between the local people and the oil companies in the Niger Delta where the bulk of oil production takes place.

Human rights violations in the Niger Delta were scrupulously studied by the Human Rights Violations Investigation Commission under the chairmanship of Justice Chukwudifu Oputa (also known as the Oputa Panel), which was established by the current Obasanjo administration with the mandate to investigate human rights abuses of previous Nigerian regimes. However, the Oputa Panel's human rights focus was very narrow, which prevented a complete discussion of human rights abuses against the Ogonis and other ethnic groups in the Niger Delta. When it convened a meeting on human rights abuses in the Niger Delta in January 2001, it disclosed that it was only concerned with two political rights: the right to personal liberty and the right to dignity of the person. All cases under investigation were categorized as murders/assassinations; abductions, torture, inhuman and degrading treatment; harassment and intimidation; prolonged detention (with or without trial); employment related issues; and attempted assassinations (Ndujihe 2001). This book conceptualizes human rights to be much broader, so – in addition to political rights – I will discuss economic and social rights and environmental rights.

I start by outlining the background to the conflicts between oil TNCs and the local people in Nigeria. The main part of the chapter is divided into a discussion of violations of political, environmental and economic and social rights. Evidence is provided from unpublished documents as well as secondary sources.

Evolution of conflicts in the oil industry

An explanation of human rights abuses must be sought in the development of oil operations and conflicts between the local people and the oil companies. While the anti-oil protests of the 1990s were relatively recent, the seeds of conflicts were sown in the early years of oil production.

Oil production in Nigeria started in December 1957 with a joint venture between the two major British oil companies, Shell and BP, and by the mid-1960s other foreign oil companies had commenced oil production. When Nigeria gained independence from Britain in 1960, crude oil production was still rather insignificant but it rose from 20,000 barrels/day (b/d) in 1960 to 540,000 b/d in 1969.[4] From then on, production increased steadily, reaching over 2,000,000 b/d in 1973, a similar production level to the late 1990s. However, the rate of Nigeria's oil production fluctuated: high points in 1974 and 1979 were followed by a decline in production between 1980 and 1983, in line with the decline in world market demand. With the introduction of better financial terms for oil companies in 1986 and 1991, and due to rising worldwide demand, Nigerian oil production began once again to rise quickly from the late 1980s onwards (Frynas 2000a, pp. 16–17).

The intensification of oil and gas exploration and production activity from the early 1970s increased the physical presence of oil companies in the oil-producing areas and thus contact with the local people. At the same time, the government and the oil companies failed to keep under control the mounting adverse effects of oil operations. This in turn increased the probability of conflicts with the local people. Rising oil production from the late 1980s was indeed followed by anti-oil protests in the Niger Delta, particularly in the Ogoni area.

As the oil industry developed, the Nigerian political landscape changed. The rise of the oil industry and the simultaneous relative decline of the agricultural sector made Nigeria's hard currency receipts almost exclusively dependent on a single commodity – crude oil. As a consequence, the interests of oil companies came to play a much greater role in government policy than the interests of farming and fishing communities in the Niger Delta and elsewhere. In this context, it is perhaps not surprising that the development of the oil industry took precedence over the interests of the local people.

The surge in oil revenues in the early 1970s coincided with increased centralization of political power in Nigeria. Until 1967, Nigeria was divided into semi-autonomous regions with considerable executive powers. During the 1967–70 civil war, Nigeria was transformed into a federation of 12 states (today 36 states), which effectively amplified the power of the central government. With regard to the oil industry, the centralization of power meant that the affairs of the local people became increasingly remote from the decision-makers in the oil industry. Two events symbolize this shift: the creation of the Nigerian National Oil Corporation (NNOC) in 1971 and the promulgation of the Land Use Act 1978.

The NNOC (which became the Nigerian National Petroleum Corporation – NNPC – in 1977) became a joint-venture partner with the foreign oil companies in Nigeria. From 1971, the government gradually set up joint ventures with oil exploration and production companies in Nigeria and acquired shareholdings in these ventures. By July 1979, the government, through the NNPC, had acquired a 60 per cent ownership in all the major foreign oil companies except for the production-sharing agreement with Ashland and the Tenneco-Mobil-Sunray venture (Frynas 2000a, pp. 31–2). The foreign oil companies retained day-to-day operational control of the joint ventures, but the Nigerian federal government became involved in key decision-making. The same oil companies thus continued their exploration and production activities in village communities, but they worked much more closely with the government than before.

The Land Use Act 1978 redefined the legal position on land ownership in Nigeria. The Act empowered state governors to acquire any land on behalf of private oil companies. At the same time, rent for land acquired for oil operations was to be paid directly to the governor and no longer to the community, as was the case before 1978. The payment of rent to the governor rather than to the actual landowners is likely to have increased dissatisfaction with oil operations in the oil producing areas.[5] Indeed, among the key demands of Nigerian pressure groups today are the abolition of the Land Use Act and, more fundamentally, the control of natural resources by the local people.[6]

These developments exemplify the way in which centralization of federal power in conjunction with the greater government role in oil industry affairs resulted in a closer relationship between the oil companies and the federal government from the 1970s, while, at the same time, the affairs of the local people became increasingly remote from the decision-makers in the oil industry.

The oil companies were partly caught up in a conflict between the local people and the Nigerian government. The oil-producing areas had been neglected by successive administrations, and resource allocation in Nigeria had been biased against the interests of the people in the oil-producing areas throughout the country's history. This was a key issue, since the most widespread demand of protesters in oil-producing areas was that a significant proportion of the oil revenues should be returned to their areas on the basis of the derivation principle (Suberu 1996, pp. 29–31). Derivation means that a fixed proportion of the revenues collected in a local area should be retained in that area. In this way, local people in oil-producing areas believe that they could benefit from the oil wealth under their land.

The Nigerian government significantly increased its contributions to oil-producing areas in the 1990s. But even increased financial flows to oil-producing states may not necessarily lead to the development of rural oil-producing areas, due to the impact of the prevalent corruption and inefficiency in Nigeria. As shown elsewhere (Frynas 2000a, pp. 49–50), government agencies charged with distributing resources to local people in oil-producing areas such as the Oil Mineral Producing Areas Development Commission (OMPADEC) often misappropriated or misspent the allocated funds. In the absence of government assistance, local people turned to the oil companies demanding compensation payments for previous environmental damage, or the construction of hospitals and other development projects. As many of their demands remained unfulfilled and oil company operations continued to damage people's livelihoods, anti-oil protests were often directed against the oil companies. These protests came to attract the wrath of the Nigerian government.

The above discussion could perhaps suggest that the oil companies had no responsibility for the rise of anti-oil protests and, by extension, no responsibility for the ensuing human rights violations by the security forces. However, there are a number of key reasons why the oil companies were directly or indirectly implicated in human rights abuses.

Above all, as mentioned earlier, the oil TNCs have retained direct operational control over the day-to-day operations of the joint ventures. They took important decisions, such as, for instance, how oil installations were to be constructed on the ground or how to respond to a protest by the local people. Therefore, oil companies could influence the human rights impact of their operations.

Furthermore, as shown below, environmental damage from oil company operations – such as through oil spills or seismic studies – both violated environmental and economic human rights and created conflicts in the oil-producing areas. Damage from oil operations could often have been avoided or considerably minimized at modest financial cost to the companies.

To sum up, the development of the oil industry in Nigeria in the last two to three decades has increased the potential for conflict and human rights violations in the oil-producing areas. In this context, the rise of MOSOP and other pressure groups in the Niger Delta in the early 1990s was perhaps not coincidental. In the early 1990s, the number of community disruptions in Nigeria rose sharply, mainly in the Ogoni area. According to Shell, the number of community disturbances increased fivefold from 34 incidents in 1989 to 169 incidents in 1993, and then fell somewhat again (quoted in Frynas 1998). In the late 1990s, community disturbances outside the Ogoni area, mainly in Ijaw ethnic areas, increased sharply. In 1997, oil companies in Nigeria reportedly lost 117 working days due to community disturbances, of which Shell reportedly lost 67 days.[7] Meanwhile, conflicts between oil companies and village communities and human rights violations look set to continue.

Human rights violations and oil TNCs in Nigeria

Political rights

By attacking critics of the oil industry, the Nigerian state breached many political rights including the right to life, the prohibition of torture and degrading treatment and the prohibition of arbitrary arrest.[8] The extent of these violations was considerable. From the beginning of serious violence in the Ogoni area in the early 1990s until the present day, thousands of local people have been killed by security forces in an attempt to quell anti-oil sentiments. Did oil companies participate or contribute to these violations?

At the most extreme, oil company staff have initiated human rights violations themselves. For instance, it has been suggested that company staff have occasionally intimidated plaintiffs who sued oil companies in Nigerian courts, or have summoned the state security forces to do so (Frynas 2001a). Various documented cases show that oil companies summoned the state security forces to deal with non-violent protesters and critics of their operations. A notable example was provided by an official inquiry into the Umuechem massacre in 1991. On 30 and 31 October 1990, local youths at Umuechem, a village East of Port Harcourt in Rivers State, demonstrated against Shell, which had been operating in the area from the late 1950s, resulting in the pollution of a stream, destruction of farm crops and other losses to property. The community had received little or no compensation, and villagers called for social amenities such as the provision of electricity. Shell did not respond to the dissatisfied community members, but decided instead to rely upon security protection. On 29 October, J.R. Udofia, Shell's Eastern Division manager wrote a letter to the Commissioner of Police in Rivers State informing him of an 'impending attack' on oil facilities allegedly planned for the next day. Udofia did not merely appeal for security protection but explicitly requested the assistance of a unit of the Mobile Police, which was well known for its brutality. Udofia requested the Commissioner to 'urgently provide us with security protection (preferably Mobile Police Force) at this location' (quoted in Rivers State of Nigeria 1991, Appendix G). In the course of the next few days, the

Mobile Police moved in with tear-gas and gunfire, killing around 80 people and destroying almost 500 houses. In the wake of the incident, a judicial commission of inquiry was set up by Colonel Godwin Osagie Abbe, the Rivers State Military Governor. The inquiry concluded that there was no imminent threat of attack and that the demonstrators were neither violent nor armed (Rivers State of Nigeria 1991).

Another example involved the Italian oil company, Agip, in a dispute with a local community in the 1980s and 1990s.[9] The company reportedly caused severe damage in the locality, including, for instance, the contamination of drinking water by oil spills. The company initially engaged in negotiations but, dissatisfied with the compensation payments offered, the local people continued to stage protests against it. In one instance in March 1984, rather than continuing to negotiate with the local people, Agip decided to call on the security forces. A district manager of Agip wrote a letter to the Commissioner of Police in Imo State, complaining about a specific family's 'unreasonable' demands and asking for 'urgent action to step into this matter so that our production could start immediately' and to 'provide a unit of your men to guard our installations in this area and to ensure that our current programmed activities are uninterrupted'. Following the company's requests for armed assistance in the 1980s and the 1990s, the local people were repeatedly harassed and intimidated by the police.

These two examples reveal how the oil companies' over-reliance on security forces – in preference to peaceful negotiations with protestors – can lead to human rights violations. There is also evidence that the oil companies actively supported the repression of anti-oil protests by providing financial and logistical assistance to state security forces. For instance, Chevron equipment such as helicopters and boats was reportedly used in attacks on anti-oil protesters in 1998 and 1999 (Pegg 1999; Human Rights Watch 1999b, 1999a, p. 151); and a secret memo from May 1994 revealed that oil companies provided the infamous Rivers State Internal Security Task Force with financial assistance. In an internal memo, Major Okuntimo called for 'pressure on oil companies for prompt regular inputs as discussed'.[10] The money was probably used for internal repression since the Task Force was mainly used in the Ogoni area to deal with anti-Shell protests. In the same internal memo, Major Okuntimo wrote: 'Shell operations [are] still impossible unless ruthless military operations are undertaken for smooth economic activities to commence.'

At the time when Okuntimo's memo was written, Shell was involved in negotiations to import light weapons into Nigeria in breach of an international arms embargo. According to court evidence, Shell sought tenders from Nigerian arms suppliers to procure weapons worth over US$500,000. These included 130 Beretta 9 mm calibre sub-machine guns, 200,000 rounds of bullets and 500 smoke hand grenades. Nigeria's Inspector General of Police approved the arms purchase under pressure from Shell managers. Following revelations in the British press on Shell's arms dealings in 1996, a Shell International spokesman admitted that one of three bids for arms purchases had been 'selected' by Shell in March 1995, although the arms deal had not gone ahead.[11]

Oil companies, of course, have a legitimate right to protect themselves against violence, particularly in an unstable region such as the Niger Delta. In the late 1990s, the number of violent attacks against oil companies increased, including incidents of kidnapping of oil company staff and sabotage of oil installations. But it must be noted that, before the spate of violence in the late 1990s, the overwhelming majority of protests in Nigeria were peaceful and that the companies' over-reliance on security forces led to unnecessary human rights abuses.

Environmental rights

Unlike civil and political rights, environmental rights are not codified in a United Nations covenant. But there is clear reference to environmental rights in the African Charter on Human and People's Rights, which pronounced that 'all peoples shall have the right to a general satisfactory environment favourable to their development' and, in the case of environmental damage, that they have a right to compensation and recovery of their property.[12] The Charter was often understood as defending the rights of local people affected by business operations in Africa.

Interpretation of the Charter is not straightforward, and it provides little guidance as to how we can measure the environmental performance of the oil industry in Nigeria. But it is clear that oil operations pose a threat to the environment at each stage of the supply chain – exploration, production, transportation and refining. During exploration for oil, environmental threats include clearance of land – which can lead to a long lasting or permanent loss of vegetation – and drilling activities, which can lead to the release of drilling fluids. Oil production activities can have an adverse impact on the environment through damage from leaking pipelines or atmospheric emissions from the flaring of gas, a by-product of oil production. During transportation, tankers release oil into the sea in the course of pumping out bilge-water or unloading cargo. The pollution from refineries can include the release of waste water containing oil residuals, solid waste disposal and atmospheric emissions. Below, I shall outline some of the major adverse environmental effects of oil operations in Nigeria at the early stages of the supply chain – that is, during exploration and production (transport and refining are relatively less important in Nigeria). Much of the following account comes from a report written by Bopp van Dessel, Shell's former head of environmental studies in Nigeria, who documented the environmental problems of oil operations in great detail (van Dessel 1995).

The first contact between oil companies and local people usually occurs during exploration for oil, which aims at locating sites with suspected oil reserves. The usual exploration method is the seismic study, in which an oil company obtains information on subsurface oil reservoirs by sending sound waves into the earth's crust. Seismic surveys involve detonating explosives on the land surface which act as the energy source, or by using small boats equipped with airguns which release compressed air into the water surface. Even before these activities can start, significant areas of land are cleared in the process of laying seismic lines. In some areas, such as farmland and uncultivated bush areas, the effect of 'line cutting' is relatively insignificant and evidence of seismic lines is short lived. In other areas, however, line cutting leaves long-term damage. The environmental impact of line cutting is particularly significant in mangrove swamps. It takes two to three years for mangrove bushes to recover after their roots are cut into, and it may take 30 years or more for mangrove trees to recover fully from line cutting. Detonation of explosives can affect the soil structure. If the holes for explosives are improperly drilled, a detonation can cause a crater. The environmental impact of seismic surveys in riverine areas is mostly restricted to sea mammals (van Dessel 1995).

The drilling for exploration and appraisal oil wells is less common than seismic studies (partly because of the greater financial cost), albeit its impact can also be damaging. Land clearance can lead to a long lasting or permanent loss of vegetation. Dredging destroys vegetation and life, especially if the dredged material is washed back into the water, which leads to further reduction of living organisms. The most damaging effect of drilling is probably the release of waste. Drilling activities require a significant quantity of 'mud' or drilling fluid. This is a special mixture of clay, various chemicals and water, which is constantly pumped down through the drill pipe and comes out through the nozzles in the cutting tool. The stream of mud returns to the surface, carrying with it rock fragments cut away bit by bit. The waste which is generated is not particularly toxic or harmful but its impact is significant because of the substantial quantities. Discharge of this waste into water leads to the degradation of living organisms in the water (van Dessel 1995, p. 16 and pp. 20–1).

Even before oil production can start, oil companies need to build the necessary infrastructure, such as access roads to production locations, pipelines and oil production installations. As shown elsewhere (Frynas 2000b), many of these activities have had important damaging effects. For instance, oil companies have occasionally blockaded creeks, ponds, lakes and other waterways by constructing access roads to oil installations. This can have a variety of negative effects: the natural course and flow of a river or a creek may be diverted; fish may no longer be able to move across the waterway; and the blockage may result in flooding on one side and drying up of water on the other. The effects of road construction or canal dredging may be more damaging than the effects of any temporary exploration activity. While plants may grow once again after a seismic survey, an inappropriately constructed road or a canal constitutes a permanent obstruction.

Once the oil starts flowing, there may be additional environmental impact, particularly through oil spills. According to the World Bank's (1995, volume II, annex M) figures, between 1991 and 1993 there were almost 300 oil spills per year in Delta and Rivers states, the main oil-producing Nigerian Federal States at the time. Depending on the location, oil spills can poison water, destroy vegetation and kill living organisms, as has been shown by various 'post impact' studies (van Dessel 1995, p. 23; Amajor 1985). The environmental impact of oil spills in the Niger Delta is increased by floods. During the rainy season, over 80 per cent of the Niger Delta is flooded (Moffat and Linden 1995, p. 527); water carries the oil into villages and onto farmlands, while floods also render the clean up of oil spills more difficult.

To sum up, oil companies have caused major environmental damage in Nigeria, as documented by an oil company itself. This is in contrast to frequent oil company assertions, which deny that oil operations have caused any major environmental effects (see, for example, Detheridge and Pepple 1998). While it is correct that environmental damage in the oil-producing areas was caused by many different sources such as over-farming, the oil industry has had a highly significant adverse environmental impact on specific areas and people.

Economic and social rights

Breaches of environmental rights led to economic and social hardship in the oil-producing areas. But were economic and social rights actually breached? Many internationally recognized rights focus on labor relations (for example, the right to work) so they cannot be applied to our case. However, there are at least two relevant rights in international agreements: the prohibition of arbitrary seizure of a person's property[13] and the right to the enjoyment of the highest attainable standard of physical and mental health.[14] Arbitrary seizure of property was legalized through the Land Use Act mentioned earlier, which resulted in de facto confiscation of land property in Nigeria, as the governor of a state was empowered to acquire any private or public land holdings for oil operations. Similarly, the physical and mental health of local people in oil-producing areas was heavily impaired by political oppression and environmental degradation. To what extent did oil companies participate in or contribute to these violations?

Oil companies in Nigeria have long argued that they do not have a social responsibility for the social and economic development of their host communities. As late as 1995, Shell's brochures stated that the company could make the 'most effective contribution to Nigeria' through the taxes and royalties it paid. The company said that it could not provide development to the host communities, which was the responsibility of the government (quoted in Boele et al. 2001). From a human rights perspective, this may be justified to some extent, as international agreements usually refer to states (not private actors) as being accountable for violations of social and economic rights. However, the UN Universal Declaration of Human Rights (while somewhat exceptional in this regard) addresses 'every individual and every organ of society'.[15] Moreover, oil companies have in a number of instances voluntarily treated the host communities in a better fashion than Nigerian regulations prescribed. Oil companies have reportedly paid higher (albeit still inadequate) compensation rates for destroyed crops and trees than prescribed by outdated Nigerian regulations, and they have voluntarily launched (although they have often failed to execute) development projects for host communities (Frynas 2001b). Nonetheless, through their conduct, oil companies have encouraged violations of social and economic rights.

Rather than working towards the enjoyment of a high 'standard of physical and mental health' in their host communities, oil companies have often impaired the social and economic development of these communities. As shown earlier, oil operations have caused considerable environmental damage. In turn, environmental damage has social consequences. An oil spill, for instance, may damage fishing and farming activities in the area and, in extreme cases, may deprive local people of any means of subsistence (Frynas 2000b).

Oil operations may also have social consequences unrelated to environmental damage, such as, for instance, the impact of inward migration of oil workers or the rise in food prices. Onyige (1979, p. 188) pointed to the effect of temporary employment of young people by oil companies during oil exploration or construction work. Those young people are highly paid for a short period of time. By increasing their spending habits and imitating a culture alien to them, their lifestyles may quickly become distinctive from the rest of the community. Both the young people and the village community as a whole may find it difficult to adjust to those sudden changes and the social fabric of a community may be severely damaged.

Using the example of Bonny Island – the site of Nigeria's largest natural gas project, Shell's own Corporate Community Development Adviser in Nigeria narrated the social problems created by oil company operations (LaPin 1999). The start of company operations and the influx of some 13,000 workers brought enormous changes. Prices of goods and rents increased, teachers abandoned schools for high-paying jobs, and public services, such as the local power generation plant, became over-stretched. The community gained from a short boom over the three years of construction but little was left once the construction teams departed and local labor contracts ended. The operating company, Nigeria Liquefied Natural Gas or NLNG (jointly owned by the Nigerian state, Shell, TotalFinaElf and Agip), finally decided to put into place social development projects. However, Shell's Corporate Community Development Adviser in Nigeria concluded that 'in many ways this movement was too late to address the very real dislocation and discomfort in social life created at the outset' (LaPin 1999).

As shown elsewhere (Frynas 2000b), many of the adverse social and economic effects of oil operations were the result of careless company operating practices, and not necessarily due to any lack of funding for the maintenance of installations and equipment. For instance, boats destroyed property, such as fishing nets, while conducting seismic studies because they failed to inform the local people of their presence beforehand. When passing through farms or constructing oil installations, oil company staff negligently destroyed crops, trees or fish ponds. As mentioned earlier, oil companies even diverted rivers or creeks, leading either to flooding or drought, which also had major social consequences (Frynas 2000b). These adverse effects could have been easily avoided at little financial cost, but the oil companies showed little interest in doing so.

Conclusion

This chapter demonstrates that oil TNCs have had a significant adverse impact on the human rights situation in Nigeria's oil-producing areas.

Over the last few years, both the Nigerian political landscape and the TNCs have changed dramatically, and the human rights situation has seen improvements. The death of General Abacha in June 1998 and the inauguration of the democratically-elected President Obasanjo in May 1999 ended 16 years of military rule in Nigeria. Many political prisoners were freed and various violations of political rights associated with military rule have ended. The people in the oil-producing areas also gained a voice in the democratically-elected institutions. With regard to the environment, the Nigerian government created an Environment Ministry, which has imposed stricter environmental regulations on the oil industry in some areas, for instance the flaring of natural gas and the discharge of waste (see also Akinmutimi 2001; Lawal 2001). In regard to economic and social development, the government has replaced the corrupt and ineffective OMPADEC with the Niger Delta Development Commission (NDDC), a new and better funded development agency for the oil-producing areas.

Under the pressure of international protests, international oil companies have also come to accept that they have a social responsibility that extends beyond making profits, paying taxes and complying with the rule of law. Most notably, the Royal Dutch/Shell Group of Companies revised its 1976 Statement of General Business Principles in 1997 to incorporate concern for human rights and changed many of its corporate policies to reflect greater concern for social and environmental issues (Boele et al. 2001). Private companies in Nigeria have reformed many facets of their operations. With regard to the environment, oil companies have committed considerable resources towards minimizing damage from their operations, for instance by replacing ageing pipelines in order to reduce the number of oil spills.[16] With regard to economic and social development, companies have also started to change their approach. The amount of money spent on Nigerian community development increased markedly in the 1990s. There was also a shift from constructing externally imposed large-scale projects such as hospitals towards development projects with a grassroots approach involving much greater consultation with the local people (Frynas 2001b).

All these developments have created a more conducive environment for human rights in Nigeria as a whole. However, there is evidence that serious human rights violations have continued in the oil-producing areas. Most notably, hundreds of people were killed and the village of Odi was destroyed by the security forces in November 1999 in retaliation for the killings of twelve policemen by an armed gang.[17] Indeed, a Human Rights Watch (2000) report concluded in general terms that 'the restoration of civilian rule in Nigeria has not seen a reduction of human rights violations in the country's oil-producing regions'. The ability of the NDDC to meaningfully develop the oil-producing areas is also questioned (Frynas 2001b).

The recent human rights performance of oil companies can also be questioned. The oil industry still relies on the infamous Mobile Police for security protection, despite its continuing disregard for human rights. For instance, Mobile Police sent by the federal government to Nigeria's Delta State to protect oil pipelines in late 2000 were reportedly involved in human rights violations including assaults, looting and burning of houses (Ogefere 2000). Oil companies are still struggling to improve their environmental and social performance. According to Shell's (2001) own figures, the company had 340 oil spills in Nigeria in 2000 alone. According to a leaked 2001 audit commissioned by Shell, less than one-third of Shell's development projects in Nigeria were fully successful. The report found that Shell is still essentially trying to buy off the local people with gifts rather than trying to offer them genuine development.[18] Therefore, despite improvements in the human rights situation, violations continue. The Niger Delta crisis still remains unresolved and oil TNCs remain implicated in human rights violations.

Notes

1. See, for instance, reports written by Bronwen Manby for Human Rights Watch (1995, 1999a,b, 2000).
2. Shell is responsible for roughly 40 per cent of Nigeria's oil production (Frynas 2000a, p. 16). Compared with the other two big oil-producing companies, ExxonMobil and Chevron, which had many offshore oil fields, a much greater share of Shell's oil production in Nigeria came from onshore areas where the potential for conflict with the local people was at its greatest.
3. 'Shell Denies Rights Abuses', *Phone News International*, 2 February 2001.
4. The 1967–70 civil war briefly disrupted oil operations, but production soon recovered.
5. On the Land Use Act, see Frynas (2000a, pp. 77–80).
6. For example, the conference of the Union of Niger Delta, an amalgam of different ethnic nationalities' organizations in the Niger Delta, called in early 2000 for 'the immediate abrogation of the Land Use Act' (*Vanguard*, 6 March 2000). Similar calls were made by many other pressure groups in the Niger

Delta. More fundamentally, the local people have demanded the control of resources on their land. A typical example of this trend was the well-known 'Kaiama Declaration' made at a gathering of Ijaw youths from different communities in December 1998. It stated that 'All land and natural resources (including mineral resources) within the Ijaw territory belong to Ijaw communities and are the basis of our survival' (quoted in Human Rights Watch 1999a).

7. *Guardian* (Lagos), 24 February 1998.
8. Articles 6, 7 and 9 of the International Covenant on Civil and Political Rights and Articles 3, 5 and 9 of the UN Universal Declaration of Human Rights.
9. Evidence on this episode was provided by the court case *Adizua v. Agip*. Unreported Suit No. HOG/22/97, Imo State High Court.
10. Memo written by the then Chairman of the Rivers State Internal Security, Major Paul Okuntimo, to the then Military Administrator of Rivers State, Lt. Col. Dauda Komo, 12 May 1994.
11. *Observer*, 11 February 1996.
12. Article 24 of the African Charter on Human and People's Rights. Article 21 further provides for the right to 'freely dispose of their [all peoples'] wealth and natural resources'. In addition, it states that 'in case of spoliation the disposed people shall have the right to the lawful recovery of its property as well as to an adequate compensation'. The Charter was ratified and made enforceable in Nigeria in 1983.
13. Article 17 of the UN Universal Declaration of Human Rights.
14. Article 12 of the International Covenant on Economic, Social and Cultural Rights.
15. Preamble of the UN Universal Declaration of Human Rights.
16. See, for instance, Shell's website at http://www.shellnigeria.com.
17. See, for example; 'Senators Find Delta Town Destroyed by Soldiers', *Phone News International*, 30 November 1999; and Adeniyi (1999).
18. Anonymous, 'Nigeria and Shell – Helping, but not Developing', *The Economist*, 12 May 2001.

References

Adeniyi, Abiodun. 1999. 'Senate Seeks Troops' Withdrawal from Odi, Probe of OMPADEC', *Guardian*, Lagos (26 November).

Akinmutimi, Tola. 2001. 'Gas Flaring: Erring Firms May Lose Licences', *Guardian*, Lagos (25 July).

Amajor, I.C. 1985. 'The Ejamah-Ebubu Oil Spill of 1970: a Case History of a 14 Years' Old Spill', in *Petroleum Industry and the Nigerian Environment*. Lagos: NNPC/Federal Ministry of Works and Housing.

Boele, Richard, Heike Fabig and David Wheeler. 2001. 'Shell Nigeria and the Ogoni. A Study in Unsustainable Development', *Sustainable Development* 9: 74–86.

Detheridge, Alan and Noble Pepple. 1998. 'A Response to Frynas', *Third World Quarterly* 19(3): 479–86.

Frynas, Jedrzej George. 1998. 'Political Instability and Business: Focus on Shell in Nigeria', *Third World Quarterly* 19(3): 457–78.

Frynas, J.G. 2000a. *Oil in Nigeria: Conflict and Litigation between Oil Companies and Village Communities*. Münster/Hamburg: LIT.

Frynas, J.G. 2000b. 'Environmental and Social Impact of Oil Operations in Nigeria – Evidence from Nigerian Court Cases', University of Leipzig Papers on Africa, Politics and Economics Series No. 33.

Frynas, J.G. 2001a. 'Problems of Access to Courts in Nigeria: Results of a Survey of Legal Practitioners', *Social and Legal Studies* 10(3): 397–419.

Frynas, J.G. 2001b. 'Corporate and State Responses to Anti-Oil Protests in the Niger Delta', *African Affairs* 100(398): 27–54.

Human Rights Watch. 1995. 'Nigeria, the Ogoni Crisis: a Case-Study of Military Repression in Southeastern Nigeria', New York: Human Rights Watch.

Human Rights Watch. 1999a. *The Price of Oil – Corporate Responsibility and Human Rights Violations in Nigeria's Oil Producing Communities*. New York: Human Rights Watch.

Human Rights Watch. 1999b. 'Nigeria: Crackdown in the Niger Delta', New York: Human Rights Watch.

Human Rights Watch. 2000. 'No Human Rights Progress in Niger Delta – Protesters in Oil Regions of Nigeria Subject to Lethal Force', New York: Human Rights Watch.

LaPin, Deirdre. 1999. 'Corporate Social Investments in the 21st Century: Multiplying Value', unpublished draft of a conference paper for a Health, Safety and Environment Conference.

Lawal, Yakubu. 2001. 'Shell Commits N700 billion to Oil, Gas Production, says Omiyi', *Guardian*, Lagos (25 July).

Moffat, David and Olof Linden. 1995. 'Perception and Reality: Assessing Priorities for Sustainable Development in the Niger River Delta', *Ambio* 24(7–8): 527–38.

Ndujihe, Clifford. 2001. 'In Port Harcourt, Oputa Panel Faces Severe Test', *Guardian*, Lagos (15 January).

Ogefere, Sunny. 2000. 'House Condemns Alleged Police Brutality on Delta Communities', *Guardian*, Lagos (4 October).

Onyige, Peter Usutu. 1979. 'The Impact of Mineral Oil Exploitation on Rural Communities in Nigeria: the Case of Ogba/Egbema District', PhD thesis at the Centre of West African Studies, University of Birmingham.

Pegg, Scott. 1999. 'The Cost of Doing Business: Transnational Corporations and Violence in Nigeria', *Security Dialogue* 30(4): 473–84.

Rivers State of Nigeria. 1991. 'Judicial Commission of Inquiry into Umuechem Disturbances under the Chairmanship of Hon. Justice Opubo Inko-Tariah', Port Harcourt: Rivers State of Nigeria.

Shell. 2001. '2000 People and the Environment Annual Report', Shell Petroleum Development Company of Nigeria Limited (April).

Suberu, Rotimi T. 1996. *Ethnic Minority Conflicts and Governance in Nigeria*. Ibadan: Spectrum.

van Dessel, J.P. 1995. 'Internal Position Paper: the Environmental Situation in the Niger Delta' (February).

World Bank. 1995. *Defining an Environmental Development Strategy for the Niger Delta*. Industry and Energy Operations Division, West Central Africa Department of the World Bank.

6
Mining and Environmental Human Rights in Papua New Guinea

Stuart Kirsch[1]

> The effective exercise and enjoyment of basic human rights for much of the world's population is prohibited by environmental problems. Water and air pollution, accumulations of solid and hazardous wastes, soil degradation and deforestation prevent many people from securing the minimum requirements for health and survival. Whether or not a basic human 'right to the environment' exists, a safe and ecologically balanced environment is necessary for the realization of all basic human rights.
>
> (United Nations Economic and Social Council 1994).

Whether transnational corporations should be held accountable for actions which violate human rights is a question which cannot be answered without consideration of new configurations of power that enable corporations to evade regulatory control.[2] Where the state is an effective regulator of transnational corporations, its own laws will be more practically enforced than the general principles of human rights (Muchlinski 2001, p. 45). But with the spread of neo-liberal political and economic policy, states have become markedly less effective as regulatory bodies, often transferring the responsibilities for monitoring and compliance to the corporations under review. Similarly, when state–corporate relationships take the form of economic partnerships, the regulatory functions of the state may fall victim to conflict of interest. Pressure from multilateral agencies may also affect state regulation of transnational corporations. Where the regulatory inclinations and capacities of the state are constrained or diminished, new ways to enforce corporate accountability are required. The recent rise of NGOs that monitor the behavior of transnational corporations is one response to these conditions (Kirsch 2002). Declarations of human rights may also constitute important political resources for persons and communities who are adversely affected by transnational corporations. The enforcement of the principles of human rights may help to regulate corporate behavior in the absence of responsible state control.

While most claims regarding human rights violations against transnational corporations are concerned with violence, militarization and forced labor, this chapter addresses the issue of environmental human rights (Popović 1996). Unfortunately, these principles remain poorly defined, lacking in both legal precedents and operational specificity. Moreover, like other human rights principles, they are constructed primarily with reference to state actors rather than corporations. While acknowledging the practical and theoretical limits of human rights regimes, including the relative weakness of enforcement schemes, Popović (1996, p. 602) is nonetheless positive about their potential application to environmental problems, concluding that 'with widespread dissemination and considered discussion, [they] have the potential to lead to a powerful and authoritative statement of international law on the connections between human rights and the environment'. In other words, increased attention to environmental human rights may expand what is regarded as normative and thus potentially enforceable as international law.

The argument that transnational corporations should abide by the principles of human rights raises the specter of a 'free-rider' problem, placing corporations which operate according to higher standards at a competitive disadvantage in relation to those which do not. These costs can be substantial in the case of environmental impacts for the mining industry. Moreover, corporate 'public standing' (Muchlinski 2001, pp. 38–9) may be of less value to the mining industry, which does not sell directly to consumers and is therefore less susceptible to public opinion. While the most common response to the free-rider problem is to reduce standards to the lowest common denominator, yielding to what critics have called the 'race to the bottom', the application and enforcement of uniform standards to the entire industry would reduce or eliminate existing economic incentives to pollute.

This case study of the Ok Tedi copper and gold mine in Papua New Guinea demonstrates that existing mechanisms for protecting the environment and environmental human rights are insufficient. This was true despite extraordinary efforts on the part of the affected communities to stop the mine from polluting their environment through riverine disposal of tailings and other mine wastes. As a shareholder in the mine, the state faced a substantial conflict of interest regarding its regulatory responsibilities. This led some observers to characterize BHP's (formerly Broken Hill Proprietary Ltd) relationship with the state in criminal terms ranging from coercion to collusion (Harper and Israel 1999). The mine's efforts to limit its own environmental impact were inadequate by any standard, ultimately prompting the corporation to acknowledge that the project was 'not compatible' with its environmental values (Barker and Oldfield 1999).[3] The Ok Tedi case demonstrates the need to hold transnational corporations accountable for their impact on environmental human rights.

The Ok Tedi mine

Located in the Star Mountains of Papua New Guinea, the Ok Tedi mine began producing gold in 1984 and copper three years later.[4] While the original Environmental Impact Assessment for the project called for the construction of a tailings dam, this work was never completed after a landslide destroyed the footings for the structure (Pintz 1987, p. 58; Townsend 1988, p. 114). Temporary permission to continue to mine using riverine tailings disposal, in which mine wastes are released into local rivers, was granted by the government of Papua New Guinea in 1986.[5] Permission was renewed in 1989 following the civil war on the island of Bougainville, which forced the closure of the controversial Panguna copper mine operated by Rio Tinto, putting enormous economic pressure on the state. While the lack of expenditure associated with tailings containment, for example, a tailings dam or a pipeline to a lowlands storage facility, made the mine a relatively low-cost copper producer, cost overruns and declining metal prices forced investors in the mine to write off much of their US$1.4 billion expenditure (Jackson 1993). The world's sixth-largest copper producer, Ok Tedi's primary markets are located in Asia and Europe.[6] Its export sales were K701.8 million in 1998, representing 19.9 per cent of Papua New Guinea's foreign exchange earnings.[7] In the same year, the mine paid K9.8 million in royalties to the government of Western Province and contributed K52 million in taxes to the Papua New Guinea government, which also benefits economically from being a shareholder in the mine (Ok Tedi Mining Ltd 2001).

The Ok Tedi mine currently releases more than 30 million tons of tailings and another 40 million tons of waste rock into the Ok Tedi River annually, causing massive environmental degradation downstream along the Ok Tedi and Fly rivers, one of New Guinea's largest and most important river systems. It is expected to operate until at least 2010, although possible extensions to the existing ore body may extend its working life.

Chronicle of a disaster foretold

From the early stages of mining it was evident that the Ok Tedi mine was problematic from an environmental point of view. After the government suspended the requirement for tailings containment, an engineer employed by the government of Papua New Guinea published a critical review entitled 'Giving Away the River' (Townsend 1988). The same year, an anthropologist who contributed to the original environmental impact studies for the mine described the project as New Guinea's 'disaster mine' (Hyndman 1988). In a newspaper editorial published in the *Times of Papua New Guinea* the following year, I described the Ok Tedi River as a 'sewer' and suggested that the entire Fly River was at risk (Kirsch 1989a). The Australian Conservation Foundation later reported that the Ok Tedi River was 'almost biologically dead' (Rosenbaum and Krockenberger 1993, p. 9).

Despite its widely-publicized environmental problems and despite enormous efforts by the downstream communities to stop the mine from dumping tailings and waste rock into their river system, the Ok Tedi mine continues to operate without any system of tailings containment. Representatives from the affected communities have sent petitions to the government, organized protests, enlisted the support of national and international NGOs, and traveled extensively throughout Europe and the Americas, presenting their case to the media at the Rio de Janeiro 'Earth Summit', the German Parliament (Schoell 1994, pp. 13–14) and the International Water Tribunal in the Hague (International Water Tribunal 1994). Their protests culminated in a high-profile lawsuit in the Victorian Supreme Court in Melbourne, where BHP is incorporated, pitting 34,000 local landowners against one of Australia's largest corporations. The case was settled out of court in 1996 for a potential US$500 million in commitments to compensation and tailings containment (Gordon 1997; Kirsch 1997).[8]

Yet following the release of more detailed environmental impact studies carried out by the mine in 1999, the managing director of the mine reported to the media that the impacts were 'much worse than previously expected', acknowledging significant discrepancies between earlier corporate representations of the mine's impacts and the assessments of local communities and independent observers. The corporate-sponsored review pointed out that even if mining at Ok Tedi were to cease immediately, the problems downstream would continue to increase due to the sheer volume of tailings already in the river and ongoing erosion from waste rock dumps adjacent to the mine in the mountains (Parametrix, Inc. and URS Greiner Woodward Clyde 1999a, p. 8). These problems are expected to continue for at least fifty years, which is as far into the future as their models can project. While 1300 square kilometers of rain forest along the river is already dead or under severe stress, this damage is expected to spread downstream, eventually covering as much as 2040 square kilometers (Higgins 2002). Even this projection may be optimistic, however, and the damage may ultimately encompass 3000 square kilometers (Parametrix, Inc. and URS Greiner Woodward Clyde 1999a, p. 8). While the changes to the river system will eventually stabilize, the local species composition is not expected to return to pre-mine conditions, with savanna grasslands replacing much of the existing rain forest (Chapman et al. 2000, p. 17).

Moreover, questions remain about toxicity at both the bottom and the top of the food chain, ranging from algae to fruit bats and marsupials (Parametrix, Inc. and URS Greiner Woodward Clyde 1999b, p. 9). While the potential health risks of exposure to heavy metals for the human populations along the river are expected to be minor (Parametrix, Inc. and URS Greiner Woodward Clyde 1999b, p. 13), these populations must be monitored for their exposure to lead and cadmium, both of which are highly toxic substances (Chapman et al. 2000, p. 14). Finally, the potential for acid mine drainage is significant, which would precipitate an even greater environmental crisis. Continued operation of the mine without effective tailings containment will increase the chance that this will occur (Chapman et al. 2000, pp. 8–9).

Indigenous responses to industrial pollution

People living downstream from the mining project on the Ok Tedi River first became concerned about environmental problems after a cyanide spill at the mine site on 19 June 1984. A bypass valve was left open for more than two hours, releasing 100 cubic meters of highly concentrated cyanide waste into the Ok Tedi River; dead fish, prawns, turtles, crocodiles and other riverine life floated downstream more than 100 kilometers from the mine (Hyndman 1988, p. 94). People in the villages along the lower Ok Tedi River recall gathering up the dead fish and animals, which they cooked and ate.

Several years after copper production began, the people living in the communities downstream began to experience problems caused by the increased sediment load carried by the river. This caused riverbed aggradation, flooding and the deposition of mine tailings and other waste material in the adjacent lowlands and rain forest. Petitions were sent by local communities to the Papua New Guinea government and the mine, expressing their concerns and demanding action. In 1988, residents of a village on the Ok Tedi River sent a petition to the North Fly Area Coordinator, describing a wide range of environmental problems which they attributed to the mine (Kirsch 1995, pp. 84–5). A letter written by people living on the Ok Tedi River to Ok Tedi Mining Ltd (OTML) expressed even more sweeping concerns about the mine's environmental impact:

> All of these things show evidence of the mine's impact: our garden crops, dogs, pigs, fish and even people becoming ill. Coconut trees have died. People are suffering from sores. Even our staple food sago is affected. The rain makes us sick. The air we breathe leaves us short of breath. And the sun now burns our skin.
>
> In the past, everything was fine. We never experienced problems like these before. But in the ten years that OTML has been in operation, all of these changes and more have taken place. Other plants in our gardens have been affected as well. We are concerned about these changes and it seems reasonable to assume that they are signs of the impact of the Ok Tedi mine. (Kirsch 1995, pp. 82–3; text modified for presentation)

When environmental impacts are evaluated from a scientific perspective, the focus is on changes in flora and fauna that can be quantified or measured. In economic terms, only those natural resources that possess value as commodities are measured. The magnitude of the loss is therefore determined by the market, rather than by local values. Neither of these perspectives captures the full range of concerns expressed by the people affected by the Ok Tedi mine. Complaints that no birds fly along the Ok Tedi are not simply references to changes in species composition or economic loss, but also symbolic representations of the environmental crisis.

An international appeal

The Wau Ecology Institute of Papua New Guinea helped several representatives from the Ok Tedi River present their grievances against the mine at the second International Water Tribunal in the Hague in 1992 (International Water Tribunal 1994, pp. 49–85).[9] The tribunal found BHP guilty of violating the rights of the people living downstream and criticized the mining company for using its foreign earning power to compel the government of Papua New Guinea to lower its environmental standards. Moreover, it was critical of the government for permitting the mine to monitor its own impacts. It advised the government to establish and enforce legally binding provisions to prevent long-term environmental damage. Finally, the tribunal recommended that if the mine could not devise a way to curtail riverine tailings disposal, then it should close its operations.

Forums of this nature, for example, tribunals and people's courts, provide important opportunities for indigenous and other politically marginalized peoples to express human rights concerns and receive a fair hearing, especially when the resources for more protracted legal procedures are unavailable. The judgment of the International Water Tribunal was significant because it internationalized and legitimated the claims of the people living downstream from the Ok Tedi mine. Unfortunately, the tribunal has no powers of enforcement and neither the government nor the mine changed their policies regarding tailings containment. In retrospect, however, the judgments of the tribunal proved to be prescient.

Documenting the problems downstream

In response to the findings of the International Water Tribunal, the Ok Tedi mine engaged a team of social scientists to carry out social impact studies of the downstream communities from 1991–94. I worked with the communities of the lower Ok Tedi River, where I had previously conducted anthropological research. As the river moves from the mountains into the lowlands, it begins to deposit its sediment load along the river banks. The lower Ok Tedi is therefore particularly vulnerable to overbank flooding and by 1992 had sustained a high level of damage from material deposited outside of the river channel.

Mine waste had been deposited onto forest and garden land, into adjacent wetland areas and upstream along the streams that flow into the Ok Tedi River. This contrasted starkly with the fertile soil that used to be deposited along the river's flood plains, permitting gardening with only a short or even no fallow period. The mine wastes had an adverse impact wherever they were deposited, killing plants and trees, and disrupting local ecosystems. The damage extended for approximately

40 kilometers along the river, with areas of dead trees along local streams as far as three kilometers from the main channel. There had been little regrowth. This land had been particularly valuable to the villages along the river because it offered resources not readily available in the rain forest interior. At the time of the social impact study, almost no formal assessment of the environmental damage along the river had been undertaken by the mine or the government, and almost no compensation had been paid. The people living in this area were plagued by frustration and despair because their efforts to obtain restitution and to stop riverine tailings disposal had been ignored.

Approximately 2000 people lived in the eight villages along the lower Ok Tedi in the 1980s and 1990s. Another thousand persons lived in adjacent refugee camps (Kirsch 1989b), all of whom depended upon local resources for the majority of their subsistence needs.[10] Pollution from the mine compromised the abilities of the people living along the lower Ok Tedi River to feed themselves and their families. The loss of garden land forced them to compete for plots in the rain forest that produced at most one or two good harvests. There were fewer fish in the river and people were often afraid to consume them. Turtles no longer migrated upriver along the Ok Tedi to lay their eggs, once an important seasonal resource. Local streams were choked with mine wastes, making it difficult to catch prawns, previously an important source of protein, especially for children. Large stands of *Metroxylon* palms, the source of sago starch that is the local staple, were also adversely affected by mine tailings.

Most of the people whom I interviewed for the study in 1992 agreed that the mine should not have begun production until a safe method for dealing with the tailings had been put in place. They complained that pollution had already 'spoiled' their land. At that particular juncture, however, they preferred that the mine stay open so that they could receive compensation for the damages that they had incurred. They also demanded that the mine stop polluting. The villagers indicated that rather than resort to violence, which had caused so much hardship and suffering during the civil war in Bougainville, they intended to enlist the support of local non-governmental organizations to bring about reform. This warning was included in the social impact study that I presented to the mine in 1993, but not heeded; local NGOs went on to file their lawsuit against BHP in the Victorian Supreme Court in Melbourne the following year.

Local concerns about pollution were largely supported by a series of NGO audits and evaluations, including the Starnberg Report commissioned by the German Lutheran Church (Starnberg Institute 1991), the review by the Australian Conservation Foundation (Rosenbaum and Krockenberger 1993), and a report issued by the International Union for the Conservation of Nature and Natural Resources (1995, p. 53), which called for a more conservative approach to the estimation of future environmental impacts. While these reviews were routinely criticized by the Ok Tedi mine for their methods, their small sample sizes and other perceived inadequacies, they proved to be much better predictors of environmental impact than the voluminous studies produced by the mine itself.

Existing international law and the failure to protect the environment

The people living downstream from the Ok Tedi mine did not receive adequate protection from the government of Papua New Guinea, which did not monitor or adequately regulate the impact of the mine.[11] Local protests and petitions were largely ignored (Burton 1997). Even though the International Water Tribunal was unable to enforce its judgment, its decision encouraged the downstream communities to seek redress through the courts. They looked to international law for support in their bid to stop the mine from using their rivers for tailings disposal.

One of the earliest expressions of international environmental responsibilities was Principle 21 of the Stockholm Declaration:

> States have ... the sovereign right to exploit their own resources pursuant to their own environmental policies, and the responsibility to ensure that activities within their own jurisdiction or control do not cause damage to the environment of other States or of areas beyond the limits of national jurisdiction. (Principle 21, Declaration of the United Nations Conference on the Human Environment, Stockholm, June 1972, cited in Hohmann 1992)

This principle has been invoked in various efforts to establish an international basis for environmental human rights, including Principle 2 of the Rio Declaration on the Environment and Development of 1992. These principles have also been cited in recent legal cases concerning foreign direct liability, the principle of holding transnational corporations accountable for their actions abroad (Kirsch 1997; Newell 2001; Ward 2001). Major cases against Texaco for its petroleum operations in Ecuador and Freeport-McMoRan regarding its copper and gold mine in Papua (formerly Irian Jaya), Indonesia, have turned on questions about the responsibilities of states not to cause environmental harm beyond their own borders (Broderick 1994, p. 16; Kimmerling 1997; Duval 1997).

Even where stringent environmental statutes or laws exist, they are often very general in nature. For example, the principle of sustainability is enshrined in the 1975 constitution of Papua New Guinea:

> We declare our fourth goal to be for Papua New Guinea's natural resources and environment to be conserved and used for the collective benefit of us all, and to be replenished for the benefit of future generations. (Papua New Guinea 1975)

Legal statutes which are consonant with the right to a clean and safe environment, such as this constitutional principle, are often too broad to be enforceable as law. For example, in *Oposa v. Factoran*, an important case in the Philippines regarding the right of the Timber Licensing Authority (TLA) to harvest the remaining rain forest in the Philippines, the judgment was based on constitutional guarantees of a 'balanced and healthy ecology' (Rosario 1993). The courts found that:

> Such a right, as hereinafter expounded, considers the 'rhythm and harmony of nature'. Nature means the created world in its entirety. Such rhythm and harmony include, inter alia, the judicious disposition, utilization, management, renewal and conservation of the country's forest, mineral, land, waters, fisheries, wildlife, off-shore areas and other natural resources to the end that their exploration, development and utilization be equitably accessible to the present as well as future generations.

However, Judge Eriberto U. Rosario (1993) later found that this claim was not enforceable because it was lacking in specificity, and thus would deprive potential defendants of the right of due process.

The lawsuit against BHP and the Ok Tedi mine

In 1994, a lawsuit representing 30,000 indigenous persons as plaintiffs against BHP and the Ok Tedi mine was filed in both the capital of Port Moresby and the Victorian Supreme Court in Melbourne, where BHP is incorporated. *Rex Dagi v. Broken Hill Proprietary Company Limited* was one of the largest claims in Australian history. It received considerable media attention and the public response to the environmental impact of the mine was overwhelmingly critical.

The case against the mine did not directly address damage to property, because the court found that it had no jurisdiction to entertain claims relating to the loss of land or damage to land (Gordon 1997, p. 153). Moreover, it did not address fundamental questions of environmental human rights, because no statutes were seen to raise the level of an enforceable international norm and because environmental laws in Papua New Guinea were insufficiently developed to be of use. Accordingly, the claims against the mine were reframed to plead loss of amenity, which embraced the subsistence economy of the plaintiffs (Gordon 1997). This was a novel concept for the court, in that it did not involve a claim for economic loss, which forms the foundation for damages in virtually all western legal systems (Victorian Supreme Court 1995, p. 59). The precedent is of considerable significance to indigenous communities internationally, for whom environmental damage has often meant the destruction or impairment of their subsistence resources.

Valuing indigenous losses

Mining companies make three major types of payments to indigenous communities in Papua New Guinea (Banks 1998, pp. 55–6). The first is known as 'compensation' and includes one-time payments for disturbance or damage to land or forest, or other improvements to the land, including houses, gardens, and 'lifestyle'. A second form of recompense called 'occupation fees' consists of annual rent for expropriated land and resulting lifestyle disruptions; these payments are calculated according to the area of land that is leased. The third category is royalty payments, which are based on a percentage of the gross value of production. More recently, as local communities have acquired equity shares in mining projects, a fourth category of dividends has emerged.

Large-scale mining operations may also be responsible for improved access to health care and education, usually according to terms spelled out in agreements between the landowners and the government, and the provision of new, although not necessarily better, housing and community infrastructure (for example, water supplies, roads and so on). These elements form a central part of compensation regimes even though substitution of a water tank for a freshwater spring, for example, while measurable on an index of modernization or development, does not necessarily translate into an improved quality of life, particularly when the introduced technology has a limited lifespan and provisions are not made for its eventual replacement.

The logic of compensation assumes that all damages have an equivalent in monetary form and that all things can be reduced to their value as commodities, which may inappropriately 'bottom-line' values that are not properly amenable to financial calculation (Rappaport 1993, p. 299). The assumptions underlying the compensation process therefore ignore the presence of other values, such as the importance of land for identity and local knowledge (Kirsch 2001). This may hold true even for indigenous communities with extensive participation in the cash economy, who may bring these resources to bear on their subsistence pursuits, which remain central to their identities and essential for social relations (Sahlins 2000). Rights to land and subsistence practices are fundamental human rights for indigenous peoples, as many scholars and advocates have observed (for example, Popović 1996, p. 541). Land is often pivotal to the historical accumulation of experience and identity; such losses must be reckoned not only in economic terms, but also in terms of the community's capacity to produce local subjects.

Provisions of the settlement

The lawsuit against BHP and the Ok Tedi mine was settled out of court in 1996. The first component of the settlement established a K110 million compensation package that is being distributed to the 34,000 people living along the Ok Tedi and Fly rivers during the remaining years of the mine. A second trust of K40 million was set up on behalf of the landowners and resource users who live along the lower Ok Tedi River where the impact of the mine is most pronounced.

The central feature of the settlement was corporate commitment to tailings containment, the most likely option for which was a tailings pipeline from the mine site in the mountains along the east bank of the Ok Tedi River to a lowland storage area. While the storage area was projected to cover between 30 and 50 square kilometers, this land could be progressively rehabilitated. The estimated cost of the pipeline ranged between US$180 and US$250 million. The lower Ok Tedi River is also being dredged at a cost of US$30 million per year; this has lowered the river bed and reduced flooding into the adjacent forests. However, it removes only a fraction of what the mine releases into the river every day. Finally, the company agreed to establish an environmental rehabilitation program for deforested land along the river. Through the settlement, BHP also committed to implement the most practicable tailings containment option on the recommendation of the Papua New Guinea government following a review of the available options.

The provisions of the accord were backed by an agreement with BHP that any disputes arising during the course of its implementation would be heard by the Victorian Supreme Court in Melbourne. The settlement also ratified the principle of alien tort claims, which seeks to hold corporations accountable in the countries in which they are incorporated and according to legal standards in their home countries. As such, the Ok Tedi case was a forerunner – and one of the most successful cases to date, even given its shortcomings – of international legal action regarding foreign direct liability, which includes cases against Freeport-McMoRan's Grasburg mine in West Papua (Indonesia) and Texaco in Ecuador, in addition to ExxonMobil's natural gas installation in Aceh (Indonesia), Unocal's oil pipeline in Burma, Chevron and Royal Dutch/Shell for their petroleum operations in the Niger Delta, Rio Tinto for its alleged military collusion in the civil war on Bougainville and British Thor Chemicals for the health impacts of mercury-based chemicals on its South African employees, all of which have recently been or are currently before the courts in the United States and the United Kingdom (Newell 2001; Pegg, Chapter 1 of this book; Ward 2001).[12]

Yet the review carried out by BHP in 1999 claimed that none of the proposed strategies for tailings containment – a tailings dam, as envisioned by the original environmental impact assessment, but never completed; dredging the lower Ok Tedi River to remove tailings and sediment; or a combination of dredging and a 100 kilometer pipeline to transport mine tailings to a lowlands containment area – will substantially mitigate the environmental processes already in train. This assertion prompted the communities downstream from the mine to return to court in Melbourne in April 2000, charging BHP with breach of the original settlement agreement. The case is expected to come to trial in 2003.

Conclusions and recommendations

The full range of factors which have influenced decision-making about the Ok Tedi mine cannot be catalogued here (see Jackson 1993; Filer 1997). Multilateral agencies guaranteed loans and provided risk insurance despite warnings and environmental problems early in the project history. Financial pressure from the unexpected closure of the Panguna mine on Bougainville in 1989 affected government decision-making regarding continued riverine tailings disposal from the Ok Tedi mine. The state faced international pressure to generate export income and had an interest in creating an investment climate that encouraged international capital, given the country's limited infrastructure, lack of skilled labor and high costs of living. The state also had a conflict of interest as a result of its investment in the mine and saw itself as 'paying double' for expenditures on environmental protection, through the loss of both royalties and taxable income.

Finally, there was an absence of binding standards, statutes or laws that could have prevented the problems at Ok Tedi from occurring. Indigenous protests and petitions were comfortably ignored, even when they entered the international arena. The findings of an international tribunal were not heeded. Criticism from scholars fell on deaf ears. Even negative media coverage had little impact until amplified by the court proceedings. Corporate policies, codes of best practice and other voluntary agreements lacking enforcement mechanisms were equally ineffective.

Perhaps the most important observation that one can make with respect to the Ok Tedi case is that despite actively pursuing all of these options, the indigenous people living downstream from the mine were not successful in stopping or even limiting the mine's detrimental impacts. It took years and a combined political and legal campaign to force the mine to take its environmental impact seriously, as indicated by their belated admission in 1999. Moreover, local efforts were largely ineffective despite advantageous circumstances. The 1990s was the UN decade of indigenous peoples and they readily found common cause with environmentalists interested in conserving biodiversity and tropical rain forests. The problems were caused by an industry strongly associated with Australian national identity and a company whose stocks were held by unions and church groups sensitive to these issues. In addition, media coverage of the legal case kept the issues in the public eye.

Despite criticism of the project almost from the outset, BHP and the Ok Tedi mine failed to implement tailings containment that would have prevented the devastation of the Ok Tedi and Fly rivers. In early 2002, BHP Billiton transferred its 52 per cent share in the mine to a trust company established in Singapore that will indemnify both the corporation and the PNG government from future environmental claims. It remains unclear whether the economic returns from this investment will be sufficient to offset the value of the losses downstream; a cost–benefit analysis of this relationship was commissioned by the PNG government and completed in 2001, although the results have not been made public. Rather than take responsibility for the long-term impacts of the mine on the downstream environment, which by their own account will last for at least 50 years and possibly much longer, BHP Billiton severed its relationship with the project and the affected communities. It is unclear how this decision, especially given the uncertain nature of the long-term impacts of the mine, corresponds to the ideals expressed in its corporate social and environmental policy.[13]

Despite the efforts of the affected communities and irrespective of their international support, the outcome at Ok Tedi was disastrous, as even BHP acknowledged in its statement that the Ok Tedi mine is incompatible with its environmental values. The process by which environmental impacts from mining projects are monitored and controlled in Papua New Guinea and elsewhere in the Third World is clearly inadequate and in need of major reform. How might the recognition and enforcement of environmental human rights help to prevent another Ok Tedi?

1. Indigenous communities should have veto power over projects which affect their land, livelihood and use of subsistence resources. To this end, governments, multilateral agencies and NGOs should formally recognize indigenous land and resource rights.[14] For these communities to exercise this power effectively, they need to be fully informed about environmental matters.
2. Independent social and environmental monitoring is required to evaluate mining and other large-scale resource extraction projects. Special efforts must also be undertaken to overcome state conflicts of interest regarding its responsibilities as a regulator on behalf of its citizens and its other economic policies and ownership interests.[15] Regular external reviews should be clearly linked to processes through which necessary changes are mandated and enforced. The review process must be open and transparent and include public participation.
3. Where appropriate, indigenous environmental knowledge should be incorporated into environmental impact assessments and monitoring of extractive industry (see Berkes and Henly 1997; Stevenson 1996).
4. There is an urgent need for full disclosure of environmental information and more effective communication between mining projects and affected communities regarding environmental impacts. Translation and explanation of scientific data and other findings may require special efforts and resources on behalf of indigenous communities.
5. Corporations are responsible for providing just and reasonable compensation for their impact on local environments and resources, local subsistence practices, sacred sites and the full costs of relocation if community permission is granted. These efforts must take cultural values into account as well as the market value of land and resources (see Popović 1996, pp. 537–9).

6. Support should be provided for mechanisms of dispute resolution at a variety of levels, including the courts. Access to international courts should not be restricted, as the government of Papua New Guinea attempted to do in 1995 by criminalizing participation in overseas legal actions against mining corporations for their operations in Papua New Guinea, claiming infringement of their national sovereignty. Nor should the countries where transnational corporations are incorporated oppose legal action when affected parties lack access to impartial courts in their home countries. Forums such as the International Water Tribunal should be supported and their verdicts linked to mechanisms of enforcement, including binding obligations on multilateral agencies that finance and insure international development projects like the Ok Tedi mine.

7. Finally, there is an urgent need for international legal precedents on environmental human rights that rise to the level of recognized standards and norms. Greater specificity is needed for the standards for environmental human rights if they are to be operationalized. Double standards which allow corporations to operate according to lower standards abroad, potentially resulting in environmental racism, should be prohibited. For example, a mine using riverine tailings disposal would not be approved in Canada or the United States, so its operation in Papua New Guinea should not be accepted even though it might comply with national standards.

The potential benefits of these recommendations include greater social and environmental justice, and the reduction in violence and conflict over resource development. Changes in how extractive industries and host governments calculate the costs of environmental degradation and pollution are also necessary; these externalities should be internalized from the outset of project planning. Moreover, mining companies need to assess their responsibilities in terms of longer time frames commensurate with the longevity of their environmental impacts, for example, at least 50 years in the case of the Ok Tedi mine (see Adam 1998). New standards for responsible mining practices must be developed, perhaps focused on mining on smaller scales with reduced throughputs. No new ore body should be exploited until reliable strategies for tailings containment have been identified. This means that some ore bodies will be off-limits to development in the immediate future, and perhaps even permanently, if no effective means of tailings disposal is available. Some strategies of waste disposal, for example, riverine tailings disposal in the tropics, as used by the Ok Tedi mine,

Freeport-McMoRan's Grasburg mine, and the Porgera mine in New Guinea, should be permanently banned.

Whether or not a basic human 'right to the environment' has been firmly established, a productive and healthy environment is clearly fundamental to the exercise of other human rights. It is imperative that these reforms be enacted and enforced, to prevent extractive industries, in their pursuit of financial gain, and host governments, in their pursuit of other development goals, from denying essential human rights to indigenous peoples. This case study also demonstrates that conflict with local communities is unavoidable until transnational corporations look beyond regulatory requirements and procedures for compensation to recognize environmental human rights and make these principles the cornerstones of industrial policy and practice.

Notes

1. This chapter is a revised and shortened version of a paper presented at a workshop sponsored by the United Nations High Commissioner for Human Rights in Geneva on 'Indigenous Peoples, Private Sector Natural Resource, Energy and Mining Companies and Human Rights' in December 2001. My research on mining in Papua New Guinea was generously supported by the Royal Anthropological Institute and Goldsmiths College Fellowship for Urgent Anthropology and the Center for International Business Education at the University of Michigan. I would like to thank the editors for their invitation to contribute to this volume and their suggestions for revisions, although I take full responsibility for any errors of fact or interpretation.
2. Critics of human rights regimes have argued that they constitute an extension of the colonial project, making universal claims for what is essentially a cultural model drawn from Euro–American intellectual traditions (Mutua 2002). The assumptions which they make about the appropriate relationship between individual rights and society, for example, run counter to many cultural traditions. Moreover, these regimes lack 'the analytical or normative tools – or even the desire and gumption – to unpack the complex oppressions which globalization now wreaks on individuals and communities' (Mutua 2002, p. 157). Critics call for new dialogues and debates that 'confront structurally and in a meaningful way the deep-seated imbalances of power and privilege which bedevil our world' (Mutua 2002, p. 157). Other scholars have written critically about how the 'market of civic virtue' shapes academic discourse on human rights (Rabinow 2002, p. 147, n. 7). While sympathetic to some of these arguments, I oppose the dismantling of existing human rights regimes in the absence of concrete alternatives. This chapter, as well as the other contributions to this volume, recommends a strengthening of these regimes through their application to corporate behavior, providing new political resources to affected persons and communities by establishing new means to hold transnational corporations accountable for their actions.

3. In its statement on environmental policy, BHP commits to: 'Comply with all applicable laws, regulations and standards; uphold the spirit of the law; and where laws do not adequately protect the environment, apply standards that minimise any adverse environmental impacts resulting from its operations, productions and services' (Anderson 1999).

4. In 2001, the shareholders in the Ok Tedi mine were BHP (52 per cent), the Independent State of Papua New Guinea (30 per cent) and Inmet Mining Corporation (18 per cent). In 2002, BHP merged with the London-based Billiton to become BHP Billiton, which divested its ownership share of the mine into a Singapore-based trust (the Sustainable Development Program Company).

5. Hyndman (1994, p. 90) notes that, 'the state renegotiated the project six times to sustain mining production, thereby canceling the environmental protection envisioned in the original OTES [Ok Tedi Environmental Study]'.

6. The production of copper concentrate in 1998 was 491,336 tons, containing 151,556 tons of copper, 413,265 ounces of gold and 838,619 ounces of silver (Ok Tedi Mining Ltd 2001).

7. The value of the Papua New Guinea kina in 1998 was US$0.4856.

8. This figure has been greatly reduced by the devaluation of the Papua New Guinea kina by more than 60 per cent (from US$0.749 in 1996 to US$0.275 in 2002), and by the failure to implement tailings containment, by far the largest expenditure envisioned by the settlement.

9. BHP declined to respond, despite being informed of the case and given ample opportunity to do so (International Water Tribunal 1984, p. 84).

10. More than 10,000 political refugees crossed the international border from Papua (formerly Irian Jaya, Indonesia) into Papua New Guinea in 1984 (Kirsch 1989b).

11. Meg Taylor (1997, p. 24) notes that 'where the state acquires equity in major resource projects, it tends to relinquish its role as an independent arbiter in matters relating to a project, especially in matters involving environmental and social impact... It is not impartial and therefore not accessible to the people whose interests are damaged'.

12. The US cases are being heard under the Alien Claims Tort Act (ACTA), a 1789 law designed to enable the United States to hear claims against sea pirates who lacked a national domicile.

13. BHP's community relations policies includes a pledge to 'work co-operatively with all communities affected by proposed or existing operations for their long term benefit and that of our shareholders', as well as the obligation to 'consult with communities, and understand and respond to their concerns and wishes about the responsible management of these impacts' (Prescott 1997).

14. The Independent Commission on International Humanitarian Issues (1987, p. 50) argues that, 'all indigenous land should be made inalienable and secure, mining operations should be re-examined and, if necessary, suspended when the indigenous community is seriously affected and so demands'.

15. Writing about the Ok Tedi case after the settlement, lawyer and former Ambassador from Papua New Guinea to the United States Meg Taylor (1997, p. 24) argued that 'it is an absolute necessity to keep environmental regulation and audit at arm's length'.

References

Adam, Barbara. 1998. *Timescapes of Modernity: the Environment and Invisible Hazards*. New York: Routledge.

Anderson, Paul M. 1999. *BHP Environmental Policy*. Mimeo.

Banks, Glenn. 1998. 'Compensation for Communities Affected by Mining and Oil Developments in Melanesia', *The Malaysian Journal of Tropical Geography* 29 (1): 53–67.

Barker, Geoffrey and Stewart Oldfield. 1999. 'BHP Admits Mine is a Mess, Downer says Dig in', *Australian Financial Review*, 12 August.

Berkes, Fikret and Thomas Henly. 1997. 'Co-Management and Traditional Knowledge: Threat or Opportunity?', *Policy Options*, March, pp. 29–31.

Broderick, Vincent L. (United States District Judge). 1994. In *Maria Aguinda et al. v. Texaco, Inc.* 93 Civ 7527 (VLB). Memorandum. 11 April: p. 16.

Burton, John. 1997. '*Terra Nugax* and the Discovery Paradigm', in Glenn Banks and Chris Ballard, eds, *The Ok Tedi Settlement: Issues, Outcomes and Implications*, pp. 27–55. Canberra: National Centre for Development Studies, Pacific Policy Paper 27 and Resource Management in Asia-Pacific.

Chapman, Peter, Margaret Burchett, Peter Campbell, William Dietrich and Barry Hart. 2000. 'Ok Tedi Mining, Ltd. (OTML) Environment Peer Review Group (PRG): Comments on Key Issues and Review Comments on the Final Human and Ecological Risk Assessment Documents', pp. 1–19. April. Available at www.oktedi.com.

Duval, J. Jr. 1997. *Tom Beanal, On Behalf of Himself and All Others Similarly Situated v. Freeport-McMoRan, Inc., and Freeport-McMoRan Copper and Gold, Inc.* [Civil Action No. 96-1474 Section K]. United States District Court, Eastern District of Louisiana. 9 April 1997.

Filer, Colin. 1997. 'West Side Story: the State's and Other Stakes in the Ok Tedi Mine', in Glenn Banks and Chris Ballard, eds, *The Ok Tedi Settlement: Issues, Outcomes and Implications*, pp. 56–93. Canberra: National Centre for Development Studies, Pacific Policy Paper 27 and Resource Management in Asia-Pacific.

Gordon, John. 1997. 'The Ok Tedi Lawsuit in Retrospect', in Glenn Banks and Chris Ballard, eds, *The Ok Tedi Settlement: Issues, Outcomes and Implications*, pp. 141–66. Canberra: National Centre for Development Studies, Pacific Policy Paper 27 and Resource Management in Asia-Pacific.

Harper, Ainsley and Mark Israel. 1999. 'The Killing of the Fly: State-Corporate Victimization in Papua New Guinea'. Australian National University Resource Management in Asia-Pacific Working Paper 22. 20 pages. ISSN 1444 187X. Available at: http://rspas.anu.edu.au/rmap/Wpapers/rmap_wp22.pdf.

Hohmann, Harold, ed. 1992. *Basic Documents of International Environmental Law*, Vol. 1. London: Graham and Trotman.

Higgins, Roger J. 2002. 'Ok Tedi: Creating Community Partnerships for Sustainable Development'. Available at www.oktedi.com.

Hyndman, David. 1988. 'Ok Tedi: New Guinea's Disaster Mine', *Ecologist* 18: 24–9.

Hyndman, David. 1994. *Ancestral Rain Forests and the Mountain of Gold: Indigenous Peoples and Mining in New Guinea*. Boulder: Westview Press.

Independent Commission on International Humanitarian Issues (ICHI). 1987. *Indigenous Peoples: a Global Quest for Justice.* A report for the Independent Commission on International Humanitarian Issues (ICIHI). New Jersey: Zed Books.

International Union for the Conservation of Nature and Natural Resources (IUCN). 1995. *The Fly River Catchment, Papua New Guinea – A Regional Environmental Assessment.* Published in collaboration with the Department of Environment and Conservation, Boroko, Papua New Guinea. IUCN: Cambridge, UK.

International Water Tribunal. 1994. 'Ecological Damage Caused by the Discharges from the Ok Tedi Copper and Gold Mine', in *Mining*, pp. 49–85. Second International Water Tribunal, Case Books. Utrecht: International Books.

Jackson, Richard. 1993. *Cracked Pot or Copper Bottomed Investment? The Development of the Ok Tedi Project 1982–1991, A Personal View.* Townsville: Melanesian Studies Centre, James Cook University.

Kimmerling, Judith. 1997. 'Oil, Lawlessness and Indigenous Struggles in Ecuador's Oriente', in Helen Collinson, ed., *Green Guerrillas: Environmental Conflicts and Initiatives in Latin America and the Caribbean*, pp. 61–73. New York: Black Rose Books.

Kirsch, Stuart. 1989a. 'Ok Tedi River a Sewer'. *The Times of Papua New Guinea*, 1–7 June, 491: 3.

Kirsch, Stuart. 1989b. 'The Yonggom, the Refugee Camps along the Border, and the Impact of the Ok Tedi Mine', *Research in Melanesia* 12: 30–61.

Kirsch, Stuart. 1995. 'Social Impact of the Ok Tedi Mine on the Yonggom Villages of the North Fly, 1992'. *Research in Melanesia* 19: 23–102. Originally distributed as 'Ok-Fly Social Monitoring Programme', Report No. 5. Port Moresby: Unisearch PNG Pty Ltd (1993).

Kirsch, Stuart. 1997. 'Is Ok Tedi a Precedent? Implications of the Settlement', in Glenn Banks and Chris Ballard, eds, *The Ok Tedi Settlement: Issues, Outcomes and Implications*, pp. 118–40. Canberra: National Centre for Development Studies, Pacific Policy Paper 27 and Resource Management in Asia-Pacific.

Kirsch, Stuart. 2001. 'Lost Worlds: Environmental Disaster, "Culture Loss" and the Law', *Current Anthropology* 42(2): 167–98.

Kirsch, Stuart. 2002. 'Anthropology and Advocacy: a Case Study of the Campaign against the Ok Tedi Mine', *Critique of Anthropology* 22(2): 175–200.

Muchlinski, Peter R. 2001. 'Human Rights and Multinationals: Is There a Problem?', *International Affairs* 77(1): 31–47.

Mutua, Makau. 2002. *Human Rights: a Political and Cultural Critique.* Philadelphia: University of Pennsylvania Press.

Newell, Peter. 2001. 'Access to Environmental Justice? Litigation against TNCs in the South', *Making Law Matter: Rules, Rights and Security in the Lives of the Poor. IDS Bulletin* 32(1): 83–93.

Ok Tedi Mining Ltd. 2001. At http://www.oktedi.com.

Papua New Guinea. 1975. *The Constitution of the Independent State of Papua New Guinea*, Port Moresby: Department of the Prime Minister.

Parametrix, Inc. and URS Greiner Woodward Clyde. 1999a. 'Draft Executive Summary: Assessment of Human Health and Ecological Risks for Proposed Mine Waste Mitigation Options at the Ok Tedi Mine, Papua New Guinea.

Detailed Level Risk Assessment'. Prepared for Ok Tedi Mining, Ltd., pp. 1–15. 6 August. Available at www.oktedi.com.

Parametrix, Inc. and URS Greiner Woodward Clyde. 1999b. 'Draft Executive Summary: Assessment of Human Health and Ecological Risks for Proposed Mine Waste Mitigation Options at the Ok Tedi Mine, Papua New Guinea. Screening Level Risk Assessment'. Prepared for Ok Tedi Mining, Ltd., pp. 1–13. 13 August. Available at www.oktedi.com.

Pintz, William. 1987. 'Environmental Negotiations in the Ok Tedi Mine in Papua New Guinea', in Charles Pearson, ed., *Multinational Corporations, Environment and the Third World: Business Matters*, pp. 35–63. Durham, NC: Duke University Press.

Popović, Neil A.F. 1996. 'In Pursuit of Environmental Human Rights: Commentary on the Draft Declaration of Principles on Human Rights and the Environment', *Columbia Human Rights Law Review* 27(3): 487–603.

Prescott, J.B. (Managing Director and Chief Executive Officer, BHP). 1997. *BHP Community Relations Policy*. Mimeo.

Rabinow, Paul. 2002. 'Midst Anthropology's Problems', The 2001 David M. Schneider Distinguished Lecture, *Cultural Anthropology* 17(2): 135–49.

Rappaport, Roy A. 1993. 'Distinguished Lecture in General Anthropology: the Anthropology of Trouble', *American Anthropologist* 95(2): 295–303.

Rosario, Judge Eriberto U. 1993. In *Juan Antonio Oposa et al. v. The Honourable Fulgencio S. Factoran, Jr*, in his capacity as the Secretary of the Department of Environment and Natural Resources, and the Honorable Eriberto U. Rosario, Presiding Judge of the RTC, Makati, Branch 66, respondents [G.R. No. 101083. July 30].

Rosenbaum, Helen and Michael Krockenberger. 1993. *Report on the Impacts of the Ok Tedi Mine in Papua New Guinea*. A report for the Australian Conservation Foundation, November.

Sahlins, Marshall. 2000. 'What is Anthropological Enlightenment? Some Lessons of the Twentieth Century', in Marshall Sahlins, *Culture in Practice: Selected Essays*, pp. 501–26. New York: Zone Books.

Schoell, Hans-Martin. 1994. 'Part One. Introduction: Controversies about Development in the Pacific', in Hans-Martin Schoell, ed., *Development and Environment in Papua New Guinea: an Overview*, pp. 9–16. Goroka: The Melanesian Institute (POINT).

Starnberg Institute. 1991. *Development and the Environment: Economic-Ecological Development in Papua New Guinea*. Commissioned by the Department of World Mission of the Evangelical Lutheran Church in Bavaria, Germany. Goroka: The Melanesian Institute for Pastoral and Socio-Economic Services.

Stevenson, Marc G. 1996. 'Indigenous Knowledge in Environmental Assessment', *Arctic* 49(3): 278–91.

Taylor, Meg. 1997. 'Putting Ok Tedi in Perspective', in Glenn Banks and Chris Ballard, eds, *The Ok Tedi Settlement: Issues, Outcomes and Implications*, pp. 12–26. Canberra: National Centre for Development Studies, Pacific Policy Paper 27 and Resource Management in Asia-Pacific.

Townsend, William. 1988. 'Giving away the River: Environmental Issues in the Construction of the Ok Tedi Mine, 1981–1984', in J.C. Pernetta, ed., *Potential Impacts of Mining on the Fly River*, pp. 107–19. United Nations Environment

Program: UNEP Regional Seas Reports and Studies No. 99 and SPREP Topic Review No. 33.

United Nations Economic and Social Council. 1994. *Question of the Realization of the Right to Development.* Commission on Human Rights, Fiftieth session, Agenda item 8: points 6–10, 10 February (E/CN.4/1994/NGO/50). Written statement submitted by Human Rights Advocates, a non-governmental organization in consultative status (category II).

Victorian Supreme Court 1995. *Rex Dagi et al. v. The Broken Hill Proprietary Company Limited No. 5782 of 1994 and others,* 24 October, pp. 58–63.

Ward, Halina. 2001. 'Securing Transnational Corporate Accountability through National Courts: Implications and Policy Options', *Hastings International and Comparative Law Review* 24: 451–74.

7
US Certification Initiatives in the Coffee Industry: the Battle for Just Remuneration

Ronie Garcia-Johnson[1]

Introduction

The value chain of coffee, the world's second most valuable commodity after oil, differs markedly between the production side and the final consumption side. At the supply end – in developing countries in Africa, Asia and Latin America – we find story after story of human exploitation and repression. When colonial powers first disseminated coffee around the globe, they also sent along slaves and indentured immigrants. People who were not forcibly or illegally removed from the land where coffee was eventually planted remained, often indebted, to cultivate a cash crop in an uncertain market instead of traditional subsistence plants and trees; this cultivation subsequently devastated the eco-systems upon which people depended, through deforestation, depletion and pesticide use. When children have not worked alongside men and women to plant, harvest and process coffee, they have suffered from poor living conditions, hunger and malnutrition, with little hope of gaining an education.

At the supply end of the chain, the state plays a major role. Coffee barons thwarted the development of unions and cooperatives as they built repressive political parties, armies and the states themselves. Non-democratic and corrupt regimes have used coffee profits to fill coffers as they engaged in civil wars or committed genocide against their own citizens. It was states that, through their coffee associations, worked to make coffee production viable within their territories. And states cooperated to build a multilateral institution, the International Coffee Organization (ICO), to stabilize world coffee prices.

At the other end of the value chain, in industrialized countries (and particularly the United States, the world's largest coffee importer) coffee availability has been taken for granted by consumers, whether it comes freeze-dried in a can and sold for pennies or freshly roasted and served in a large mug for as much as five dollars. In contrast to the supply end of the value chain, the state does not usually intervene in the market. Instead, enormous conglomerate TNCs dominate; the industrial roasters that they own market their coffee blends under familiar brands such as Folgers and Maxwell House. During the past few decades, smaller, gourmet roasters have emerged to cater to consumers longing for quality coffee and a more genteel retail experience. More recently, on this end of the value chain, in industrialized countries, non-governmental organizations (NGOs) have appeared to challenge the TNCs and small roasters alike to address the needs of those at the supply end of the value chain.

The story of coffee told in this chapter begins in 1989 with the collapse of the 1963 International Coffee Agreement (ICA), to which both producer and consumer countries belonged. The price stabilization it created benefited coffee growers, and, we might argue, positively affected basic human rights including 'just and favourable remuneration' and 'a standard of living adequate for the health and well-being of himself and of his family' (Universal Declaration of Human Rights articles 23 and 25, United Nations 1948) in coffee-growing countries around the world. With the collapse of this institution in 1989, and, later, a coffee glut, prices fell dramatically. In a buyers' market, large TNCs have purchased coffee at prices that have left growers without sufficient income; human rights problems endemic to the industry have been exacerbated.

For the first time in the history of the global coffee industry, it seems, private actors – NGOs and smaller roasters, *instead of the state*, and instead of intergovernmental organizations, have stepped in to build institutions to check the market. This time, organizations in consuming countries, rather than producing countries, have taken action to address market-driven inequities. Instead of working to protect an industry within a country, these private groups have worked to protect individuals and communities. And instead of lobbying governments to take action on human rights issues (Keck and Sikkink 1998; Risse et al. 1999; Risse 2000), these private groups have created certification institutions. Similar institutions have emerged in other industries, among them apparel and footwear, architecture and construction, chemical, fishing, forest products, mining and petroleum (Garcia-Johnson 2001).

Environmental and social certification institutions, designed with the expressed purpose of protecting the environment or human and labor rights, incorporate two fundamental components: a 'set of rules, principles or guidelines' (usually in the form of a code of conduct, environmental management system or a more general set of policies) and a 'reporting or monitoring mechanism' (a corporate environmental report, audit or labeling scheme) (Gereffi et al. 2001). Whether they are created by business firms, industry organizations, NGOs or governmental actors, social and environmental certification institutions are designed to provide information (as a kind of public good) to producers and consumers; that information, ideally, guides the behavior of both groups (Garcia-Johnson 2001).

Certification institutions fall roughly along a spectrum of ideal types. In first-party certification institutions, a firm or other organization generates rules internally and itself reports conformity; in second-party institutions, a firm works with other firms (usually through a trade association) to generate rules and to report conformity; in third-party institutions the firm or organization *voluntarily* agrees to allow one or more external, functionally distinct governmental or non-governmental group to generate rules and to report compliance beyond the firm. Fourth-party certification institutions involve universally imposed standards set and/ or overseen by government or international regulatory regimes (Gereffi et al. 2001).

Certainly, in some coffee-growing communities that participate in certification institutions, coffee certification is successfully providing growers with enough money to feed their families. Yet currently, coffee certification misses the mark, in that it has yet successfully to engage producers in contexts where human rights violations are likely to be prevalent. The largest coffee roasters have not been persuaded to participate. Instead, TNCs are developing their own initiatives to protect human rights and the environment. In this chapter, I briefly explain the structure of the coffee industry and the role of major TNCs in it. I explore the battles between NGOs and TNCs on human rights issues, and explain the development of three coffee certification initiatives in the United States. Finally, I discuss the prospects for certification to further the protection of human rights (in particular, just remuneration) in the coffee industry.

From TNCs to specialty roasters: shaping the coffee market

Some fifty countries around the world export the coffee that is eventually sold in a $55 billion market (Neuffer 2001). Brazil is the world's largest coffee producer, and Colombia – until recently, when Vietnam took its place – has been the second largest. Yet Brazil is much less dependent on coffee than it used to be, and is also less dependent than many smaller producers in Latin America and Africa. For instance, in Uganda and Burundi, the percentage of export earnings from coffee has been over 70 per cent (Dicum and Luttinger 1999, p. 100). Coffee production is organized differently around the globe. One 'very rough estimate' suggests that some 70 per cent of the world's coffee comes from small farms of less than 10 hectares; in some countries, these small farms dominate, while in others, including Brazil, Guatemala, India, Kenya and Vietnam, large plantations are more common (Van de Kasteele and Zeldenrust 2000, p. 5).

The United States is the world's leading coffee importer. According to Dicum and Luttinger (1999, p. 38), the US consumed one-fifth of the world's coffee in 1996, with Germany importing over 14 per cent and Japan and France importing over 7 per cent each in the early 1990s (Coffee Research Institute 2002). For the better part of the twentieth century, a handful of coffee brands have dominated the coffee market in the United States. Folgers has generally led the pack, followed by Maxwell House, Hills Brothers and Chock Full O'Nuts. Today, these coffee brands and others are owned by major TNCs: Procter & Gamble owns Folgers; Kraft, which is majority owned by Philip Morris, owns Maxwell House; Nestlé owns Hills Brothers; and the Sara Lee Corporation owns Chock Full O'Nuts (see Dicum and Luttinger 1999, pp. 130–1, 128). These TNCs 'account for 60 per cent of US retail sales and 40 per cent of worldwide sales' (Neuffer 2001) (see Table 7.1). Starbucks, a company that differs greatly from the large conglomerates, can also be considered a TNC given its global operations; it is described in more detail below.

The largest coffee roasters in the United States, working through a system of brokers, import and roast some 80 per cent of the country's coffee. The major roasters then blend it according to secret brand formulas. Through their many brands, the conglomerates aggressively compete with one another for supermarket sales (where 64 per cent of US coffee sales took place in 1998) (see Dicum and Luttinger 1999, pp. 68, 71).

As the coalition that held the ICA together was deteriorating, the specialty coffee industry in the United States emerged, with companies including Starbucks, Peet's Coffee and the Coffee Connection. While at first, the specialty industry was dwarfed by the traditional one (Starbuck's 1988 sales of $10 million were a drop in the bucket in a $5 billion US industry), ten years later 'retail specialty beverage sales in the United States … passed $3 billion … with another $2 billion of roasted beans sold. This new U.S. industry suddenly consumed 5 per cent of the world's coffee output' (Dicum and Luttinger 1999, pp. 147–8). The 'specialty

Table 7.1 TNCs and their major coffee brands

TNC	Philip Morris (Kraft General Foods)	Procter & Gamble	Sara Lee	Nestlé	Starbucks
Coffee brands	Brim, General Foods International Coffees, Gevalia, Jacobs, Maxim, Maxwell House, Sanka, Yuban	Folgers, High Point, Millstone	Chock Full O'Nuts, Douwe Egberts, Maison Du Café, Pilao, Superior Coffee	Hills Brothers, MJB, Nescafé, Taster's Choice	Starbucks Coffee (various blends) and Frappuccino
US coffee market share in 1996; coffee related revenues	Philip Morris – 30%; $1.2 billion	35%; less than $1.5 billion	Figures not available	10%; $400 million	$967 million (1997)
Global market share	24%	7%	7%	25%	1%
Scope of sales	Kraft – sales in 140 countries	Sales in 140 countries	Sales in over 180 countries	Sales in over 80 countries	Customers in 23 countries
Total revenues in millions of dollars (2001)	Kraft – 33,900	39,224 (net sales)	17,204	50,254	2649 (net)

Sources: Dicum and Luttinger 1999, pp. 121–56; Pendergrast 2000; Van de Kasteele and Zeldenrust 2000, p. 14; Kraft 2001; Nolan 2001; Starbucks 2001a, 2002; Maitland 2002; Sara Lee 2002; Standard and Poor's Market Insight 2002.

revolution', as it is known, did not immediately change the structure of the industry. Instead, some argue, it is a 'new industry' that is 'represented by its own trade groups contending with its own unique issues' (Dicum and Luttinger 1999, p. 145).

The specialty coffee industry quickly moved beyond the United States. By May 2000, Starbucks had between 2900 and 3000 fully-owned stores in 15 countries. As he finished opening Starbucks stores in Hong Kong, Seoul and Shanghai, company CEO Howard Schultz was struck by the realization that 'we had achieved the status of a worldwide enterprise and a global brand ... We are no longer just an American company but something truly international'. Schultz explained, 'Our aim is to see more people drinking coffee than eating hamburgers. McDonalds has 25,000 outlets around the world ... we are going to get there too' (Gumbel 2000). In 2002 Starbucks operated over 5400 stores around the globe (Jung 2002) and was purchasing 1 per cent of the world's coffee supply (Maitland 2002).

Still, the specialty coffee industry differs from the traditional one in several important ways. It prefers mild arabica beans to harsh and often bitter robusta: the quality of beans, judged subjectively by master roasters who travel the world in search of perfection, matters more than quantity. It pays special attention to the origins of coffee (buying, for the most part, from estates and small cooperatives). The specialty coffee industry is also devoted to the careful preparation of coffee. It offers freshly roasted beans, and incorporates point-of-sale retail sites, primarily targeted at consumers with higher income and education levels – people who care less about the cost of their coffee.

Targeting TNCs: from Folgers to Starbucks

Two major types of human rights concerns involving the cultivation and production of coffee have prompted activists to focus on the role of transnational corporations in the industry during the past three decades. One of them focuses on political human rights; the other on social and economic rights. The first type of concern addresses government repression, torture or genocide, especially in war-torn countries, or in countries dominated by non-democratic and corrupt governments. The second main area of concern revolves around the industry's effects on small farmers, laborers and children in coffee-dependent regions; the rights for fair compensation, sound working conditions and the right to organize are most salient. While the first type of concern has earned attention over time, the latter has won increased attention since the collapse of the International Coffee Agreement, the resulting fall in prices, and the growth of the specialty coffee industry.

Government atrocities

In 1977, news stories that the US was purchasing one-third of Uganda's exports, which directly profited the dictator Idi Amin caused a stir.

Reports that 93 per cent of Amin's export earnings came from coffee, and claims that his regime was engaged in human rights violations including genocide, prompted TNC roasters to comment about the percentage of Ugandan robusta they used, or to dismiss a focus on roasters. One Nestlé official complained, 'This is not a question for us; it's a question of U.S. foreign policy' (cited in Morgan 1977). As activists supported a bill in the House of Representatives to boycott Ugandan coffee, the National Coffee Association, representing TNCs, demanded a uniform government policy on the issue. Yet once Congress seemed likely to pass a resolution in support of an embargo, Procter & Gamble broke ranks and announced that it would not buy coffee from Uganda; Nestlé and General Foods soon followed, only they claimed that they had already stopped buying it (Pendergrast 2000, pp. 327–9; Tofani 1978). Congress imposed an embargo later in 1978 (Pendergrast 2000, pp. 327–9).

Over ten years later, just as coffee roasters were contending with the collapse of the ICA and a liberalized coffee market, a Californian NGO with 52,000 members, run by an activist who had worked with Chico Mendes during the grape boycott of the 1960s, called attention to human rights violations closer to home: the US-supported military regime's death squad attacks on rebels and civilians alike in the context of the bloody civil war in El Salvador. At the time, El Salvador exported 60 per cent of its coffee to the United States. Activists argued that the government, and its military death squads, were funded in part by coffee exports. Roasters of Salvadoran coffee and, by implication, Salvadoran coffee drinkers were supporting a violent, repressive regime and its atrocities. In November 1989, after the murder of six Jesuit priests, Neighbor to Neighbor began to leaflet and threaten boycotts against the industry. Together with over 50 church, consumer and humanitarian organizations, it placed full-page ads in the *New York Times* naming Folgers, Hills Brothers and other companies (Pendergrast 2000, p. 355; Stein 1989; *St Louis Post-Dispatch* 1989).

In response, union dockworkers on the West Coast refused to unload Salvadoran coffee shipments, and General Foods, Procter & Gamble and Nestlé were forced to receive their shipments elsewhere. In early December 1989, Hills Brothers (the third largest US coffee company) decided to suspend new coffee contracts from El Salvador for thirty days. Nestlé, which had suffered from a consumer boycott of its infant formula, announced that it would also suspend coffee purchases from El Salvador for thirty days (Pendergrast 2000, p. 355; Stein 1989; *St Louis Post-Dispatch* 1989).

But the San Francisco NGO made no headway with Procter & Gamble's Folgers (Pendergrast 2000, p. 355). It developed a television commercial, narrated by actor Ed Asner, that specifically named Folgers. The commercial linked the war and oppression of coffee workers to the company and demanded an end to US military aid to the government of El Salvador. A Boston CBS affiliate ran the commercial, and shortly afterwards, on 11 May 1990, Procter & Gamble pulled their advertising from the station. The company did not seem too concerned about being singled out for its use of Salvadoran beans, and claimed that, as less than 2 per cent of the brand's coffee came from that country, 'Folgers contains less coffee from El Salvador than the average American cup of coffee' (Ramirez 1990).

Neighbor to Neighbor called for a boycott of Folgers. The boycott gained speed, and spread to retailers serving or offering Folger's coffee. It was supported by a Gamble heir (Cuff 1990) and the mayor of Boston, who ordered a ban on it in city departments and agencies (*Boston Globe* 1990). Procter & Gamble eventually renewed its advertising on the Boston television affiliate (Associated Press 1990), and the *Wall Street Journal* reported that Folgers was developing a Salvadoran-bean-free coffee blend (Stern 1991). But the boycott continued until a peace accord was signed in El Salvador (*Columbus Dispatch* 1992).

Fair wages, working conditions, and the right to organize

As the collapse of the ICA took its toll, and coffee prices fell during the mid-1990s, gourmet coffee consumers continued to pay high prices for their coffee drinks. Noting this trend, a group of activists inspired by the writings of Nobel Peace Prize winner Rigoberta Menchu began to demand fair wages, standard working conditions and the right to unionize for Central American coffee workers. By late 1994, the Guatemala Labor Education Project (US/GLEP, now US/Labor Education in the Americas Project, or US/LEAP) was demanding that Starbucks adopt a code of conduct like those created by Levi Strauss and Reebok. 'We are requesting that Starbucks adopt a CODE OF CONDUCT setting forth basic conditions (E.G. no child labor, compliance with labor law, no repression against workers who organize unions, fair wages) that must be met by their business partners who produce the coffee these retailers sell. These codes of conduct establish the fundamental principle that companies can and should take responsibility for the working conditions of their suppliers, whether at home or abroad', read an 'Urgent Action Guatemala' e-mail alert describing the new campaign (Shniad 1995).

Coordinated through a Seattle-based umbrella group, the Coalition for Justice for Coffee Workers, the activists began publicizing the news that Central American coffee workers were underpaid, and that they did not earn enough money to feed and clothe their children. Coffee workers in Guatemala earned a minimum wage of just $2.50 a day, when the government estimated it would take $7.25 to feed a family of five (Nogaki 1995). To make matters worse, those who worked for change within Guatemala – by going to the courts or organizing in unions – faced repression and violence (US/GLEP 1996). Focusing on issues in Guatemala, the coalition sent letters to Starbucks' Howard Schultz requesting fair wages, sound working conditions and the right to organize for coffee workers. On 11 February 1995, activists handed out leaflets at 75 Starbucks stores in 25 cities across the United States and Canada. Four days later, on 15 February, Starbucks announced its intention to develop a code of conduct (Makower 1995; US/GLEP 1996).

Starbucks' 'framework for a code of conduct' (what we would consider an incomplete, first-party certification institution) was unveiled some six months later, in late October 1995. The document's 'Statement of Beliefs' addressed the 'human rights and dignity' issues of forced labor, freedom of association, child labor, wage levels and basic needs, and asserted the company's dedication to non-hazardous working conditions, educational opportunities and clean and safe housing and facilities. It also addressed cultural and environmental issues. The document's guidelines for coffee selection indicated that Starbucks would purchase quality coffee that enhanced its 'competitiveness in the world market', and coffee that came from people who 'share our commitment for treating employees with respect and dignity', and grow coffee 'in a manner that reflects our environmental mission' (Starbucks 1995). Starbucks' spokeswoman Jeanne McKay explained, 'To our knowledge, we are the first coffee company attempting to improve the conditions in the coffee-origin countries through a code of conduct.' *The Wall Street Journal* reported the belief that the guidelines were the first of a large 'US importer involving an agricultural commodity' (Zachary 1995).

Despite the fanfare, the 'framework for a code of conduct' was immediately criticized by the International Labor Rights Fund and other groups for its lack of verification or enforcement mechanisms. Jeanne McKay responded to criticism that the code was not strong enough by noting that Starbucks purchased under 'half of one per cent of the world's coffee' and did not have enough leverage to force plantation owners to change their treatment of workers. Moreover, the company did not want to make promises that it could not keep (Lim 1995).

In June 1996, Starbucks received the Corporate Conscience International Human Rights Award from the Council on Economic

Priorities in recognition of its code. But critics argued that Starbucks had not done enough to implement the code as a pilot in Guatemala and threatened to renew their campaign. Although the company announced an agreement to work with Appropriate Technology International, a non-profit organization established by Congress in the 1970s to make change on the ground in Guatemala (Moriwaki 1997) the Coalition for Justice for Coffee Workers was not satisfied, and renewed its campaign against Starbucks in 1997. At a press conference called by the coalition, various groups explained that they wanted Starbucks to monitor suppliers (Solomon 1997; DiBenedetto 1997). Starbucks argued once again that it did not have the capacity – with just 5 per cent of the market share of coffee in Guatemala – to do so (DiBenedetto 1997).

Yet by July 1997, US/GLEP had suspended the campaign that it had renewed in March. Starbucks had begun a dialogue with US/GLEP and other human rights and labor groups, and was interested in working to implement a pilot incentives program in Guatemala (US/GLEP 1997). In early 1998, the company released a 'Framework for Action for Improving the Lives of People Who Grow, Harvest and Process Coffee' which outlined its implementation plan (although this fell short of US/GLEP's expectations) (US/GLEP 1998). Starbucks also funded a 2000 Commission for the Verification of Codes of Conduct (COVERCO) study of general working conditions in the Guatemalan coffee industry that uncovered labor law violations on coffee plantations (and that is now often cited by NGOs as they describe human rights problems in the industry). Starbucks also began to discuss the issue of monitoring (US/LEAP 2001a).

While US/LEAP worked to move Starbucks forward with its initial code of conduct, others – notably San Francisco-based Global Exchange – began an aggressive campaign targeting the company. Global Exchange was founded in 1988 by Kevin Danaher and Medea Benjamin. The origins of the group can be traced to the anti-Apartheid movement. Danaher explained, 'We forced over 200 U.S. corporations to pull out of South Africa, which was one of the most profitable markets ... You raise the hassle factor enough, and they bail' (Mann 2000).

The emergence of social certification and the fair trade movement in the US

Since 1985, NGOs and firms have emerged in the United States to shape production and consumption in the industry through innovative trade programs. For example, in recognition of the relationships linking coffee to the revolution in Nicaragua, Paul Katzeff of California's Thanksgiving Coffee began selling Nicaraguan coffee beans as 'Coffee for Peace', and contributed 50 cents for every pound he sold to the Sandinista rebels (Pendergrast 2000, p. 353). In 1986, in Massachusetts, three former food co-op workers established Equal Exchange to buy coffee from co-ops in Nicaragua at a consistent price for sale to co-ops in the US; coffee growers were encouraged to grow their beans in an ecologically sensitive fashion (Pendergrast 2000, p. 354). Fair trade programs (explained in more detail below) shape trade to alleviate the widespread human rights problem of unjust remuneration in the coffee industry: small coffee farmers around the world are not fairly compensated for their investments and labor, and as a result, they cannot provide appropriate food, clothing, shelter or educational opportunities for their families.

Fair trade in coffee began in the Netherlands after Bert Beekman, who had worked in Latin America, challenged the country's top roaster (owned by US-based Sara Lee) to work on a fair trade scheme. When the roaster, Douwe Egberts, failed to pursue a serious agreement, Beekman and others made a deal with the smaller competitors of Douwe Egberts; the activists would create a certification label, and the roasters would get the beans to market. In November 1988 Max Havelaar Quality Mark Coffee was launched. The name of the coffee, taken from a Dutch novel of the mid-nineteenth century that criticized the treatment of Javanese coffee growers, resonated well with Dutch consumers. By the end of its first year, the brand had captured 1.6 per cent of the market. It soon spread to other European countries, but in Germany and Austria it was known as Transfair Coffee (Pendergrast 2000, pp. 354–5).

Paul Rice established TransFair USA in 1999, in Oakland, California, to certify fair trade products. Basing his organization on the European Fair Trade model (Burgess 2000), Rice began to work with the coffee industry. 'Coffee was far and away the hottest market we could plug into' he later explained. 'It's a high-growth, high-margin business with a consumer profile nearly identical to that of socially conscious consumers' (Alden 2000).

Fair trade, as it is implemented in the coffee industry, assists family farmers with credit and other forms of support as they organize in democratic cooperatives and sell their beans directly to roasters (avoiding the middlemen who have traditionally taken much of the profit). Coffee growers receive $1.26 per pound (an amount that was decided upon after consideration of the cost of living and cost of coffee production in various regions of the world). Although the focus of TransFair is ensuring a wage that will allow growers to provide for their basic needs (food, shelter, clothing and educational opportunities for their children), the environment is important, too. Coffee growers are encouraged to certify organic beans with an additional $0.15 per pound (Rice 2001).

The Fair Trade Federation and its system of certifiers have forged a third-party certification institution. The rules include four basic guidelines and 'Fair Trade Federation Principles and Practices', which focus on fair wages, cooperative workplaces, consumer education, environmental sustainability, financial and technical support, respect for cultural identity and public accountability. The reporting mechanism is the certification provided by certifiers like TransFair USA and other members of the Fair Trade Labeling Organization. As a certifier, TransFair monitors the supply chain by auditing the movement of each 150-pound burlap coffee bag from the farmer to retail, and certifies coffee for which growers received a fair price with the fair trade label (see North American Commission on Environmental Cooperation 2002 for a succinct description of the Fair Trade process).

In addition to providing certification services, TransFair actively promotes the fair trade model by educating and recruiting individuals and groups at various points of the supply chain. Rice began by enlisting specialty roasters and retailers in the San Francisco area, contracting with them to buy fair trade coffee (Alden 2000). TransFair convinces companies that working with them will do more than bring growers a fair wage: as consumers are increasingly concerned about social and environmental justice, the Fair Trade label will add value to their coffee product, and improve their public relations and community standing (Hirsch 2001). TransFair also engages the customers of roasters, by explaining why and how they should demand fair trade coffee at their favorite points of sale.

NGOs including Global Exchange and Oxfam have mobilized student and faith-based groups around the country into a growing movement in support of fair trade. Student groups have been particularly active. Referring to non-fair trade coffee as 'sweatshop' coffee, passing petitions and hosting fair trade days, they have replicated the success of the anti-sweatshop campaigns on campus after campus. By demanding fair trade coffee in campus cafeterias and coffee shops from vendors like ARAMARK and Sodexho, student groups have made fair trade coffee available at some 200 college campuses across the United States, including Berkeley, Brown, Columbia, Cornell, Duke, Harvard, UCLA, the University of Puget Sound and the University of Washington (TransFair USA 2002; Batsell 2002).

Finally, the fair trade movement linked the major intergovernmental organizations to the coffee crises (and the anti-globalization movement) by pointing to the story that coffee production in Vietnam had occurred through World Bank support. The World Bank asserted that the story was not true: 'none of its investments have been designed to promote coffee production' in Vietnam (World Bank 2002a). The World Bank also explained its efforts to address the coffee crisis in Central America with the Inter-American Development Bank and the United States Agency for International Development in April 2002 (World Bank 2002b).

The fair trade campaign, Starbucks and other TNCs

A major challenge of the fair trade movement was how to persuade major brands to make use of fair trade coffee. Once again, Starbucks was targeted by activists. Given its rapid expansion, and what some called predatory tactics, Starbucks was increasingly seen as the Wal-Mart of coffee, moving into town after town and ruining small, local business people serving up local color. In November 1999 protesters attacked a Starbucks store (Alden 2000) during the Seattle WTO riot. By May 2000 new store openings had been challenged in California, New York, Oregon and Wisconsin (Gumbel 2000). Then, much as Beeker had met with Douwe Egberts a decade before to discuss fair trade coffee, representatives from Global Exchange met privately with Starbucks' executives (Salter 2000). Winning little ground with them, Medea Benjamin took her case to Starbucks shareholders at the company's 14 February 2000 annual meeting (Global Exchange held 100 shares of Starbucks; Nelson 2000b). Calling upon the company to buy fair trade coffee, Benjamin warned that if the company stayed its course, Starbucks coffee would become known as 'sweatshop coffee' (Nelson 2000b). She also threatened to organize a campaign against Starbucks similar to the campaign against Nike (Durhams 2000). In response Orin Smith, the president and chief operating officer of Starbucks, explained that the company had been taste-testing fair trade coffee and would buy it if it met company quality standards.

Although the company announced that it had bought 75,000 pounds of fair trade coffee in mid-February (Nelson 2000a), Global Exchange wanted more. It planned a 30-city protest campaign called 'Roast Starbucks'. Protests in Washington DC were planned for the second week of April, for the meetings of the World Bank and IMF (Mann 2000). Global Exchange was rallying various groups, asking them to sign an open letter to the CEO of Starbucks, Howard Shultz; the group wanted

Starbucks to sell fair trade-certified coffee in its stores and on college campuses (Nelson 2000b). Global Exchange expected the campaign to continue for 'most of the year' (Lee 2000).

Three days before the scheduled protests on 10 April, the company announced that it had made an agreement with TransFair USA to buy fair trade coffee beans from certified wholesale sellers (Reuters 2000) and to sell the coffee at its stores and on its internet site. While Starbucks 'completely caught the group by surprise', Global Exchange spokesman Janson Mark stated 'There is no question that the upcoming protests prompted Starbucks to make this move' (Lee 2000).

Starbucks put fair trade coffee on its store shelves on 4 October 2000. But NGOs continued their campaign, claiming that Starbucks could do much more to promote fair trade. Over the course of the next year and a half, the company made fair trade coffee available to hotel, restaurant and university accounts (in the university market, demand had tripled for such coffee in 2001) and announced that it would expand the Starbucks Fair Trade Certified coffee program. Furthermore, in the US, fair trade-certified coffee would be offered as 'Coffee of the Day' in Starbucks stores in the Spring of 2002 (Starbucks 2002, p. 7). Although activists pointed out that Starbucks' commitment meant that under 0.10 per cent of its beans would be certified fair trade, company executives made no apologies. CEO Orin Smith challenged the activists: 'They provide us with the quality of coffee that we're looking for instead of blowing their horns, we'll take it' (Zwerdling 2001). Later, he challenged the fair trade movement to move beyond cooperatives, and to simplify the certification process (Reuters 2002).

In November 2001, Starbucks announced an initiative that it had developed with Conservation International's Center for Environmental Leadership in Business: the Starbucks Green Coffee Purchasing Program. This pilot program, based on the Conservation Principles for Coffee Production (which Starbucks had helped create; see Consumer's Choice Council 2000), offers a set of quality, environmental, social and economic criteria and a point system that suppliers can use to earn up to 10 cents more for each pound of coffee. And those suppliers with more points receive purchasing preference. Each supplier is expected to obtain verification of its claims by a third party (Starbucks provided a sample list of verification organizations). By May 2002, around 60 vendors had applied to participate in the program (Clifford 2002).

When the company announced the program, Scott McMartin of Starbucks explained that it hoped to influence other TNCs. 'We feel that we're playing a leadership role in the industry, trying to move it in a way it hasn't moved before' (Batsell 2001). While the company asserted 'it is not our intention to create a new certification and labeling program within the coffee industry' (Starbucks 2001b), the initiative can be considered a mixed-type certification institution, with first-party rules (although these were shaped in part by a third party, Conservation International) and third-party conformity reports.

Citing the importance of public disclosure, Global Exchange was not yet convinced that these measures were adequate. Deborah James was quoted as saying, 'If they say they're doing it and there's no proof of it ... then it only becomes an exercise in public relations' (Batsell 2001). While Paul Rice described the guidelines 'as a great first step', and found the principles 'complementary to Fair Trade to help farmers get a decent price', he argued that 'Fair Trade is a stronger standard on the social side'. Others found the guidelines weighted more heavily towards environmental, rather than social, concerns (Clifford 2002). The industry, however, seemed to be impressed: Starbucks won the Coffee Quality Institute's first Humanitarian Medal of Merit in May 2002 for its efforts.

The fair trade movement met success with one other TNC besides Starbucks. Student activists at UCLA demanded fair trade coffee, and to stay on campus, Sara Lee, a vendor owner (and owner of Chock Full O'Nuts) signed on with TransFair USA in March 2001 (Schweisguth 2002; Luttinger 2002). This was a great victory, as Sara Lee had been unsuccessfully targeted by European groups since before the fair trade coffee model had emerged (Rice 2001).

Despite its success with specialty coffee, and in getting grocery store chains like Safeway to sell fair trade-certified coffee (Mulady 2001a) fair trade activists had much work to do in 2001. Starbucks was just one important coffee brewer/retailer. Dunkin' Donuts sold two million cups of coffee each day, the largest number of cups of coffee sold in the United States (Neuffer 2001). And specialty coffee, sold at the retail level (as beans or beverages), was worth $5.4 billion compared with an estimated US retail coffee market of $17.9 billion in 1998 (Specialty Coffee Association of America 1999, pp. 3–4).

Still concerned about the 60 per cent of the US coffee market held by Folgers, Maxwell House and Nestlé coffees (*Seattle Post-Intelligencer* 2001), activists were ready once again to take on Folgers and its parent, Procter & Gamble. Global Exchange sent Folgers a letter in late September, asking the company to purchase 5 per cent of its annual coffee in fair trade beans. Shareholders organized to make demands at the P&G shareholders meeting on 9 October 2001 (Global Exchange 2001). Student groups mobilized to approach supermarket store managers, to explain that they would like Folgers coffee (and Millstone, Procter & Gamble's gourmet coffee) to be fair trade certified (Schweisguth 2002).

Yet Procter & Gamble declined, explaining that fair trade would not work for the company. 'The way we buy beans is very complex, through brokers. The market is not set up to trace back to the source. The way the coffee is traded, it's not possible to do that. It's really an industry issue' (Bock 2001). The company cited its own efforts to assist communities and to support education initiatives. 'Fair-trade coffee is just one element', said a spokeswoman for the company. 'If you look at the big picture, there are a lot of ways to do it' (Nolan 2001). Procter & Gamble would give aid instead, or try to work with groups that could help farmers move on to other crops (Finley 2001). In January 2002, the company announced that it would work with Technoserve, an NGO dedicated to assisting development through business and technology in Latin America and Africa, to help small-scale coffee growers. It contributed $1.5 milion to the NGO (*Specialty Coffee Retailer* 2002; Technoserve 2002).

In the meantime, the campaign to bring TNCs to the fair trade table even spread to the House of Representatives. Democratic Congressman George Miller (who had previously worked on anti-sweatshop issues) and some colleagues successfully demanded fair trade coffee in House cafeterias, dining halls and cafés from Guest Services. In early 2002, Miller also wrote a letter to Proctor & Gamble, Kraft Foods, Sara Lee and Nestlé USA, explaining that they could 'make a significant contribution to the stability and prosperity of the region by purchasing premium, high-quality, sustainable coffees…such as fair trade, organic and shade-grown coffees'. The letter explained that low coffee prices were jeopardizing years of US work to stabilize economies and to promote democracy in Central America and Africa, and threatening 'U.S. national security interests'. Miller concluded, 'We look forward to receiving your help in creating a stable and prosperous coffee market in Latin America, Africa, and in other parts of the developing world. Please let us know your plans to incorporate sustainable coffees into your product line' (Miller 2002). Kraft, Nestlé USA, and Procter & Gamble responded to the letter with expressions of concern and explanations of their own initiatives. 'There are many ways to promote sustainability – we believe that our approach works best for the farmers we do business with as well as for our consumers', wrote Nestlé USA's Director of Government Relations (Hilsen 2002).

Evaluating certification initiatives and institutions: the prospects for the protection of human rights

Small growers and coffee-dependent regions suffered as a result of the collapse of the ICA in 1989 and increased coffee cultivation in Asia (in Vietnam, which produced cheap robusta, in particular). A coffee glut early in the twenty-first century sent prices below $0.50 per pound, and some farmers, at the mercy of their middlemen, were reportedly receiving less than $0.20 per pound by late 2001 (Mulady 2001b). The mainstream media, scholars and activists alike communicated alarming reports of famine, displacement and violence. Coffee prices, along with a drought, had caused a 'worsening disaster in rural Guatemala, El Salvador, Honduras, and Nicaragua' (Edelman 2002). The link between the viability of coffee production and coca production in Colombia was drawn again (Case 2002). Some 300,000 coffee workers were estimated to have abandoned rural Mexico; 14 men who died working their way into the United States in May 2001 were said to have come from coffee country (Neuffer 2001). The executive president of the Mexican Coffee Council, a government agency, exclaimed, 'This is the worst crisis in the history of the coffee industry – not just in Mexico, but in the whole world' (Case 2002).

The failure of the ICA to provide a fair and consistent price for coffee, and the more recent failure of consumer country governments to attend to the issue (despite a growing crisis that moves beyond hunger and suffering to the drug trade, terrorism and political instability) suggests the need for alternative approaches to the problem of inadequate remuneration. To date, the best-developed approach is certification, dominated by the fair trade groups. Starbucks has provided two additional alternatives for itself, if not for the rest of the industry, with its 1995 'framework for a code of conduct' and its 2001 purchasing guidelines and the requirements that participants provide verification. Will fair trade certification, Starbucks' 1995 framework, or Starbucks' 2001 purchasing program change the way coffee growers are compensated, elevate their standard of living, and protect basic human rights?

Starbucks' initiatives

Starbucks' initial 'framework for a code of conduct' has been implemented on a small scale in Guatemala (US/LEAP 1999), but not independently verified: 'Starbucks refuses to disclose the location of the plantations from which it buys, making independent monitoring impossible' (James 2000). Although it is continuously referenced by NGOs, Starbucks' 'framework for a code of conduct' is no longer high-lighted among the company's social and environmental initiatives. There is little evidence that the framework code itself – apart from dona-tions that the company has made – has affected conditions on the ground in Guatemala.

Still, this initial effort seems to have had a lasting effect on certifica-tion in the coffee industry and subsequent initiatives. With it, in the words of one of Starbucks' strongest critics, US/LEAP, 'Starbucks became the first commercial coffee company to accept the principle that it has responsibility for the wages, working conditions and the basic rights of coffee workers on plantations from which it buys' (US/LEAP 2001b). Other, more critical NGOs have used the code as a launch pad for cam-paigns to push the company further, a form of what Keck and Sikkink (1998, p. 24) term 'accountability politics'. More substantively still, an incentive program created by Starbucks after US/LEAP renewed its cam-paign against the company for not implementing the initial code seems to have formed a foundation for the new sourcing guidelines (US/LEAP 2001b). And Starbucks seems to have learned what is and is not accept-able from the perspective of NGOs like US/LEAP and Global Exchange.

It is too soon to evaluate the effectiveness of the Starbucks' 2001 purchasing program initiative, but NGOs like US/LEAP have already pointed out its potential benefits and shortcomings. US/LEAP appreci-ated Starbucks' acceptance of 'the principle that retailers have a finan-cial responsibility to suppliers who pay their workers the legal minimum wage (as inadequate as it may be), provide legal benefits, meet health and safety standards and provide adequate living conditions'. It also lauded the incorporation of a transparency component into the guide-lines; the company would find it more difficult to argue that it cannot know where its coffee comes from (US/LEAP 2001b). Yet US/LEAP, like Global Exchange, found fault with the verification component, and wondered if it would be truly independent. Finally, given Starbucks' lack of progress with the initial 1995 framework code of conduct, US/LEAP wondered if the company would implement this new scheme any more efficiently (US/LEAP 2001b).

TransFair USA

TransFair USA has already demonstrated progress towards reaching its goals. Bolstered by the fair trade movement, it has managed to overcome enormous barriers to span the value chain. It has convinced 140 roasters and importers, and 10,000 retail outlets, to offer fair trade-certified coffee. In 1999, TransFair USA's first year, it certified 2.1 million pounds of coffee, and in 2001, it tripled that amount. Overall, in just three years, it certified more than 13 million pounds (TransFair USA 2002).

In the United States, the share of all certified coffee is still small. TransFair USA's 2001 figures – 6.7 million pounds of certified coffee, out of the US's 2.5 billion pounds of coffee – is less than half of 1 per cent of the market. TransFair USA hopes to reach 1 per cent by 2005 (Hudson 2002). Yet fair trade certification has spread to 17 countries. Fair trade-certified coffee had retail sales of $64.4 million in 2000 (Fair Trade Federation 2002). And sales of fair trade coffee in Europe alone were $300 million; 6 per cent of the Swiss coffee market has been won by fair trade coffee.

Critics have argued that the fair trade movement is creating more demand than supply, but Fair Trade Federation members are working on that end of the value chain as well. By Spring 2002, TransFair USA was working with 300 fair trade cooperatives (comprised of over some 550,000 farms and families) in 22 countries in Latin America, Asia and Africa. (TransFair USA 2002). This effort has generated $10 million in additional income for these coffee growers. On the ground, that $10 million seems to make a big difference in the standard of living for coffee growers.

Case studies suggest that each TransFair co-op provides an oasis for coffee growers in a desert of misery. For example, Fair Trade farmers in the *Promotora de Desarollo Cooperativo* (PRODECOOP) in Esteli, Nicaragua, get 91 cents a pound for their fair trade beans, while their neighbors sell theirs for 45 cents a pound. PRODECOOP children can eat rice and corn, and go to school (Finley 2001). On the other side of the world, the leader of a cooperative in Uganda explained to the *Independent* newspaper that coffee market liberalization led to the dominance of multinational corporations who, in an attempt to streamline production, mixed 'all the five different grades we once produced ... But of course the coffee's quality suffered, and the people working in the fields became dispirited ... and pride was lost'. Fair trade has not only brought back that pride, it 'has helped the whole community ... we took the money we had accumulated through the Fairtrade premium, contributed some of our own money saved through working for Fairtrade and built our own parent-run school' (Ram 2002).

Yet despite considerable success on both ends of the value chain, TransFair USA may bump against some limits as it intends to continue to work in the specialty coffee industry (TransFair USA 2000). Many specialty roasters are wary of the fair trade movement. Fair trade coffee imposes limits on the autonomy of roasters looking for that special crop of beans. Roasters worry about the quality of fair trade coffee. Because fair trade cooperatives could count on the $1.26 floor, they have incentives to sell their lesser quality coffee as fair trade, while selling better quality coffee beyond the auspices of the program for the best price they can get. Although 85 per cent of the fair trade-certified coffee sold in the United States is organic as well (TransFair USA 2002), it does not guarantee the environmental benefits of certified organic or shade-grown coffee (a guarantee that many roasters were prioritizing). Some argue that TransFair certification may also be too expensive for some smaller roasters to afford. Most troublesome of all, to work with TransFair, roasters must commit to purchasing 5 per cent of their coffee as fair trade. But given the quality concerns of many roasters, the supply of acceptable fair trade coffee is still limited; fair trade coffee may have to work with suppliers to enable their participation in the program.

Finally, some roasters resented being targeted by the movement. The student campaigns mean that fair trade-certified brands get free publicity, and brands that are not certified get negative publicity; specialty brands may feel forced to certify. 'It's curious', explained the SCAA's executive director, 'When it comes time to pick on an industry for not doing anything, they pick on specialty coffee, particularly Starbucks. The segment doing the most to help the farmers is specialty coffee. And the industry that continues to sit on its hands is the commercial sector' (Bock 2001). 'We can't do what we need to do with fair trade', explained the director of the SCAA. 'We can't get consumers to connect with the issue fast enough to make a real difference for the farmer' (Finley 2001).

A drop in the cup?

The two Starbucks' initiatives and the fair trade certification initiative are just three among many proposals (albeit three of the best known) that are competing for legitimacy with NGOs and within the industry, for space on the label of a coffee bag, for recognition by consumers, and, of course, for market share (see, for a partial list of some of these, the North American Commission on Environmental Cooperation 2002; Van de Kasteele and Zeldenrust 2000). As these initiatives emerged, environmental certification institutions – focusing on organic or shade-grown coffee – grew in strength and multiplied. This competition shapes certification institutions, which evolve in reference to one another.

In the forest-products industry and the chemical industry, for example, second-party certification institutions moved towards third-party certification as competing third-party institutions grew in strength (Garcia-Johnson 2001). We can see a similar evolutionary path in the creation of Starbucks' 2001 purchasing program, which provides more opportunity for third-party verification than its 1995 'framework for a code of conduct'. On the other hand, industry insiders worry that competition among certification initiatives, given their number, complicates matters for producers and consumers alike.

Also, the human rights concerns addressed by the three initiatives are much narrower than those of earlier coffee and human rights campaigns. None of these initiatives aggressively addresses political rights, and while they do have implications for working conditions and child labor, their human rights focus is on just compensation. Despite the logic of the argument that fair wages and sound working conditions will bolster other human rights, there is no guarantee that this will in fact happen. Rather than moving towards a more comprehensive human rights agenda, these institutions are working to demonstrate how well they address environmental concerns.

Neither do the fair trade and Starbucks' initiatives cast a broad net in terms of targeted groups or membership. Fair trade certification is limited to groups of small farmers – excluding individual farmers who cannot form cooperatives and larger plantations (for this reason, groups like US/LEAP (2002) see fair trade initiatives as complementary to initiatives that have the potential to address problems at 'medium and large plantations'). Cultivators of robusta coffee, or those who do not cultivate high quality arabica, are explicitly excluded by the Starbucks' 2001 purchasing program (but not by fair trade).

Because cheaper, canned coffee makes up over 80 per cent of American coffee consumption (Finley 2001), even if all the specialty coffee worldwide were certified fair trade or taking advantage of the Starbucks' supplier incentives, much of the activity in the value chain would take place as usual. Despite activist campaigns and high-level support in the US, major brand-owning TNCs continue to resist the pressure to join extant certification initiatives. In the meantime, the coffee crisis is deepening, and activists seem far from giving up their campaign against the major TNCs. It is not inconceivable that, following Starbucks' lead, the big roasters will develop their own certification mechanisms. Nonetheless, even if such mechanisms do develop, they are unlikely to be effective in the absence of governmental or intergovernmental efforts to protect basic human rights.

Note

1. This chapter emerges from the Duke Project on Social and Environmental Certification, generously funded by the Ford Foundation. I wish to thank colleagues Gary Gereffi and Erika Sasser and research assistants Sara Eisenstat, Christopher Galik and Veronica Muñoz. I am grateful also to Peter Giuliano, Bill Mace and Steve Moody for sharing their understanding of the fair trade movement and the coffee industry.

References

Alden, Edward. 2000. 'US Offered Coffee with Conscience', *Financial Times*, 4 October, p. 14.

Associated Press. 1990. 'Dispute Over a Coffee Commercial is Ended', *New York Times*, 14 December, p. A20.

Batsell, Jake. 2001. 'Starbucks to Pay for Fair Play', *Seattle Times*, 13 November, p. C1.

Batsell, Jake. 2002. 'Coffee in Good Conscience', *Seattle Times*, 17 March, p. D1.

Bock, Paula. 2001. 'Ground Zero', *Seattle Times*, 12 August.

Boston Globe. 1990. 'El Salvador Coffee Hit with City Ban', 17 November, p. 34.

Burgess, John. 2000. 'Deal Brews to Give Fairer Deal to Farmers; Coffee at Premium Price Improves Growers' Lot', *Washington Post*, 13 May.

Case, Brendan. 2002. 'Bitter Days for Coffee Producers', *Dallas Morning News*, 7 February.

Clifford, Bill. 2002. 'Starbucks' Struggle for Moral Ground', *CBS MarketWatch.com*, 2 May.

Coffee Research Institute. 2002. 'Importation Statistics'. Available at http://www.coffeeresearch.org/market/importations.htm.

Columbus Dispatch. 1992. 'El Salvador Accord Ends Coffee Boycott', 21 March, p. 1C.

Consumer's Choice Council. 2000. 'Conservation Principles for Coffee Production'. Available at http://www.consumerscouncil.org/.

Cuff, Daniel F. 1990. 'P. & G. Heir Leads Effort for Salvador Boycott', *New York Times*, 21 September, p. D3.

DiBenedetto, William. 1997. 'Labor, Churches Roast Starbucks; Firm Defends Conduct Overseas', *Journal of Commerce*, 7 March.

Dicum, Gregory and Nina Luttinger. 1999. *The Coffee Book: Anatomy of an Industry from Crop to the Last Drop*. New York: New Press.

Durhams, Sharif. 2000. 'Students, Labor Keep Heat on Apparel Makers', *Milwaukee Journal Sentinel*, 9 April, p. A1.

Edelman, Marc. 2002. 'Price of Free Trade: Famine', *Los Angeles Times*, 22 March.

Fair Trade Federation. 2002. '2002 Report on Trends in the Fair Trade Industry'.

Finley, Bruce. 2001. 'Millions of Producers in Third World Mired in Poverty', *Denver Post*, 21 October.

Garcia-Johnson, Ronie. 2001. 'Certification Institutions in the Protection of the Environment: Exploring the Implications for Governance'. Paper presented at the 23rd Annual Research Conference of the Association for Public Policy, Analysis and Management, Washington DC, 1 November 2001.

Gereffi, Gary, Ronie Garcia-Johnson and Erika Sasser. 2001. 'The NGO–Industrial Complex', *Foreign Policy* (July–August): 56–65.

Global Exchange 2001. 'Socially Responsible Investors Will Attend Proctor & Gamble Shareholder Meeting', Press Release, 8 October. Available at http://www.globalexchange.org/economy/coffee/news2001/gx100801.html.

Gumbel, Andrew. 2000. 'Interview: Howard Schultz Has Made a Fortune', *Independent*, 24 May, Business, pp. 1–2.

Hilsen, Louise. 2002. Letter to The Honorable George Miller, 5 March.

Hirsch, Deborah. 2001. Telephone interview with the author, 14 August.

Hudson, Repps. 2002. 'Activist Takes Up the Battle to Promote Fair Trade', *St Louis Post-Dispatch*, 2 January.

James, Deborah. 2000. 'Justice and Java: Coffee in a Fair Trade Market', *NACLA*, September/October.

Jung, Helen. 2002. 'Starbucks Culture: Coffee is Grounds for Much More', *Seattle Times*, 28 May, Business and Technology.

Keck, Margaret and Kathryn Sikkink. 1998. *Activists beyond Borders: Advocacy Networks in International Politics*. Ithaca: Cornell University Press.

Kraft. 2001. *2001 Annual Report*. Available at http://164.109.67.247/pdfs/AR-01.pdf.

Lee, Thomas. 2000. 'Starbucks Gives in to Coffee Activists, Fair Trade Deal Averts Protests', *Seattle Times*, 10 April.

Lim, Paul J. 1995. 'Starbucks' "Code" for Suppliers is Criticized', *Seattle Times*, 24 October.

Luttinger, Emily. 2002. E-mail communication to the author, 15 May.

Maitland, Alison. 2002. 'Bitter Taste of Success', *Financial Times*, 11 March, p. 14.

Makower, Joel. 1995. 'Attitudes Percolate as Code of Conduct Brews at Coffee Firms', *Houston Chronicle*, 16 April.

Mann, Judy. 2000. 'Standing Up for the Victims of Globalization', *Washington Post*, 26 April.

Miller, George. 2002. Letter to Proctor & Gamble, Kraft Foods, Sara Lee, and Nestlé USA, 28 January. Available at http://edworkforce.house.gov/democrats/fairtrade.html.

Morgan, Dan. 1977. 'U.S. Coffee Companies Major Source of Amin's Revenue', *Washington Post*, 5 November, p. A2.

Moriwaki, Lee. 1997. 'Starbucks, ATI to Aid Guatemalan Growers', *Seattle Times*, 28 February.

Mulady, Kathy. 2001a. 'Seattle Coffee's Fair Trade Product Coming to Safeway', *Seattle Post-Intelligencer*, 18 August.

Mulady, Kathy. 2001b. 'Starbucks Buying More Fair Trade Coffee Beans', *Seattle Post-Intelligencer*, 19 October.

Nelson, Robert T. 2000a. 'Starbucks Buys Politically Correct Beans', *Seattle Times*, 19 February, B1.

Nelson, Robert T. 2000b. '"Roast Starbucks", Group Says', *Seattle Times*, 24 March, p. D2.

Neuffer, Elizabeth. 2001. 'The Shadows of Globalization', *Boston Globe*, 29 July.

Nogaki, Sylvia Wieland. 1995. 'Coffee's Code of Conduct – Starbucks to Adopt Standards for Wages, Work Conditions for Guatemala Workers', *Seattle Times*, 16 February.

Nolan, John. 2001. 'P&G Eschews Fair-Trade Coffee Offered by Some Sellers', Associated Press.

North American Commission on Environmental Cooperation. 2002. The Coffee Certification Program Database. Available at http://www.cec.org/programs_projects/trade_environ_econ/sustain_agriculture/databases/index.cfm?varlan=english.

Pendergrast, Mark. 2000. *Uncommon Grounds: the History of Coffee and How It Transformed Our World*. New York: Basic Books.

Ram, Harry. 2002. 'Fair Trade: Just Reward Encourages Even Greater Endeavour', *Independent*, 9 March, pp. 6–7.

Ramirez, Anthony. 1990. 'Procter & Gamble Pulls Some TV Ads Over Slur to Coffee', *New York Times*, 12 May, p. 1.

Reuters. 2000. 'Starbucks Will Buy Beans at Premium', *New York Times*, 11 April, p. C2.

Reuters. 2002. 'Coffee Industry under "Threat"', *Seattle Times*, 7 May, C3.

Rice, Paul. 2001. Presentation at 'Certification Institutions and Private Governance', The Seventh Annual Colloquium on Environmental Law and Institutions, Duke University, 7 December.

Risse, Thomas. 2000. 'The Power of Norms versus the Norms of Power: Transnational Civil Society and Human Rights', in Ann M. Florini, ed., *The Third Force: the Rise of Transnational Civil Society*, pp. 177–209. Washington: Carnegie Endowment for International Peace.

Risse, Thomas, Stephen C. Rop and Kathryn Sikkink. 1999. *The Power of Human Rights: International Norms and Domestic Change*. Cambridge: Cambridge University Press.

St Louis Post-Dispatch. 1989. 'Nestlé Halts Purchase of Salvadoran Coffee', 13 December, p. 11C.

Salter, Stephanie. 2000. 'Mm, Fair Trade Certified to the Last Drop', *Star Tribune*, 18 April.

Sara Lee. Available at http://www.saralee.com/brands.

Schweisguth, Melissa. 2002. Telephone interview with the author, 4 June.

Seattle Post-Intelligencer. 2001. 'Coffee Glut, Feudal Traditions Combine to Starve Communities', August 28.

Shniad, D. 1995. E-mail message to pen-l@anthrax.ecst.csuchico.edu, 2 February. Available at http://lanic.utexas.edu/la/region/news/arc/lasnet/1995/0048.html.

Solomon, Christopher. 1997. 'Group: Coffee Giant Slow to Keep Guatemala Promise', *Seattle Times*, 6 March.

Specialty Coffee Association of America. 1999. '1999 Coffee Market Summary'. Available at http://www.scaa.org.

Specialty Coffee Retailer. 2002. 'P&G Technoserve Helping Smaller Coffee Roasters', 13 March, p. 9.

Standard and Poor's Market Insight. 2002. Available at: http://umi.compustat.com.

Starbucks. 1995. 'Starbucks Commitment ... To Do Our Part', October. Available at http://www.usleap.org/Coffee/coffeetemp.html.

Starbucks. 2001a. *Starbucks 2001 Annual Report*. Available at http://www.starbucks.com/aboutus/ar01_financials.pdf.

Starbucks. 2001b. 'Starbucks Green Coffee Purchasing Program'.

Starbucks. 2002. 'Corporate Social Responsibility Annual Report: Fiscal 2001'. Available at http://www.starbucks.com/aboutus/CSR_FY01_AR.pdf.

Stein, Mark A. 1989. 'Coffee Seller Suspends Deals in El Salvador', *Los Angeles Times*, 9 December, p. D4.

Stern, Gabriella. 1991. 'P &G, Pressured by Boycott, to Market Coffee Blend without Salvadoran Beans', *Wall Street Journal*, 15 November, p. B5.

Technoserve. 2002. Available at http://www.technoserve.org/P&G.htm.

Tofani, Loretta. 1978. 'U.S. Companies Ask Uganda Coffee Import Ban', *Washington Post*, 22 June, p. A20.

TransFair USA. 2000. 'Market Opportunity Assessment'. Available at http://www.transfairusa.org/about/reports/moa.html.

TransFair USA. 2002. 'Update Spring 2002'. Oakland, CA: TransFair USA.

United Nations General Assembly. 1948. *Universal Declaration of Human Rights*. Available at http://www.un.org/Overview/rights.html.

US/GLEP. 1996. 'Justice for Coffee Workers Campaign'. Available at http://www.usleap.org/Coffee/justiceforcoffee.html.

US/GLEP. 1997. 'Starbucks Reconsiders; Campaign on Hold', July newsletter. Available at http://www.usleap.org/Coffee/SBcampaignonHold%2797.html.

US/GLEP. 1998. 'Starbucks Moves Forward', April newsletter. Available at http://www.usleap.org/Coffee/sbMoves%2798.html.

US/LEAP. 1999. 'Starbucks Issues New Report', December newsletter. Available at http://www.usleap.org/Coffee/SBIssuesNewReport12-99.html.

US/LEAP. 2001a. 'Guatemalan Coffee Growers Agree to Discuss Monitoring Options with Starbucks', May newsletter. Available at http://www.usleap.org/Coffee/ANACAFETalktoSB5-01.html.

US/LEAP. 2001b. 'Starbucks Issues New Sourcing Guidelines', December newsletter. Available at http://www.usleap.org/Coffee/SBNewGuide12-01.html.

US/LEAP. 2002. 'Coffee Worker Campaigns'. Available at http://www.usleap.org/Coffee/coffeetemp.html.

Van de Kasteele, Adelien and Ineke Zeldenrust. 2000. 'Controlling the Coffee Supply Chain?', January. Available at http://www.eftafairtrade.org/pdf/Coffeechain-aangepast.doc.

World Bank. 2002a. 'No World Bank Role in Vietnam's Expansion of Coffee Production', Press release 18 March.

World Bank. 2002b. 'Central America to Discuss Responses to Coffee Crisis in Conference Sponsored by IDB, USAID, and World Bank', Press release, 2 April.

Zachary, G. Pascal. 1995. 'Starbucks Asks Foreign Suppliers to Improve Working Conditions', *Wall Street Journal*, 23 October, p. B4.

Zwerdling, Daniel. 2001. 'The Campaign to Humanize the Coffee Trade', NPR/American Radio Works. June 8. Available at http://www.americanradioworks.org/cgi-bin/htsearch.

8
The Transnational Garment Industry in South and South-East Asia: a Focus on Labor Rights

Jedrzej George Frynas

In the last few decades, labor-intensive industries such as garment production have increasingly been relocated from developed countries to developing countries with lower labor costs, such as China, the Philippines and Indonesia (Dicken 1998, pp. 290–1). In many of these developing countries, human rights standards are lower, and garment firms violate some of the key internationally accepted human rights. This chapter examines the impact of transnational garment firms on human rights in South and South-East Asia by focusing on labor rights.

For the purpose of a systematic inquiry, the chapter focuses explicitly on clothing production, which starts with the cutting of fabric and ends with the selling of products to intermediaries or retailers.[1] I exclude the earlier stages of production (for example, cotton farming or textile weaving), as it would be difficult, if not impossible, to establish a link between these earlier production processes and the transnational corporations (TNCs). Therefore, I focus on the stages of the production process, over which TNCs have greater control. I also exclude (except for two references to Nike) the discussion of other related industries (for example, footwear), as they involve somewhat different working environments and different concerns.

The chapter focuses entirely on labor rights as opposed to, say, environmental rights. This is not to say that environmental rights are unimportant in the clothing trade. But pressure groups have found that labor rights are the main human rights concern in the garment industry. Environmental concerns play an important role in earlier phases of the production process including textile production (for example, the dyeing of textiles) and agriculture (for example, the use of pesticides in cotton farming).[2] Nonetheless, I exclude those concerns here.

UN human rights standards and International Labor Organization (ILO) norms form the basis in this chapter for analyzing the impact that garment firms have on human rights. Combining a number of core labor rights stipulated by the UN and the ILO, the chapter focuses on the following ten rights and prohibitions:

- the right to form and join trade unions[3]
- the right to freedom from discrimination[4]
- the prohibition of forced or compulsory labor[5]
- the prohibition (or limitation) of child labor[6]
- the right to leisure and rest during work[7]
- the right to equality of treatment between home workers and other wage earners[8]
- the right to an 8-hour day or a 48-hour week[9]
- the right to a healthy and safe working environment[10]
- the right to a minimum wage[11]
- the prohibition of firing a worker without a valid reason related to the quality of his/her work[12]

The selection of these ten rights is partly arbitrary, as certain rights could perhaps be included or excluded. However, it is hoped that a focus on a core number of accepted labor rights will allow a more systematic investigation of the performance of TNCs in the garment industry.

This chapter is predominantly based around evidence on garment production in Asia collated by the Clean Clothes Campaign (CCC) and the Centre for Research on Multinational Corporations (SOMO) in Amsterdam between 1994 and 2000 as well as interviews with staff of CCC and SOMO. Sources have only been used where interviews were conducted with both factory managers and workers in a given locality and where a personal visit to the manufacturing site was made by SOMO, CCC or a CCC member organization. Using these sources, evidence from 73 clothing manufacturers was analyzed. However the majority of the names of the manufacturers are not disclosed in order to protect the individuals working there.[13]

The chapter starts by describing the trade patterns in the international garment industry. This sets the background for the subsequent analysis of the human rights impact of TNCs, the main part of the chapter. This analysis is followed by a brief discussion of the indirect impact of TNCs on human rights, a discussion of the retailers' ethical policies towards their clothing suppliers and concluding remarks.

Trading patterns in the international garment industry

In order fully to understand the human rights implications of garment TNCs, it is illuminating to outline the basic trading patterns in the international garment industry. Figure 8.1 presents three different trading patterns.

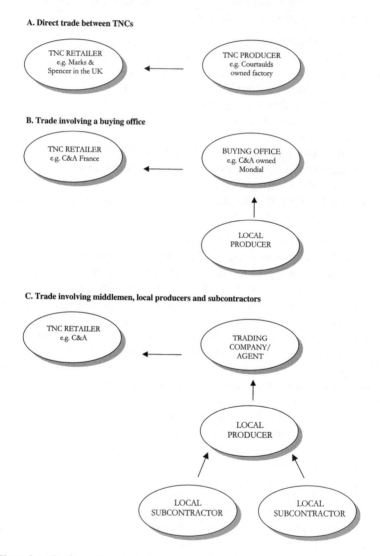

Figure 8.1   Trading patterns in the garment industry

The simplest relationship occurs when a clothing retailer buys directly from the producer (A in Figure 8.1). For example, Marks & Spencer, which buys a large proportion of its clothes from transnational manufacturers such as Coats Viyella, Courtaulds, William Baird and Dewhirst, may import clothes directly from a Courtaulds-owned factory in Thailand. In such an instance, it is relatively unproblematic to establish a link between TNCs and the human rights implications of their activities.

Nonetheless, the simple relationship described above rarely occurs and the clothing trade typically involves middlemen, local producers and subcontractors. Some clothing retailers have buying offices in Asia, which buy directly from local producers (B in Figure 8.1). For example, C&A France purchases clothes through Mondial, a 100 per cent C&A-owned venture with offices in a number of countries, such as Hong Kong, which in turn buy clothes from the local manufacturers in a country or in an entire geographic region.

However, trading patterns are usually more complex than the two examples mentioned above. In many cases, a retailer employs an intermediary, which can range from a single local agent to an international trading company with wholly-owned or controlled clothing factories (C in Figure 8.1). The intermediary can, at one extreme, merely facilitate a business deal between a buyer and a manufacturer or, at the other extreme, can offer a range of services including placing orders with the local producer as well as managing the quality control process. The services of an intermediary may reduce the profit margins for the retailer or the manufacturer but they offer a number of advantages, especially in terms of providing the retailer with local knowledge and contacts. The intermediary may buy or facilitate a purchase from a manufacturer. In some cases, the manufacturer may subcontract part or all of the output. All of the Indonesian clothing manufacturers visited by CCC in 1995, for example, subcontracted part of their production. In the Philippines, manufacturers reportedly subcontract as much as 75 per cent of their garment production. Studies show that garments produced in the parent factory can be up to three times more expensive than those subcontracted out, although subcontracting decreases the reliability of quality and delivery (quoted in Green 1998).

Trading patterns can be more complex still. A TNC retailer may procure clothes through a buying office from an intermediary. The intermediary may buy from a local producer, who buys from a subcontractor, who in turn subcontracts the work. The TNC retailer may never learn the names of the subcontractors involved. In addition, an independent firm may be hired to manage the quality control process, such as SGS, a Swiss firm specializing in quality control.

In view of the complex trade relationships between the retailer and the local producers, one may encounter specific difficulties in attributing the retailer's responsibility for human rights abuses committed by the local producers, especially if the same local manufacturer produces clothes for a large number of different clients, in which case the manufacturer's ethical conduct is affected by a greater variety of different influences.[14]

Nonetheless, TNC retailers have retained a certain measure of control over manufacturing operations. This can be seen, above all, in relation to monitoring the quality of the clothes produced. While manufacturers usually have an internal system for monitoring the quality of clothes, the buyer tends to have an additional form of quality control. These additional controls may be carried out at different stages of the production process, either by the final buyer, an intermediary or a specialized firm. The manufacturer's failure to meet specified criteria can lead to financial penalties or, in an extreme case, to a withdrawal of orders. In general terms, the closely supervised quality control systems indicate that TNC retailers have a large measure of control over the local manufacturers, even if they do not own the production sites or if intermediaries are involved.

Indeed, most manufacturers visited by SOMO or CCC staff reported many visits by representatives of TNC retailers or intermediaries. Final buyers often dictate conditions to the local manufacturer, including specifying the number of fire extinguishers in a factory. The manufacturers, who are dependent on orders from the buyers, have difficulty in rejecting these demands, especially if a substantial proportion of their orders comes from a single buyer. The buyers' main 'weapon' against suppliers is their ability to switch orders from one supplier to another and from one country to another. As mentioned in the next section, buyers sometimes switch suppliers where a trade union has been established or where the labor standards have been raised, or more recently, away from suppliers who violated a TNC's code of conduct. In this context, a TNC – which can exert influence upon dozens of manufacturers in different countries – is likely to have a greater impact upon the human rights situation in a given locality than a local manufacturer who competes against other local manufacturers on the basis of cost, which may include the cost of implementing social improvements in the workplace.

In conclusion, despite the complex trading patterns in the garment industry, there is some basis to argue that TNCs can have a direct, albeit sometimes unintended, impact on human rights standards.

Human rights and the garment industry

In this section, I attempt to confront the ten rights and prohibitions mentioned earlier with the reality of garment production on the ground. As a starting point, I have analyzed the appeals received by CCC between January 1999 and July 2000 from the representatives of garment workers and CCC member organizations worldwide, with a view to identifying some of the key labor rights-related concerns of worker representatives.

Judged by these appeals, the main concern of workers appears to be related to trade unions and collective bargaining rights. Of the total number of appeals received in 1999 (25) and 2000 (17), 12 and 10 deal with these issues (see Table 8.1). These requests are likely to be biased in favor of organized workers as opposed to less organized groups such as child workers and home workers, who lack access or resources to seek external assistance from non-governmental organizations or other bodies. However, the right to form trade unions is often seen by workers as a vehicle or a precondition for obtaining other rights related to working conditions, so its importance to Asian workers cannot be overestimated.

The second and third main concerns of appeals relate to unjust dismissal and wages. Of the appeals received in 1999 and 2000, 12 and 7 deal with unjust dismissal while 10 and 6 deal with wages (see Table 8.1).

Table 8.1 Nature of appeals received by CCC in 1999 and 2000

	1999	2000*
Trade unions and collective bargaining	12	10
Unjust dismissal	12	7
Wages	10	6
Healthy and safe working environment	5	3
Working hours	5	2
Workplace discrimination	4	2
Leisure and rest during work	1	1
Home workers	0	0
Child labor	0	0
Forced or compulsory labor	0	0

Note: * January–July

Working conditions are seen as less important, while no appeals were received with regard to child labor, home workers or forced labor.

These results suggest that when external assistance is sought by worker representatives the key issues raised are related to how they are represented, how they can avoid arbitrary dismissal and how much they earn. The conditions of work, albeit crucial, are relatively less important if compared to the issue of bare survival. This could be due to the fact that workers are much more concerned about having a job rather than the nature of this job.

Nonetheless, as the above hierarchy of problems is far from perfect, I attempt below to establish whether the ten rights and prohibitions mentioned earlier have been a matter of concern to workers by analyzing the evidence on 73 clothing manufacturers and providing specific examples from factories in South and South-East Asia.

The right to form and join trade unions

Based on this evidence, trade union activities are frequently hampered. Among the typical concerns voiced by union activists are intimidation, physical violence, financial penalties at work, assignment to more strenuous jobs and the unfair dismissal of union members.

The formation of a trade union is often hampered or forcefully prevented by employers. For instance, in the case of one clothing factory in Bogor/Java, Indonesia, the workers registered an independent trade union in August 1998. The employers refused to acknowledge the union. Following a strike in May 1999, the company subsequently signed an agreement with the union, but later sacked the union's chairman and other union members. The union's complaint to the Manpower Department in Bogor did not lead to a resolution of the dispute. Indeed, there were indications that the Manpower Department was biased against the union. For example, when the department organized a legal assistance program for workers in Bogor, union members were prohibited from taking part. In another case, when workers attempted to form a union in a factory in Bangladesh, the employer hired a group of men who visited the factory and made threats to workers. When the union finally went on strike, all 350 workers were fired.

In the most extreme cases, the formation of a trade union could lead to the closure of a factory and relocation of production elsewhere. In one case, Splendid – a German leather manufacturer – became involved in a labor dispute in a Thai manufacturing subsidiary producing leather jackets, which centered around the workers' demand for a wage increase and the firm's subsequent attempt to ban the factory's union. Under pressure from workers, the local trade unions and non-governmental organizations, the manufacturing subsidiary was forced to pay compensation to 130 unjustly dismissed workers. However, Splendid subsequently decided to close down the Thai subsidiary and relocate production.

Considering the above difficulties, it is perhaps not surprising that the majority of firms analyzed did not have a trade union. However, even if a trade union exists, the management may try to dominate it. This was perhaps best illustrated in Indonesia where, until mid-1998, the only legal trade union was the government-approved SPSI, which had close links to the Indonesian military and did little to champion labor rights.[15] In various cases from Indonesia, SPSI collaborated with employers rather than representing its members. For instance, during a strike in a clothing factory in Java in 1999, workers sought the support of SPSI for their demands. Rather than supporting the workers' demands, SPSI officials signed a letter calling for the suspension of 42 workers. Perhaps not surprisingly, in a number of Indonesian firms studied for this research, one of the workers' demands was to abolish the SPSI branch in the factory. In cases where the local SPSI branch genuinely attempted to represent the workers, its activities were often hampered by management, as in the case of independent unions mentioned earlier.

In general terms, the above discussion suggests that the right to form and join trade unions is frequently breached in the clothing industry.

The right to freedom from discrimination

Based on the analysis of clothing manufacturers, there exist a number of discernible forms of discrimination in the garment industry. The most pertinent form of discrimination in the garment industry is that against women, who make up the majority of workers in Asia's garment factories. For instance, it was reported that more than 80 per cent of the workers in the Malaysian textile industry are female (Rudnick 1995).

Among the typical concerns voiced by female workers are lower pay than men or inferior contract terms, no provision for, or difficulties in obtaining, maternity leave, sexual harassment by supervisors, forced pregnancy tests and dismissal of pregnant women. In addition, there are specific concerns in some countries. For example, in Indonesia, an Islamic country where the menstruation period has a special significance, employers often refuse to grant women the statutory right to menstruation leave. In one analyzed case, a clothing firm in Indonesia did not grant any women's rights such as maternity leave, menstruation leave and breast-feeding leave despite the fact that more than 97 per cent of the factory staff were women.

The importance of women's rights, such as maternity leave in the garment industry, can be seen in their principal position in labor disputes. For example, when a dispute between workers and the management started in one Indonesian factory in 1998, workers named three reasons for the strike: the firm's refusal to acknowledge an independent trade union, the refusal to provide a statutory pension scheme and the refusal to grant a number of women's rights. Refusal to grant women's rights such as the failure to implement the statutory menstruation leave played an important part in the dispute.

Discrimination against women or other groups of workers may arise if employers feel that they can gain advantages in terms of saving cost and increasing the number of working hours. For example, in one Indonesian factory, pregnant women were not granted maternity leave by the employer if they were unmarried, in order to keep production running.

Apart from discrimination against women, there are other types of discrimination, such as discrimination against foreign migrant workers.[16] Rudnick (1995) reported that Bangladeshi workers in Malaysia worked longer hours than locals, were paid less money for the same job, received worse treatment in the workplace and were unrepresented or barely represented in the Malaysian trade union movement. Another type of discrimination may be on the grounds of age. During recessionary periods, a number of manufacturers visited by CCC and SOMO tended to dismiss older and more experienced workers, perhaps because they were entitled to greater social benefits than younger workers or had dependants and therefore required better wages than young workers without dependants.

The list of groups discriminated against is, of course, not exhausted here. In the firms analyzed, apart from frequent evidence of discrimination against women, there was relatively little evidence of discrimination against other groups of workers. A broader survey would probably have uncovered a greater variety of discrimination. Nonetheless, if we base our considerations solely on discrimination against women, a significant number of firms have systematically breached the right to freedom from discrimination.

The prohibition of forced or compulsory labor

In the analyzed firms, there was no evidence of forced or compulsory labor, as stipulated in Article 8 of the International Covenant on Civil and Political Rights (ICCPR).

However, if 'forced labor' is more widely defined as any work performed under duress, one finds many instances of such work in the analyzed firms. One form of labor under duress refers to foreign migrant workers. Those workers are often attracted by promises of high wages and pay a fee to job agencies in return for finding work. Once they start work, the actual conditions can be considerably worse than previously promised, so many workers decide to leave. However, in a number of cases analyzed, the employer refused to let a worker leave or tried to induce workers to stay by withholding payments. For instance, in a clothing factory in Macao, more than 60 workers decided to leave in July 1999, but the employers refused to pay them their due wages. Under pressure from a labor organization, the factory decided to repay the wages. Subsequently, all remaining workers were ordered by management to sign a guarantee stating that they would not apply to leave before February 2000 at the earliest. This example is indicative of the compulsion used against migrants in the clothing industry, which has also been reported elsewhere.[17]

Another form of labor under duress is forced overtime. In the clothing factory of a Gap supplier in Jakarta, workers who opposed overtime were intimidated and, in some cases, locked in a separate room as a disciplinary measure. In many clothing factories, there are specific procedures to ensure that workers cannot refuse overtime. For example, in a factory controlled by the William Baird Group in the Philippines, a worker who refuses overtime receives a verbal warning. After the second refusal, a worker receives a written warning. After the third refusal, a worker is suspended from work. These two examples, among many others, suggest that garment workers may often be forced to perform work beyond their regular duties.

Nonetheless, as there is no evidence of illegitimate practices such as forced prison labor or government schemes for compulsory labor in the clothing industry, the human right stipulated in the ICCPR Convention was not breached.

The right to a healthy and safe working environment

Of the ten rights and prohibitions discussed in this chapter, the right to a healthy and safe working environment is perhaps the most difficult to interpret in practice, as there may be ambiguity with regard to certain expressions used by ILO Convention No. 155, such as 'safe' or 'without risk to health'. Nonetheless, using the convention as a guideline and based on our evidence, specific unhealthy and unsafe conditions in the garment industry include, among others, lack of ventilation, inappropriate lighting, unsuitable seating, noise, insufficient protection from dangerous chemicals, insufficient safety measures for fire emergencies, lack of protective clothing or insufficient number of toilets.[18]

In many cases, an unsafe or unhealthy working environment can lead to occupational diseases. Among others, the use of chemicals in garment production – for example, cleaning solvents – can lead to different illnesses ranging from a sore throat to cancer, while repetitive strenuous work – for example, repeated use of scissors – can lead to muscular-skeletal strain. For instance, in one clothing factory in the Philippines in 1999, roughly 30 per cent of the workforce suffered from TB, most probably as a result of overwork and exhaustion combined with overcrowding in the workplace and high air humidity that enabled the quick spread of this highly contagious illness. An unsafe or unhealthy working environment can also lead to preventable injuries, such as those involving scissors or industrial sewing machines. Long working hours may aggravate some of these problems due to loss of concentration.

At the most extreme, an unsafe or unhealthy working environment can lead to the death of workers. For instance, during a fire in the Rose Knitting Garment Factory in Bangladesh in July 1999, five people died because the factory had no fire exits. Of ten clothing manufacturers visited by CCC staff in Bangladesh in 1995, at least five did not have a fire exit (in two cases, it was not clear from the sources whether a fire exit existed).

Workers are often aware of the negative effects of such working conditions and call for improvements. For example, in an Indonesian subsidiary of a Japanese clothing manufacturer, one section of the plant utilized old and rusty machinery. The workers in the section had to carefully arrange 200 layers of thread on the machine for each piece of cloth. They were not allowed to talk, take a break or even turn their heads. Workers in that section complained of work-related illnesses including headaches, back pain and stiffness in their arms. The management transferred workers to that section of the plant as punishment for union activities. During subsequent industrial action, the main demand of the workers was to shut down that specific section of the plant, demonstrating the workers' preoccupation with unhealthy working conditions.

In general terms, while the right to a healthy and safe working environment leaves room for a certain measure of ambiguity, the majority of analyzed firms appeared to breach this right in at least one of the ways suggested above.

The right to an 8-hour day or a 48-hour week

Amongst the firms analyzed, there are many examples of factories which considerably exceeded the 48-hour week. In one Bangladeshi factory, the normal working hours were 8 am until 9 pm, seven days a week with no overtime payments. This factory was unusual, as workers in clothing factories usually receive some form of overtime payment, although it must be remembered that overtime is often compulsory. For instance, in another Bangladeshi factory, the normal working hours were 8 am until 4.30 pm, seven days a week. However, overtime lasted until 7.30 pm every day. On busy days, workers were forced to work until 9.30 pm and sometimes even until 3 am, which would amount to a 19-hour working day. A worker who had to stay until 3 am would still be expected to start at 8 am the next working day. The number of hours worked were related to excessive production quotas set for individual workers in many factories, which could only be obtained with considerable strain and which were sometimes periodically raised, resulting in additional stress and physical exhaustion as well as even longer working hours.

In general terms, it appears that workers in the majority of the clothing factories work for considerably more than 48 hours a week. Of ten clothing manufacturers visited by CCC staff in Bangladesh in 1995, at least eight had a normal working week of more than 48 hours, while seven had a working week in excess of 60 hours (in two factories, the working hours were not clear). All nine manufacturers visited in the Philippines in 1995 had a normal working week of more than 48 hours, while six had a working week in excess of 60 hours. In some factories, the number of hours was much higher than 60 hours per week.

While workers in developing countries may sometimes prefer to work long hours in order to earn extra money, particularly if the basic wage is insufficient, there is evidence that workers on occasion opposed long working hours, for example, by resisting forced overtime. In any case, the above discussion suggests that the working hours in the clothing industry were excessive by any standards. The right to an 8-hour day or a 48-hour week was clearly breached.

The right to leisure and rest during work

Closely related to working hours is the right to leisure and rest during work. Among the typical concerns related to leisure and rest voiced by workers in different countries are: long working hours with few breaks; work on public holidays; restrictions regarding going to the toilet; and difficulties in obtaining sick leave. In extreme cases, workers may receive no proper rest during the working week. In one garment factory in the Philippines, for instance, the workers worked seven days a week for two months without a single day of rest. In addition, there are specific concerns in some countries. In Indonesia, an Islamic country, workers may not be able to perform regular daily prayers due to work pressure and no allocated breaks for praying.

Rest during work is often highly restricted. For example, in one Bangladeshi factory, when a worker went to the toilet, the time was measured with a watch and restrictions on going to the toilet were imposed. As a result, workers would often decide not to go to the toilet. In some cases, the lack of rest may contribute to illnesses. For example, in the Philippines' clothing factory mentioned earlier where roughly 30 per cent of the workforce suffered from TB in 1999, one of the contributing factors was the fact that most workers diagnosed with TB only received 30 days' sick leave, while it can take 6 months or even several years of treatment to cure TB, which, if untreated or insufficiently treated, can be terminal. In various other firms, workers faced difficulties in obtaining sick leave or their statutory annual holiday leave. This, combined with long working hours, may have had repercussions on their health.

If we base our considerations on 'the right to rest and leisure, including reasonable limitation of working hours and periodic holidays with pay' stipulated by the UN Universal Declaration of Human Rights,[19] the majority of firms analyzed appear to breach this right in at least one of the ways suggested above.

The prohibition of firing a worker without a valid reason related to the quality of his/her work

From the evidence analyzed, the most common ground for unjust dismissal was union activity or participation in a strike. Union members or other workers may be dismissed using fabricated excuses. For instance, in one factory in the Philippines, five workers were dismissed on charges of 'sabotage' when they tried to form a trade union. In the same factory, more workers, including union officers, were subsequently dismissed due to alleged cost cutting at a time when the factory was actually hiring extra workers to meet client orders. One factory in the Philippines dismissed workers who were diagnosed with TB.

In various clothing factories, unfair dismissal is also practiced systematically in order to circumvent various statutory labor provisions or other workers' entitlements. For instance, in one factory in Sri Lanka, the management tried to dismiss all workers before their fifth year of work because, after five years of work, workers would be entitled to one-and-a-half times their monthly salary if dismissed.

In order to avoid the charge of unfair dismissal, employers use a number of tactics. For instance, in one Thai clothing factory, workers were forced to sign letters of resignation in advance of commencing their employment. In one factory in Bangladesh, workers did not receive letters of appointment, even though some of them had been working for the company for more than a year. In this way, a company may attempt to ensure the legality of any potential unfair dismissals in advance.

In general terms, a significant number of the firms analyzed practiced unfair dismissal. This would suggest that the prohibition of firing a worker without a valid reason related to the quality of his/her work was frequently breached in the clothing industry.

The right to a minimum wage

The evidence analyzed suggests that clothing firms sometimes pay less than the statutory minimum wage. For instance, in the Dhaka Export Processing Zone in Bangladesh, the minimum monthly wage for unskilled and skilled workers was Tk. 1200 and Tk. 3360 respectively in early 1999. A Wal-Mart supplier in the zone paid only Tk. 900 and Tk. 2000 for unskilled and skilled workers respectively. In other countries, clothing firms also pay less than the statutory minimum wage. A survey for the US trade union office AAFLI in Jakarta and the Indonesian official trade union SPSI in 1996 revealed that roughly 20 per cent of workers in Java were paid less than the legal minimum (quoted in Burns and Mather 1999).

As jobs are scarce in many Asian countries, many workers are prepared to work for less than the statutory minimum wage. For example, one study on women dismissed from factories in Thailand found that roughly half of the women surveyed stated that they would agree to work for less than the minimum wage under health-hazardous working conditions (Ekachai 1999).

Even if all workers were to receive a minimum wage, it could still be far below subsistence level in many of these countries. For example, while most workers in Jakarta and West Java received the minimum wage of 172,500 rupees in 1997, this was deemed to be below subsistence level and the SPSI recommended a figure of 300,000 rupees per month (quoted in Burns and Mather 1999). Following the Asian financial crisis, the gap between minimum wages and the actual subsistence level has increased further. In this context, the inadequate level of minimum wages in countries such as Indonesia could perhaps be construed to contravene Article 3 of the ILO Convention No. 131 which stipulated that the minimum wage should include 'the needs of workers and their families, taking into account the general level of wages in the country, the cost of living, social security benefits, and the relative living standards of other social groups'.[20]

Even if the employer formally agrees to pay the minimum wage, he/she may arbitrarily delay or reduce payments so that effectively the employees earn less. Among the typical complaints voiced by garment industry workers in different countries are non-payment of bonuses, allowances and termination benefits and, in some cases, deferred wage payments lasting for weeks or months. For example, one Bangladeshi factory visited by CCC in 1995 was two months behind with paying the regular wages and nine months behind in terms of paying overtime.

Furthermore, wages may be kept low as the result of various deductions such as strict fines for mistakes made by workers or compulsory payments to a factory fund. For instance, in the clothing factory of a Gap supplier in Jakarta, loss of a tool resulted in a 25,000 rupee fine, a sewing mistake cost a worker 5000 rupees and coming late to work was punished with a 5000 rupee fine. In comparison, the minimum wage was 7000 rupees per day in early 1999.

Last, but not least, irregular work as a result of fluctuations in company orders may keep the actual wages below the minimum wage. For instance, in one factory in the Philippines, a collective bargaining agreement (CBA) was in place in a factory and workers formally received a wage above the statutory minimum wage. However, as a result of falling orders, workers were asked to work only three days a week and actually received only half of the normal salary. Furthermore, wages were paid irregularly or payment was often delayed. In effect, the CBA was not effectively implemented and workers earned less than the minimum wage.

In general terms, the above discussion suggests that the right to a minimum wage has been violated by a significant number of clothing manufacturers.

The right to equality of treatment between home workers and other wage earners

In a number of the clothing factories analyzed, there is a striking difference between the conditions of regular workers and those who work from home. For instance, in a clothing factory in the Philippines, home workers were not entitled to any sick leave or holiday leave, and only a minority were entitled to social security, while regular workers received those benefits. In contrast to regular factory workers who received a bonus for fulfilling the production quota, home workers received disciplinary action for not fulfilling the quota.

Home workers may be disadvantaged in many other ways. For example, many home workers do not receive a regular wage but rather work on a piece rate, which means that they are paid per finished piece of clothing. As a result of inadequate rates and periodic drops in orders, their hourly earnings may, on average, be lower than those in factories.

Perhaps the home workers' main disadvantage is that they tend to have fewer legal rights than those workers employed in factories. For instance, one Indonesian factory, which used roughly a dozen subcontractors with a total of approximately 200 home workers, did not have fixed contracts with any of its subcontractors. If there was no work, the home workers were simply not paid, albeit this practice was also reported of factory workers elsewhere. These problems were compounded by the fact that unionization of home workers is considerably more difficult, if compared with regular workers.

Unfortunately, in the firms analyzed, there was relatively little evidence of the working conditions of home workers as external observers usually visit factories as opposed to home workers. Therefore, any general conclusions on the working conditions of home workers should be avoided here.

The prohibition (or limitation) of child labor

Based on our sources, there is some evidence of child labor. Of ten clothing manufacturers visited by CCC staff in Bangladesh in 1995, for example, two used child labor, although in some other cases it was not entirely clear from the sources whether child workers were employed or not, partly because of practices such as hiding child workers during a visit by foreign observers to a factory or concealing the actual age of child workers. Where child workers were used, this was usually because they tended to be cheaper than adult workers and factories sometimes preferred children for certain types of jobs. For example, in one Bangladeshi factory, a child helper earned between Tk. 400 and 700 per month in 1995, while adult workers earned a minimum of Tk. 1800.

Nonetheless, the issue of prohibiting child labor is arguably very complex, particularly with regards to alternative occupations for children. A 1998 report on child labor in the garment industry in Bangladesh by a non-governmental organization remarked that 'The garment industry employs only a tiny fraction of the total number of child workers. The vast majority of children work in the informal sector where conditions are far worse' (Bangladesh People Solidarity Centre 1998). Some of the alternative jobs for children in Bangladesh include domestic servants, vendors and waste collectors. Some work is much more hazardous than that in the garment industry such as making brick or stone chips, working in plastic, rubber or glass factories and prostitution.

The above discussion of Bangladesh, where child labor is particularly prevalent, cannot necessarily be applied to every Asian country. In Malaysia, for instance, jobs in the garment industry compete with better-paid jobs in the computer industry and child labor appears to be less prevalent than in Bangladesh. However, even if jobs in the clothing industry are not as well paid as other employment opportunities, children may still prefer to work in clothing factories than to have alternative jobs or to have no occupation at all. As families may be too poor to send their children to school, the alternative of not having a clothing industry job for a child may simply be to stay at home and do nothing. A report by the India Committee of the Netherlands, which advocated the elimination of child labor, found that 'abolition of child labor was not favored by the children for economic reasons and because they did not like to attend school', albeit the majority of children would have preferred to receive education if circumstances permitted (Kruijtbosch 1996, pp. 37 and 41). This is why certain organizations and firms advocated a limitation of child labor rather than an outright prohibition or a payment of children's education by employers as opposed to an outright dismissal of child workers.

In conclusion, the available evidence suggests that a significant number of clothing manufacturers violated the prohibition of child labor. Nonetheless, if judged by the relatively low number of local complaints by those affected, an elimination of child labor does not appear to be a significant preoccupation of garment industry workers themselves. In this context, it is difficult to dispel the impression that until poverty alleviation measures are able to raise the income of parents or compulsory education can effectively be implemented, the demand for the total elimination of child labor remains perhaps more of a western preoccupation than a local concern. This raises the question of to what extent do certain international human rights perhaps mirror western concepts of human rights rather than the real-world concerns of some people in developing countries.

Indirect impact of garment firms on human rights

In addition to the above instances of the direct impact on human rights, garment firms may also have an indirect impact on human rights, albeit this is even more difficult to establish and usually impossible to quantify.

While any conclusions on the indirect impact of garment firms must be tentative, the most likely impact of company activities is the influence on government policy in a given country. The activities of TNCs may persuade a government to change its policies with the aims of preventing the relocation of production activities to other countries and encouraging further investment in the local clothing industry. Many Asian countries have been able to attract foreign investment in labor-intensive industries such as clothing manufacturing thanks to low wages as well as to little or poorly-enforced legislation in the area of labor rights. In pursuit of further savings on operational costs, many TNCs may relocate some of their manufacturing plants from one developing country to another or shift to sourcing their supplies from a different country.

Indeed, clothing firms have already relocated part of their production activities away from countries such as Hong Kong and Taiwan towards countries with lower wages where trade unions have less of an influence, such as Vietnam and mainland China (FHKI 1990; Khanna 1993). There may also be regional differences within countries in terms of pay and working conditions, which is why clothing manufacturers may choose to avoid certain areas such as Kerala in India in favour of low-wage and less union-organized regions. As the clothing industry does not require major fixed investment or sophisticated technology and the required manpower is abundant in many developing countries, relocation of production activities is relatively unproblematic and therefore a constant threat.

Faced with this threat, governments may perceive the need to hamper the functioning of trade unions, to prevent a rise in wages and an improvement in working conditions in order to keep operational costs to a minimum, as a means of attracting foreign investors. As a result, the minimum wage may be set at a relatively low level, labor legislation may be weak or remain unenforced. The state apparatus may also actively be used to suppress workers' protests. For instance, Indonesian legislation provided the military with an active role in labor matters including a role in settling disputes between management and workers (SÜDWIND 2000, p. 15). In practice, the Indonesian security forces (both the military and police) suppressed labor strikes, intimidated workers, placed secret agents in factories to monitor union activities and arrested workers or forced workers to resign, a situation which has changed little since the start of the country's transition to civilian rule in 1998 (SÜDWIND 2000, pp. 15–17 and 48; Burns and Mather 1999, pp. 12–13). There is also evidence that the government hampers the functioning of organizations which sympathize with or support workers.

While the responsibility for the above-mentioned repressive and anti-labor measures must rest primarily with governments, there is evidence of linkages between TNCs, their local business partners and state policy. Indeed, in the case of Indonesia, there are indications that manufacturers actively encouraged the repression of workers' protests by making payments to the Indonesian police and the military. Among others, manufacturers reportedly make payments to 'Koramil' (local military commands) for 'protection' during labor strikes, which could cost the company US$1000 per day for even a small strike, while a large strike could reportedly cost up to US$1 million (SÜDWIND 2000, p. 17; Burns and Mather 1999, p. 13). Yet Nike, for instance, claimed that the presence of Indonesian 'Koramil' at their Indonesian manufacturing sites was benign and was indeed welcomed by the workers.[21]

The brief discussion above indicates that TNC involvement in the clothing industry may have a considerable indirect impact on human rights, albeit much more research is needed on this issue.

Ethical policies of TNCs

Many western retailers have developed some sort of an ethical policy related to their suppliers, in the form of a code of conduct or written ethical statements, frequently as a response to pressure from non-governmental organizations such as CCC, trade unions and other organizations.[22] While TNC codes of conduct do not have the power of law, it was found that clothing suppliers often paid considerably more attention to their transnational clients' codes of conduct than to national labor laws, despite the fact that they tended to be more familiar with national laws (Musiolek 1999, p. 167). This further underlines the influence of TNCs over their clothing suppliers and highlights some of the advantages of codes of conduct noted in Chapter 3.

There are a large variety of codes of conduct and social label systems. These can range from codes designed solely by one large TNC to agreements negotiated between non-governmental organizations, trade unions, governments and the clothing firms. The contents of the codes of conduct also differ significantly between firms. For example, Littlewoods' ethical policy covers nine out of the ten rights and prohibitions discussed in this chapter, while Storehouse Group's (which includes BhS) ethical code only covers six out of the ten rights and prohibitions. In general terms, an ILO survey of over 200 codes of conduct and social label systems in November 1998 found that well over 60 per cent of these referred to the issue of discrimination and roughly 50 per cent referred to child labor, but less than 20 per cent included the rights to freedom of association and bargaining (European Commission 1999).[23]

The use of codes of conduct is not without difficulties. Among others, stakeholders may not be properly consulted or there may be implementation problems (for example, poor communication or lack of involvement of employees). Based on research on UK companies in Indonesia, Burns and Mather (1999, p. 37) found that a great majority of workers interviewed were unaware that the firms they worked for, or supplied goods to, had a code of conduct or written ethical statements. Last, but not least, codes of conducts often do not involve any effective penalties for non-compliance, either in the form of fines or withdrawal of orders.[24]

As a result of the above limitations, some of the best codes of conduct may not be enforced in practice. For instance, while Levi Strauss pioneered the use of the code of conduct in the clothing industry, a number of its suppliers visited by SOMO and CCC failed to meet many, if not most, of the ten rights and prohibitions discussed in this chapter. A Levi Strauss supplier in Jakarta, Indonesia, visited in 1998 did not respect women's rights or the right to form and join trade unions, the wage was below the legal minimum wage, workers worked 75 hours per week and had little, if any, time to rest. Although the factory was founded around 1990, none of the workers interviewed knew about the existence of Levi Strauss' code of conduct. According to interviews with workers, when Levi Strauss representatives visited the factory, they only checked the cleanliness and pleasantness of the workplace and examined the quality of production. If they asked to talk to workers, the management selected those most loyal to the enterprise. Despite the violation of many sections of Levi Strauss' own code of conduct, the firm continued to order its clothes from the factory. Judged by this example, even the best code of conduct may remain a dead letter unless it is communicated to all workers and its implementation is properly monitored. In a paper on the Thai footwear and garment industries, Yimprasert et al. (1999) concluded in general terms that the 'enforcement of codes of conduct in the apparel industry is very weak and performed only on a voluntary basis'.

The above-mentioned difficulties would point to the conclusion that a code of conduct is of limited value unless it is effectively implemented and monitored. As with the written ethical codes, there are a large variety of implementation and monitoring procedures in the clothing industry, ranging from 'in-house' monitoring systems to independent monitoring by external bodies such as non-governmental organizations. As an example of the former, C&A founded a wholly-C&A owned monitoring subsidiary called SOCAM (Service Organization for Compliance

Audit Management) in 1996 and, by May 1999, it had already made roughly 3700 visits to suppliers and their subcontractors.[25] As an example of the latter, the Fair Trade Charter in the Netherlands – a body comprising of clothing sector employers, trade unions, non-governmental organizations and the state – introduced independent monitoring systems. Monitoring can have a major impact on a supplier. As Musiolek (1999, p. 167) found, suppliers attached considerably more importance to a code of conduct as a result of a monitoring visit and a threatened cancellation of orders by a client.

Nonetheless, unless there is independent and transparent external monitoring, the audit reports of bodies such as SOCAM and external auditors selected single-handedly by the firms can be questioned; reports are usually kept secret and are not available to outsiders, and it is impossible to check on the validity of the methodology utilized and the findings of inspections.

Evidence of secrecy surrounding the human rights situation in the clothing industry suggests that TNCs may attempt to conceal certain facts regarding their suppliers. This is exemplified by a confidential Ernst & Young audit of labor and environmental conditions inside Tae Kwang Vina Company (a Nike subcontractor in Vietnam), which was leaked to the Transnational Resource and Action Center (TRAC). This was the first time that an accounting firm's labor and environmental audit of the clothing and footwear industries was made public. The audit observed widespread violations of labor law on issues such as working hours, unprotected chemical exposures and trade union rights. This was despite the fact that Tae Kwang Vina Company was reportedly the most technically advanced of Nike's subcontractors in Vietnam and that it largely complied with Nike's own code of conduct. Furthermore, the audit report had methodological shortcomings; among them a failure to provide information on important labor issues such as health and safety and a reliance on data mainly provided by management.[26] In essence, the audit report indicated that TNCs may have reasons to conceal the nature and content of their monitoring reports.

This secrecy renders any inter-firm comparisons of the actual ethical performance of TNCs (as opposed to their formal policies such as codes of conduct) very difficult. However, perhaps one indication of the firms' performance is their relative openness to external scrutiny. Out of 11 UK clothing retailers I contacted for this research, only four firms sent details of their ethical policies, and two of these firms – Marks & Spencer and Littlewoods – are regarded as being among the above-average UK performers in terms of their ethical stance on clothing suppliers. Above all, both firms are members of the Ethical Trading Initiative (ETI), a multi-sector coalition of companies, non-governmental organizations and trade union organizations backed by the UK government.[27] Both firms were more open with regard to answering questions on their performance than most other firms surveyed. In contrast, several firms regarded as average or under-performers appeared secretive about their ethical policies. The press office of Next refused to send me the company's code of conduct claiming that this was confidential information.[28] The above discussion could perhaps indicate that there is a correlation between a firm's openness to external scrutiny and its actual ethical performance.

In conclusion, it appears that the ethical policies and monitoring techniques of clothing firms are not in themselves sufficient to raise actual ethical performance. Indeed, the gap between formal policy measures and the situation on the ground could perhaps explain the secrecy of clothing retailers with regard to their suppliers in Asia.

Conclusion

This chapter investigated the impact of transnational garment firms on human rights in South and South-East Asia by focusing on labor rights. Our findings suggested that in the case of at least eight out of the ten rights and prohibitions analyzed, there was evidence of serious violations.

Among the arguments defending TNCs and questioning our findings there may be suggestions that there is a weak link between the local human rights situation and a TNC's own policy or that a TNC cannot influence the human rights situation in a local clothing factory, especially if a supplier has many other buyers. However, despite the complexity of trading networks in the clothing trade, suppliers are highly dependent on their transnational clients. As Dicken (1998, p. 306) stated: 'Major international retail chains and buying groups exert enormous purchasing power and leverage over clothing manufacturers. Although the production and retailing of clothing may be fragmented in individual markets, international buying operations are highly concentrated.' By implication, TNCs have considerable influence over the local human rights situation in clothing manufacturing. Indeed, transnational buyers are able to dictate many conditions regarding working practices to the local manufacturer; and suppliers appear to be even more likely to abide by the TNCs' codes of conduct than their national labor laws.

In addition, there are indications that there is a large measure of variation in terms of observing human rights between manufacturers of the same country and between different countries. The position of the clothing industry in relation to other local industries also varies. For example, in Bangladesh the working conditions in the clothing industry are said to be better than in other national industries (Bangladesh People Solidarity Centre 1998), while in Malaysia, the opposite seems to be the case (Rudnick 1995). These variations suggest that individual TNCs have a choice in terms of selecting countries or specific suppliers who are above-average performers in terms of respecting human rights. In practice, the opposite frequently appears to be the case. Research indicates that, in pursuit of profit, some firms intentionally relocated their operations towards countries or specific plants with lower wages, lower labor rights standards and a lesser degree of unionization.

Many clothing TNCs have developed some sort of an ethical policy related to their suppliers, although there are still few common standards and many implementation problems remain. As a result of corporate secrecy, it is difficult to make any inter-firm comparisons, albeit it was suggested that there are differences in the human rights impact of different companies. Littlewoods[29] and Marks & Spencer, for instance, which helped to found the ETI in the UK, appear to perform better in terms of human rights than a number of rival firms. In this context, while methodology for measuring the human rights impact of firms requires further refinement and more research is needed on the clothing industry, this chapter indicates the different ways in which TNCs have adapted to the world of international sourcing strategies.

Notes

I am very grateful for the kind assistance rendered by CCC staff, especially Ineke Zeldenrust, in the course of this research. Many thanks also to Joris Oldenziel of SOMO and Martin Pepper of Littlewoods for their kind assistance. Last, but not least, the author would like to thank the Coventry Business School for generous funding of this research.
1. The production process itself usually involves cutting, stitching, washing, ironing and packaging.
2. See CleanClothesCampaign website at http://www.cleanclothes.org/.
3. Articles 20 and 23 of the Universal Declaration of Human Rights (hereafter UDHR) and article 8 of the International Covenant on Economic, Social and Cultural Rights (hereafter ICESCR).
4. Article 2 of the UDHR, article 2(2) of the ICESCR and articles 2(1) and 3 of the International Covenant on Civil and Political Rights (hereafter ICCPR). All of these instruments provide that there should be no discrimination of any kind as to race, color, sex, language, religion, political or other opinion, national or social origin, property, birth or other status.
5. Article 8 of the ICCPR.

6. According to the 1989 UN Convention on the Rights of the Child, a child is defined as a person under the age of 18. In accordance with article 32, children have the right to be protected from work that threatens their health, education or development.
7. Articles 23 and 24 of the UDHR and articles 6 and 7 of the ICESCR.
8. Article 4 of the ILO Home Work Convention, 1996 (No. 177).
9. Article 2 of the ILO Hours of Work (Industry) Convention, 1919 (No. 1).
10. Articles 4 and 16 of the ILO Occupational Safety and Health Convention, 1981 (No. 155).
11. Article 1 of the ILO Minimum Wage Fixing Convention, 1970 (No. 131) obliges states, which ratified the Convention, to establish a system of minimum wages for all groups of wage earners.
12. Article 4 of the ILO Termination of Employment Convention, 1982 (No. 158) stated: 'The employment of a worker shall not be terminated without a valid reason for such termination connected with the capacity or conduct of the worker or based on the operational requirements of the undertaking, establishment or service.' According to articles 5 and 6, valid reasons for termination exclude union membership, filing a complaint against the employer, acting as a worker representative, race, color, sex, marital status, family responsibilities, pregnancy, religion, political opinion, national extraction, social origin, absence from work during maternity leave or temporary absence from work because of illness.
13. In addition, a questionnaire on the ethical policy of clothing retailers towards suppliers was sent to the UK's 11 top clothing retailers (out of 15 clothing retailers targeted). However, most firms failed to respond to the questionnaire so the results are not reproduced here.
14. As a corollary, if the same local manufacturer produces clothing for a large number of different clients and the firm's size is relatively large, the firm is more likely to reject a client's demands for implementing any changes to ethical policies, as the bargaining power of a single client is smaller. Based on their research in Thailand, Yimprasert et al. (1999) found a contrast between the footwear and the clothing industries. In the footwear industry, which is more capital-intensive than the clothing industry, a local manufacturer tends to rely on a smaller number of buyers and the relationships between the TNCs and their local suppliers tend to be more stable. As a result, the effective implementation of TNC codes of conduct was less problematic in the footwear industry.
15. Following General Suharto's fall from power in 1998, the Indonesian government under President Habibie ratified the ILO Freedom of Association and Protection of the Right to Organize Convention, 1948 (No. 87) and the formation of independent trade unions was legalized. However, despite the formal legalization of trade unions in Indonesia, union activity is still hampered by employers and state officials (Burns and Mather 1999, pp. 12–13).
16. The use of foreign migrant workers is primarily restricted to countries which face internal labor shortages, such as Malaysia where the garment industry competes for workers with other industries with better working conditions and better pay, especially the electronics industry. For instance, of 16 Malaysian textile and garment firms analyzed by Rudnick (1995), at least nine reported labor shortages, 11 employed foreign workers and a further

three had applied for foreign workers who were expected to shortly arrive. Overall, foreign workers comprised 29 per cent of the total labor force of those 16 firms. Well over 90 per cent of these foreign workers were Bangladeshi.

17. For example, Rudnick (1995) reported that Malaysian employers frequently withhold the passports of migrant Bangladeshi workers – in violation of Malaysian law – in order to prevent them from leaving.

18. Provision of protective clothing, for instance, was explicitly covered in article 16, section 3 of the ILO Occupational Safety and Health Convention, 1981 (No. 155). Certain other sources of unsafe or unhealthy conditions such as insufficient safety measures for fire emergencies or lack of ventilation could arguably be covered by article 4 of the same ILO Convention which aims 'to prevent accidents and injury to health arising out of, linked with or occurring in the course of work, by minimizing, so far as is reasonably practicable, the causes of hazards inherent in the working environment' (where the term 'health' was defined by the Convention as 'not merely the absence of disease or infirmity; it also includes the physical and mental elements affecting health which are directly related to safety and hygiene at work', article 3, section e) as well as article 16 of the same ILO Convention.

19. Article 24 of the UDHR.

20. Article 3 of the ILO Minimum Wage Fixing Convention, 1970 (No. 131).

21. Source: CCC documentation.

22. On codes of conduct and their effectiveness, see, for example, Blanpain (2000) and Seyfang (1999).

23. *European Social Dialogue*, a Newsletter of the European Commission, 'Special Edition: Codes of Conduct and Social Labels', May 1999.

24. For instance, Emmelhainz and Adams (1999) conducted an analysis of 27 out of 34 codes of conduct of a leading group of US clothing firms – including prominent TNCs such as Gap and Levi Strauss – called 'Trendsetters', which pledged to work together to eliminate sweatshops. In spite of the fact that these were supposedly more progressive codes of conduct, it was found that only 17 of the 27 codes included any reference to sanctions for non-compliance, some of which were very weak, with one code including the simple term 'strongly object'.

25. *European Social Dialogue*, a Newsletter of the European Commission, 'Special Edition: Codes of Conduct and Social Labels', May 1999.

26. Source: CCC documentation.

27. ETI members are committed to the adoption of the ETI code of conduct based on core ILO conventions for all or part of their business, which must be defined from the outset. Furthermore, they are committed to participation in pilot studies with other members designed to test monitoring and verification systems, and to providing an annual report of their progress. The ETI claims it is unique 'because it is an ongoing collaboration between industry, non-governmental organisations, Trades Unions and Government which will develop practical tools for developing best practice in the field of ethical trading' (ETI website at http://www.eti.org.uk, 30 July 2000).

28. Phone conversation with Natalie Pead, Next Press Office (8 June 2000).

29. After this book went to print, Littlewoods was taken over by two British billionaires, the Barclay brothers. The new owners announced the loss of over

200 jobs, which includes ten staff employed to check that the firm's suppliers meet ethical standards. Littlewoods is also to withdraw from the ETI.

References

Bangladesh People Solidarity Centre. 1998. 'Unstitching the Child Labor Debate', Amsterdam: Bangladesh People Solidarity Centre.

Blanpain, Roger, ed. 2000. *Multinational Enterprises and the Social Challenges of the XXIst Century*. Dordrecht: Kluwer Law International.

Burns, Maggie and Celia Mather. 1999. *UK Companies in Indonesia – Responses to Ethical Trade Issues*. London: CIIR.

Dicken, P. 1998. *Global Shift: Transforming the World Economy*. Third edn. London: Paul Chapman.

Ekachai, Sanitsuda. 1999. 'A Life of Hard Labor', *Bangkok Post*, 15 April.

Emmelhainz, Margaret A. and Ronald J. Adams. 1999. 'The Apparel Industry Response to "Sweatshop" Concerns: a Review and Analysis of Codes of Conduct', *Journal of Supply Chain Management* (Summer).

FHKI. 1990. 'Hong Kong's Offshore Investment', Hong Kong: Industry and Research Division, Federation of Hong Kong Industries.

Green, Duncan. 1998. *Fashion Victims: Together We Can Clean Up the Clothes Trade – the Asian Garment Industry and Globalisation*. London: CAFOD.

Khanna, S.R. 1993. 'Structural Changes in Asian Textiles and Clothing Industries: the Second Migration of Production', *Textile Outlook International* (September).

Kruijtbosch, Martine, 1996. 'Child and Adult Labor in the Export-Oriented Garment and Gem Polishing Industry of India', Utrecht: India Committee of the Netherlands.

Musiolek, Bettina. 1999. 'Die Debatte um Verhaltenskodex und unabhängiges Monitoring: eine kritische Zwischenbilanz', in Bettina Musiolek, ed., *Gezähmte Modemultis*, Frankfurt a.M.: Brandes & Apsel.

Rudnick, Anja. 1995. 'The Thread of Life – Malaysia's Textile Industry and the Plight of Bangladeshi Workers', Masters Thesis at the Department of Human Geography, University of Amsterdam (December).

Seyfang, Gill. 1999. 'Private Sector Self-Regulation for Social Responsibility: Mapping Codes of Conduct', School of Development Studies, University of East Anglia, Norwich.

SÜDWIND Institut für Ökonomie und Ökumene. 2000. *Das Kreuz mit dem Faden – Indonesierinnen nähen für deutsche Modemultis*. Siegburg: SÜDWIND.

Yimprasert, Junya, Christopher Candland and Walden Bello. 1999. 'Can Corporate Codes of Conduct Promote Labor Standards? Evidence from the Thai Footwear and Apparel Industries', unpublished draft, Hong Kong: Hong Kong Christian Industrial Committee and Asia Monitor Resource Centre.

9
Timber Logging in Clayoquot Sound, Canada: Community–Corporate Partnerships and Community Rights

Heike Fabig and Richard Boele

Introduction

Clayoquot Sound, an area of about 265,000 hectares[1] on the central west of Vancouver Island (known as the Central Region), is the largest contiguous area of temperate rainforest in the world. With 75 per cent of its ancient forest still intact, it is the region with the largest biomass of any intact forest system remaining on earth. Clayoquot Sound is special because of its size but also because of its relative rarity, as temperate rainforests comprised less than 0.2 per cent of the earth's land surface before clearing commenced (FOCS 2001a–f). Clayoquot Sound was declared a United Nations Biosphere Reserve in January 2000.[2]

The Canadian Province of British Columbia (BC), where Clayoquot Sound is situated, holds about a quarter of the world's remaining temperate rainforest, about half of which (53 per cent) has been logged already (FOCS 2001d, p. 1). Clayoquot lies on Vancouver Island, which has been cut extensively in the past. Seventy-four per cent of old-growth forest on the island has been logged, and only ten out of 170 large valleys are still pristine. Six of these remaining old-growth forest valleys are located in the Clayoquot Sound area – two valleys are protected, and four are not.[3] Of Clayoquot Sound land protected by parks, 62 per cent was designated open for logging. The end result is that of all the productive ancient forest in Clayoquot, 74 per cent was opened for logging (FOCS 2001d, p. 2).

The Clayoquot Sound (known locally as Tla-o-qui-aht[4]) area comprises ten First Nations reserves on 220 hectares, some small towns (mainly Tofino and Uclulet) and the Pacific Rim National Park (Ministry of Aboriginal Affairs 2001). Almost 90 per cent of Clayoquot Sound is on Nuu-chah-nulth land.

The impact of corporate logging activity in the Clayoquot Sound area on indigenous lives is significant.[5] Before colonization by the Europeans, the Nuu-chah-nulth people lived self-sufficiently, utilizing forest and sea produce. European appropriation of land and the commercial activities introduced since, especially logging (Marchak 1983), significantly changed the basis of aboriginal economic life. As the Nuu-chah-nulth Tribal Council states, 'In the few short generations following European contact, Nuu-chah-nulth people suffered almost incalculable losses. Many of those losses were and continue to be associated with high-volume, and often destructive logging practices' (Nuu-chah-nulth Tribal Council 2001, p. 2). Many Nuu-chah-nulth found employment with logging companies and their contractors as tree fellers and in other manual work. Technological modernization, however, has put many people out of jobs, while still enabling big expanses of forest to be logged. Few Nuu-chah-nulth people work for the big timber corporations active on Vancouver Island (Nuu-chah-nulth Tribal Council 2001, p. 2).

In 1993, Clayoquot Sound became the site of the largest civil disobedience protests in Canadian history. While historically significant for Canada, the conflict in Clayoquot Sound between logging company MacMillan Bloedel and the environmental movement represented by a number of environmental non-governmental organizations (eNGOs) and the Nuu-chah-nulth First Nations, is of wider interest and has potential ramifications beyond Canada. What makes the case particularly interesting is the unique way in which it was eventually solved. After years of confrontation the key actors moved beyond the traditional positions of conflict, distrust and hostility and devised a unique and innovative solution to the apparently intractable community–corporate conflict discourse. In an unprecedented move, a logging company joint venture was created between the local indigenous communities and a multinational corporation, with the support of key eNGOs.

Partnerships between civil society and corporations

This book presents several case studies of human rights problems and challenges posed by corporate activities. Yet, while there are many as yet unresolved conflicts, there have also been interesting solutions. This chapter aims to show that creative answers benefiting both civil society and corporations can be found. While there is considerable pressure by civil society organizations, notably non-governmental organizations

(NGOs) on corporations to improve their track record on human rights, the realm of conflict has been transcended by new and innovative partnerships between civil society and corporations, especially in the environmental arena.

This is indeed a remarkable development, which represents a marked contrast with corporate–NGO relations only two or three decades ago. For instance, Vogel (1978) extensively studied movements of corporate accountability in the United States from the 1950s to the late 1970s, particularly the black civil rights movement and the anti-Vietnam war movement. As Vogel showed in the cases of Kodak's and General Motors' reactions to challenges by the US civil rights movement regarding equal opportunities for African Americans, these companies were in favor of some of the suggested changes. Yet business was not prepared to 'give in' to NGO demands, fearing loss of power and legitimacy (Vogel 1978, pp. 30–5 and pp. 71–89). The attitude of business has changed significantly since then. Now some companies think it is acceptable to cede some power and legitimacy to NGOs where this is seen as beneficial for the company. Indeed, in a radical shift, many scholars and business leaders now reason that it is in companies' long-term economic interests to enter into relationships with NGOs to confer legitimacy upon their operations. If planned and implemented carefully, such partnerships can offer both actors useful tools to discuss and promote global corporate responsibility and sustainable development. As Murphy (1997, p. 17) argues:

> By entering into partnerships with NGOs, some businesses are calling for a broader interpretation of global civil society. In response to their critics, a growing number of TNCs are seeking out NGO partners to help global business enhance its image and contribution to fair trade and sustainable development.

Chairman of consultancy group SustainAbility John Elkington examined the growing number of business/NGO relations and distinguished between the four types of NGO approaches to business (Elkington 1997, p. 229). Elkington's typology, which will be useful to our discussion later, centers around the following two axes:

> Polarizors/integrators: integrators place high priority on developing productive relationships with the corporate world, while polarizors are of a more ideological nature who made strategic decisions not to develop working relationships with businesses and prefer to expose corporate practice.

Discriminators/non-discriminators: discriminators discriminate between companies within an industry depending on the perceived and real social and environmental performance, while non-discriminators focus on the social and environmental performance of industry in general.

Integrators aim to reward good business practice with an endorsement or cooperation. Such NGOs might engage in dialogue with companies about how products are produced, and encourage the idea of the consumer's 'market vote' to encourage the corporate world to be more socially and environmentally responsible. In some instances, NGOs and companies may get together in a product collaboration or in establishing informal codes of conduct or stewardship regimes.

Polarizors fundamentally question the role and purpose of corporations in society, and aim to change the corporate capitalist system. They argue that green consumerism is still consumerism, and reduces power to purchasing power, while leaving aside issues such as economic growth in a finite planet, the power and influence of TNCs and the way that power is structured in society (Plant and Plant 1991; Haynes 1991).

The two models outlined here are ideal types and must be taken as such. Furthermore, the confrontational NGOs often create the space for others to engage with business. For example, long-term campaigns against McDonalds on environmental issues set the scene for the company to enter into partnership with the Environmental Defense Fund (see Murphy and Bendell 1997). In some cases, both strategies may be pursued by the same NGO on the same issue, or even against a particular company on different issues. The Greenpeace PVC-free credit card made of biodegradable material is produced by Monsanto, the company targeted by Greenpeace with heavy criticism over genetically engineered foods. Asked about these 'double standards', a Greenpeace spokesperson explained on a UK radio program that where companies do well, Greenpeace will work with them, and where companies behave badly, they will be criticized.

At the same time, more pragmatic approaches – sometimes by the very same individuals and organizations that radically question businesses' license to operate – try to alleviate the immediate situation and aim to make business more socially and environmentally sustainable and more transparent and accountable (see Estes 1996; Elkington 1997; Wheeler and Sillanpää 1997). Simultaneously, many neoliberal governments (national and transnational) increasingly define the corporate world as a social and political agent without whom society will not function optimally.

In a few cases, the dialogue between business and civil society has moved further, forging partnerships between traditional enemies. This has been most visible on the environmental front where companies have invited non-commercial organizations to help solve business problems, often after a period of prolonged action from pressure groups. Focused towards creating solutions based on common grounds and common aims, these partnerships between civil society and corporations could be labeled 'practical partnerships'. Examples include the cooperation between the German fridge-manufacturer Foron and Greenpeace to build a CFC-free fridge (Porter and van der Linde 1996, p. 74; Stafford et al. 2000; Stafford and Hartman 2001), the Forest Stewardship Council (analyzed in detail in Murphy and Bendell 1997, pp. 96–142 and Bendell and Murphy 2000), the Marine Stewardship Council (studied by Weir 2000 and Fowler and Heap 2000) and the UK-based Ethical Trading Initiative (Murphy and Coleman 2000).

There are a small number of outstanding cases of corporate–community engagement that have partnerships focused on capacity building at the core of their success. Cameco's operation in Northern Saskatchewan (Canada) is one of these. The company – the world's largest uranium producer – has focused on ensuring the core activities of the company directly benefit the indigenous communities. Among their solutions they concentrated on public education, indigenous labor force development and increasing indigenous business capacity so they can supply the company's operations. They have appointed a Chief of the largest First Nation to their board and have Elders on their mining sites on five days every month to be cultural advisers and counsellors to both management and indigenous employees. Cameco has also been instrumental in nurturing a mining and construction services joint venture between a consortium of indigenous partners (Wayne Dunn Associates 2001). However, the most impressive case of a company and a community moving beyond conflict and towards collaboration is found in Clayoquot Sound.

Conflict and collaboration in Clayoquot Sound

Chronology of events

The conflict in Clayoquot Sound first ignited in the late 1970s, when Canadian logging company MacMillan Bloedel (MB) planned to log a small island in Clayoquot Sound, Meares Island, located in Tofino harbor.[6] The First Nations laid claim to the Island, and indeed most of the Sound, and took their case to court. Meanwhile, environmental organizations were vigorously opposed to logging the pristine wood in the entire Clayoquot Sound area and sprang into action to halt the logging plans. Opposition to logging activities took various forms, including building a hiking trail on the island to encourage eco-tourism, and physical occupation of the island by activists in 1984 in what became the first ever logging blockade in Canadian history. The environmental activists disbanded their blockade in 1985 when the First Nations were granted an injunction by the court which prevented any logging on Meares Island pending the outcome of the First Nations' land claim on the island, an injunction which is still in force today.[7]

After this temporary halt, the conflict flared up again in the early 1990s and gained an international dimension in 1993 when various eNGOs initiated an international market and education campaign to steer worldwide wood consumers away from old-growth forest from BC, and Clayoquot Sound in particular. That summer 12,000 people participated in a blockade at the Kennedy Lake Bridge, the largest peaceful civil disobedience action in Canadian history. Almost 1000 people were arrested, and some jailed, for non-violent road blockades. The efforts of the eNGOs and the high national and international media attention for Clayoquot Sound mobilized worldwide public opposition to the clearcutting of old-growth forests.

Due to the negative publicity and concerted action by eNGOs disrupting logging operations and targeting MacMillan Bloedel's buyers, MB was facing serious financial losses. Firstly, the company was confronted with a figure of upwards of C\$20 million (Chow 2000, p. 3) in lost revenue on its tenure. Secondly, under the volume-based tenure system of BC, companies who do not meet minimum harvest volumes risk losing their timber rights and thus effectively have their tenure revoked (Chow 2000, p. 5). Furthermore, 'in 1996, MacMillan Bloedel lost 5 per cent of its sales when two of its customers in the UK, Scott Paper and Kimberly-Clark, cancelled their contracts. Employee morale at MB was at an all time low' (Svendsen 2000, pp. 3–4). Under pressure, MB closed its operations at Kennedy Lake in Clayoquot Sound in January 1998. With further threats of international boycotts of BC timber products, and no waning of energy from environmental activists in sight, the government of British Columbia and MacMillan Bloedel realized they had no alternative than to take some sort of proactive initiative.

While awaiting the finalization of the nationally initiated treaty negotiations (see below), the government of British Columbia signed an initial two year Interim Measures Agreement (IMA) with five First

Nations of the Nuu-chah-nulth Central Region in 1994. The IMA stipulated and formalized joint management of the Nuu-chah-nulth land until the treaty negotiations were complete, and 'acknowledged that the Ha'wiih (Hereditary Chiefs) of the First Nations have the responsibility to conserve and protect their traditional territories and waters for generations which will follow' (Iisaak 2000b, p. 1). The IMA created a Central Region Board (CRB) with equal aboriginal and non-aboriginal membership to promote sustainable resource use in Clayoquot Sound (Iisaak 2000b, p. 2) and provided the opportunities for joint ventures between industry and First Nations. In 1995, the government of British Columbia appointed a Scientific Panel for Sustainable Forest Practices in Clayoquot Sound to detail how and where sustainable logging could take place in the region. The panel's recommendations, which will revolutionize logging in BC when fully implemented, were accepted by the BC government in July 1985.[8] By 1996, treaty negotiations were still incomplete and a three-year extension was established in the Interim Measures Extension Agreement (IMEA). As little progress had been achieved on the joint ventures, the IMEA specifically committed MacMillan Bloedel and the Nuu-chah-nulth to establish a joint-venture logging business to operate in the Clayoquot Sound area (Iisaak 2000b, p. 2). Ma-Mook Development Corporation was created in 1997 by Ucluelet, Tha-o-quit-aht, Toquaht, Ahousat and Hesquiaht First Nations (Nuu-chah-nulth Tribal Council 2001, p. 8) to represent the collective economic interests of the five Central Region Nuu-chah-nulth (Chow 2000, p. 4; Iisaak 2000b, p. 2).

On 16 November 1998, Iisaak Forest Resources was established as a joint-venture logging company between MacMillan Bloedel, owning 49 per cent, and the Nuu-chah-nulth First Nation of Clayoquot Sound represented by the Ma-Mook corporation, owning 51 per cent.[9] The Iisaak Board of Directors consists of two company representatives and three Nuu-chah-nulth First Nations' representatives (Iisaak 2000f, p. 4). Pronounced 'E-sock', Iisaak means 'respect' in the Nuu-chah-nulth language. The company is 'committed to Hishuk-ish ts'awalk (pronounced "He-shook ish sha-walk"), the Nuu-chah-nulth belief of respecting the limits of what is extracted and the interconnectedness of all things' (Iisaak 2000a). The Clayoquot Sound part of the MB tenure was passed on to Iisaak by the Ministry of Forests, thus giving the new joint venture an immediate working base.[10]

Iisaak is to be in line with the recommendations set out by the Scientific Panel. The company has made one of the panel's recommendations, the shift from volume-based to value-based harvesting, a key point in its mission statement and working practices. As the company states:

> Iisaak is committed to making Clayoquot Sound a leading global example of ecologically sensitive forest management. The implementation of the Clayoquot Sound Scientific Panel recommendations form the technical basis for Iisaak's approach to forest management in Clayoquot Sound. Iisaak recognises that the application of the Scientific Panel is a continuous learning process and that based on what is learned, the process of adaptive management will be applied. (Iisaak 2000d, p. 3)[11]

A Memorandum of Understanding (MOU) was signed in 1999 by Iisaak Forest Resources and four environmental NGOs (Greenpeace International and Canada, Western Canada Wilderness Committee, Sierra Club of BC, and the US-based Natural Resources Defense Council). The Memorandum[12] contains commitments from Iisaak to respect the role of First Nations in resource management activities, achieve certification under the Forest Stewardship Council (FSC),[13] refrain from logging pristine areas in its tenure and eventually phase out old-growth logging. In return, the eNGOs will support Iisaak's operations, actively engage in promoting markets for Iisaak's products and develop ongoing mechanisms for sustaining operations (Iisaak 2000b, p. 2). One eNGO involved in the confrontation with MacMillan Bloedel, the Friends of Clayoquot Sound (FOCS), chose not to sign the Memorandum of Understanding.[14] A further Memorandum of Understanding was signed in September 1999 between Iisaak and the unemployed forest workers of the Clayoquot Sound South Community, in which Iisaak agreed to provide opportunities to local contractors and individuals from the community (Iisaak 2000b, p. 3). Iisaak committed 30 per cent of timber volume harvested to local value-added businesses (for example saw mills and transport companies) in Ucluelet and Tofino (Iisaak 2000f, p. 7).

In November 1999, only days after the MOU was signed, US logging giant Weyerhaeuser International bought MacMillan Bloedel and took over the minority shareholding in the joint venture. MB is now wholly owned by Weyerhaeuser, which assumed all MB's commitments.

In August 2000, Iisaak commenced its operations in Clayoquot Sound. That year, Iisaak cut approximately 10,000 cubic metres of old growth in Clayoquot – it logged 53 small patch cuts each of less than 1 hectare using variable retention systems (Iisaak 2000c). Variable retention systems are defined as logging in which at least 15 per cent of the forest is retained. The retained trees are dispersed across the harvest area, concentrated in patches, or distributed in a combination of both (Iisaak 2001). Iisaak's approach resulted in an average retention level of 75 per cent in its logging licenses (Iisaak 2000c). The company's logging plan for 2001–2003 aims at an estimated 106,000 cubic meters of old growth wood from nine cutblocks in four areas of Clayoquot Sound (FOCS 2001d, p. 3).[15]

In 2001, Iisaak obtained the FSC certification stipulated in the first Memorandum of Understanding. This makes Iisaak the first Tree Farm License holder in British Columbia certified to FSC standards, and the largest certified forest operator in Canada (Iisaak 2001).

From conflict to collaboration

The formation of this joint venture between a local community and a corporation, supported by civil society organizations, suggests a new and innovative model for addressing the needs of indigenous peoples faced with extractive industries. Given the more positive human rights impact than in many other TNC practices, and conflicts between civil society and corporations (as we have seen through case studies in this book), it is imperative to understand how this solution came about. Svendsen (2000) and Boutilier and Svendsen (2001) have extensively studied the process by which the key actors in this case moved from conflict to collaboration, and have comprehensively analyzed management processes and the case's lessons and implications. Their research into the 'evolution of relationships between companies and their stakeholders' conducted a 'detailed case study of the interpersonal and inter-organisational relationships that developed between ... MB and six environmental groups between 1993 and 1999' (Svendsen 2000, p. 1).

Svendsen identified a number of reasons why collaboration was eventually possible between what seemed arch-enemies. Suffice it here to outline a selection of key issues relevant for our further analysis.

Of crucial importance in this case was the role of the First Nations. The First Nations leaders of Clayoquot Sound found themselves in an awkward position between the warring parties, yet also in a position of power in relation to both the company and the environmental organizations. They were caught in the middle of a battle that threatened, on the one hand, their land and natural environment, and on the other, their timber resources and income. The First Nations insisted that a solution to the stand-off between MB and the NGOs was found, yet made a conscious decision not to take sides in the debate.[16] They did, however, play an important role in the negotiations between both parties. Not only did they insist that the conflict be solved, they requested that the environmental community speak with one voice and even informally appointed a representative for the eNGOs (Svendsen 2000, p. 6). Furthermore, they convened a series of meetings between the company, the environmental organizations, local community representatives and loggers.

A stalemate was reached in 1994. Faced with serious local opposition, an international campaign that was losing the company customers, and a set of scientific recommendations calling for a radically different approach to logging in Clayoquot Sound, MacMillan Bloedel accepted that change was necessary.

Svendsen describes how a slow process of building trust took place over an extended period, with the aid of the meetings initiated by the First Nations. The process was further helped by a number of gestures and initiatives taken by the company and the growing interpersonal contact between representatives of the company and the environmental NGOs (see Svendsen 2000, pp. 4–8). MacMillan Bloedel's new CEO, recruited from outside the company and the country in late 1997, believed the company needed to transform its forest management values to become the safest, most respected and most profitable forest company in Canada (Svendsen 2000, p. 5). He announced a number of initiatives, including the company's decision to phase out clearcutting in June 1998.[17] Crucially, when MB announced its radical decision on clearcutting, Svendsen notes, the environmental leaders 'agreed to actively co-operate with MB to develop the plan to end clear-cutting across all of MB's operations, not just in Clayoquot Sound' (Svendsen 2000, p. 6). This was a significant step which allowed the eNGOs which signed the MOU – to use Elkington's (1997, p. 229) classification – to move from non-discriminator to discriminator positions, making it possible for them to work with MB while maintaining their hostile stand towards other logging companies. Thus, working together, the environmentalists and company representatives learned more about each other's perceptions, values, and concerns, and both trust and value-sharing slowly intensified and matured. This trust-building and learning allowed the eNGOs, with the exception of FOCS, to shift their position from polarizors to integrators.

It must also be noted that the Canadian federal and provincial governments, although reluctantly, provided considerable financial support for change in Clayoquot Sound. The government was further crucial in the creation of the Interim Measures Agreement (IMA) and the Interim

Measures Extension Agreement (IMEA), which specifically committed MacMillan Bloedel and the Nuu-chah-nulth to establish a joint-venture logging business to operate in the Clayoquot Sound area.

There remain some questions regarding the future of Iisaak. While funding from the Canadian government for new initiatives in Clayoquot Sound has been considerable, it is not open-ended. Iisaak needs to attract investors to succeed commercially. As Chow argues: 'without a formal business plan and an estimated three years before Iisaak will turn a profit and approximately five years before an overall profit is realized, any traditional investments are unlikely' (Chow 2000, p. 8). Due to its unusual history, its commitment to environmentally and culturally sensitive logging, sustainable manufacturing, support from environmental organizations, and the unique competitive advantage of Iisaak's FSC certification, Iisaak should be attractive to non-traditional investors. In late 2000, Iisaak 'received line credit financing from Ecotrust Canada and Shorebank Enterprise Pacific, two organisations that have developed a revolving loan fund for conservation based businesses on Vancouver Island' (Iisaak 2001).

From an ecological point of view, scattered tenure makes an ecosystems approach difficult, if not impossible. The parts of Clayoquot Sound logged by Iisaak make it a minor player and, with other logging companies not using variable retention logging, a patchy approach is inevitable and the overall positive environmental impact questionable. Furthermore, the transition to phase out old-growth cut will not be an easy one, especially in the context of the current policy of volume-based tenures. 'While current tenures require management for non-timber values such as recreation, wildlife and biodiversity, companies are not allowed to realise returns from these management activities. Furthermore, revenue streams for non-timber forest products such as mushroom or berry collecting are not allowed under TFL's; only timber flows are permitted' (Chow 2000, p. 9).

While the analyses by Svendsen (2000) and Boutilier and Svendsen (2001) are very useful in helping us to understand *how* the Clayoquot Sound solution came about, our experiences with other community–corporation conflict situations – particularly the case of Shell and the Ogoni people in Nigeria – makes us interested in understanding *why* the solution was possible. We believe the key to the transition from conflict to collaboration in Clayoquot Sound was only possible, and effective, because of the implicit recognition by all key actors (local government, logging companies and environmental organizations) of the rights of the First Nations. As we have demonstrated elsewhere (Boele et al. 2001b) we hope that applying a rights-based perspective on sustainable development to conventional notions of corporate social responsibility and 'stakeholder management' may allow new insights into how conflicts over natural resources may arise and how they may eventually be solved. Thus, we advocate a rights-based approach to understanding this case in order to be able to draw lessons from this example and apply them elsewhere.

A rights-based approach to development

What is a rights-based approach to development

Article 2 of the United Nations Declaration on the Right to Development (UNDRD) places the human person as the 'central subject of development'. Human beings should be the 'active participants and beneficiaries of the right to development', and states should ensure their 'active, free and meaningful participation in development and the fair distribution of the benefits resulting thereof'. However, not all actors advance the same definition of development, which raises particular difficulties for the corporate sector when it is engaged in activities which might be described as development by some, but not all, stakeholders.

Western notions of development or 'progress' have been framed largely in rational, economic terms. While the semantics have changed over time (from 'progress' to 'modernization', 'development' and 'growth') and the legitimations have evolved (from 'civilizing mission' to 'economic efficiency'), the underlying ideology of progress persists. This idea of progress lies at the heart of the classification of the world's countries into 'developed' and 'underdeveloped' (Shanin 1997).

Yet conflicting values and perceptions of 'progress' and 'development' have become apparent when, for example, transnational companies have entered a previously industrially underdeveloped area with a view to maximizing development in the rational, economic sense. This view of progress does not necessarily account for the world's human cultural diversity and ecological complexity, and may be challenged by stakeholders outside the mainstream (ranging from religious revivalists to ethnic minorities) who hold a different idea of 'progress' – perhaps focused on moral, cultural and spiritual growth (Gandhi 1997). More recently the notion of development has been elaborated to 'sustainable development', a concept that embraces environmental, social and economic aspects of development. In addition, there is a growing awareness that development must be culturally sensitive and initiated and controlled by the people themselves. Current thinking in the development field takes a step further and advocates a rights-based approach to development.

A rights-based approach to development sets the achievement of human rights as both a *method* and an *objective* of development. It uses thinking about human rights as the scaffolding of development policy. It invokes the international apparatus of human rights accountability in support of development action. In all of these, it is concerned not just with civil and political rights (for example, the right to a trial, the right not to be tortured), but also with economic, social and cultural rights (such as the right to food, housing, a job) (ODI 1999, p. 1). The United Nations High Commissioner for Human Rights (UNHCHR) defines a rights-based approach to development as follows:

> A rights-based approach to development is a conceptual framework for the process of human development that is normatively based on international human rights standards and operationally directed to promoting and protecting human rights. Essentially, a rights-based approach integrates the norms, standards and principles of the international human rights system into the plans, policies and processes of development. (UNHCHR 2001a)

In addition, the right to development is mentioned specifically as a fundamental human right (UNHCHR 2001e), rooted in the provisions of the United Nations Charter, and expressed in the Universal Declaration of Human Rights (UDHR), the International Covenant on Civil and Political Rights and the International Covenant on Economic, Social and Cultural Rights, made explicit in the United Nations Declaration on the Right to Development, and affirmed by consensus at the 1993 World Conference on Human Rights. These documents encompass issues ranging from health and education to housing and governance. The international standards expressed in treaties, declarations and guidelines thus offer public and readily accessible tools describing both the institutional and developmental requirements of these rights, and thus making monitoring progress clearer.

A rights-based approach to development therefore is not just concerned with economic growth but equally 'involves equitable distribution, enhancement of people's capabilities and widening of their choices' (UNHCHR 2001b). The hope and aim of this approach is to avoid some of the mistakes made by previous development theories and practices. By putting beneficiaries in charge of development, a more sustainable and more genuine development is to be achieved (UNHCHR 2001c). A rights-based approach to development also allows for easier focus on the rights of vulnerable groups in society, such as women,

minorities and indigenous peoples (UNHCHR 2001b). In particular relation to the development concerns of indigenous peoples:[18]

> National development processes have often failed to include the free
> and meaningful participation of indigenous peoples. As a result,
> national development objectives and policies, as conceived by
> national-level officials and processes, have not always been consis-
> tent with the views, wishes and interests of indigenous peoples
> affected by them. Some have had a serious negative impact on
> indigenous peoples, including displacement, loss of livelihood,
> destruction of local environments, damage to sacred sites and, from
> the perspective of indigenous peoples, an intrusive, unsustainable and
> unplanned influx of outsiders into traditional territories ... Experience
> has shown that conflicts arise when development projects take place
> without an understanding of, or respect for, indigenous peoples'
> strong spiritual attachment to and traditional association with their
> lands and territories. (UNHCHR 2001d)

Consistent with Nobel Prize Winner Amartya Sen's analysis of development as freedom (Sen 1999), we would contend that an expansion of
people's rights should be both the principal *means* and primary *end* of
development. The key argument in a rights-based approach centers
around the definition of increased human rights as both ends and
means to development, in that human rights are both an outcome and
a constitutive part of the process of development. We believe the
Clayoquot Sound case is a useful demonstration of this approach, in
that recognizing the rights of the First Nations was a necessary *means* to
transcend the conflict and bring increased economic development,
while providing the *end* of greater self-determination for the Nuu-chah-
nulth people.

Indigenous peoples and the rights-based approach

Since the acceleration of economic globalization through giant transnational corporations, indigenous people have articulated an increasing
confrontation with private corporations, especially those engaged in
resource extraction (Burger 1987; Rival 1993; Young 1995; Hitchcock
1997). A 1993 report by the United Nations Transnational Corporations
and Management Division noted that indigenous nations were being
harmed more often by private corporations than by governments
(UNTCMD 1993).

The flip-side of the phenomenon of globalization is the increasing organization of indigenous peoples in social movements, connected via global communications technology with other, like-minded organizations.[19] In addition, a globalization of the rights discourse has occurred, and the language of rights is not applied only by western development specialists or social advocates but is also increasingly adopted by Aboriginal peoples. Indeed, many marginalized communities around the world now actively engage in the rights debate and frame their struggles and demands in a language of rights (see Cowan et al. 2001; Morris 1992; Tennant 1994; Wilson 1997).

The situation in the oil-rich delta of Nigeria (discussed in Chapter 5 of this book) and the process of the Ogoni people of the delta asserting their rights via a social and cultural challenge to dominant power structures (which we have analyzed in Boele et al. 2001a,b) is illustrative in this regard. If we examine the Movement for the Survival of the Ogoni People (MOSOP)'s statements, they express an unambiguous assertion of rights in the context of development, with demands to 'end political marginalisation, economic strangulation and environmental degradation' (Saro-Wiwa 1995). The influential Ogoni Bill of Rights of October 1990 is clearly framed in rights-based language (Boele et al. 2001b). The title of the document explicitly refers to rights, and much of the content deals with rights to development. The structure of the Bill follows closely that of international rights documents, such as the Universal Declaration of Human Rights. Furthermore, by articulating their cultural identity in terms of being 'indigenous people', the Ogoni took a further significant step towards selecting a rights discourse to their struggle. Contact with international human rights organizations – such as the United Nations Working Group on Indigenous Populations – was crucial in this regard. After discovering the work of the United Nations, MOSOP sent regular missions to the United Nations Working Group on Indigenous Populations, the UN Sub-Commission on the Prevention of Discrimination and the Protection of Minorities and the UN Committee for the Elimination of All Forms of Racial Discrimination, based in Geneva. MOSOP representatives also attended the United Nations Conference on Human Rights in Vienna. Not only did the rights terminology provide the Ogoni with a broader framework in which to place their situation; the fact that the UN is working on indigenous peoples' rights – such as the drafting of a Declaration of the Rights of Indigenous Peoples – made 'being indigenous' a politically advantageous position.

In the framework of British Columbia, the major expression of aboriginal rights is in the context of land rights, and the right to self-government. The situation of indigenous peoples' land rights in British Columbia is unusual in the Canadian context (Cassidy and Dale 1988). While most Canadian provinces have historical treaties with indigenous nations, the BC government never negotiated treaties with its first inhabitants.[20] 'British Columbia is not the only portion of Canada in which aboriginal title was not extinguished and in which aboriginal peoples have been pressing their claims in recent times. British Columbia is, however, virtually alone in continuing to refuse to acknowledge aboriginal land claims or to negotiate' (Tennant 1990, p. 227). Consequently, there has been much debate about the exact legal situation regarding indigenous land rights in BC. In the Royal Proclamation of 1763, the British laid claim to the territories to the west of their existing colonies. The Proclamation 'asserts that the Indians are not to be interfered with; and it acknowledges the Indians as continuing to own the lands which they have used and occupied' (Tennant 1990, p. 10).

The federal government does acknowledge aboriginal land claims and is prepared to negotiate them in all its provinces. Yet the Provincial government of British Columbia 'has always denied the existence of aboriginal title and has declined to negotiate' (Tennant 1990, p. 13). This is felt as particularly hurtful because:

> For Indians, land claims negotiations are important not only because of the land, but also because they will signify that governments, and the non-Indian public, are acknowledging something of the historic and the present importance of Indian peoples ... Government refusal to negotiate is thus taken as being much more than a refusal to talk about land; it is taken as belittling the worth and identity of Indian peoples. (Tennant 1990, p. 14)

The aboriginal peoples of BC argue that they have never signed any of their lands' ownership to the government of British Columbia, and hold full and continuing title to their lands. In reality, having signed no land treaties, this legal uncertainty meant that 'aboriginal peoples had negligible property rights or control over resources' (Barnes and Hayter 1997, p. 4) until the 1970s. By the mid-1980s, many groups, including the Nuu-chah-nulth, 'had prepared and submitted land claims [in order to] protect the lands and the resources until the claim was settled' (Tennant 1990, p. 207).

In the 1997 Delgamuukw Decision, 'the Supreme Court of Canada held that the provincial government never extinguished aboriginal title in BC because it did not have the jurisdiction to do so' (quoted in Forest Futures 2001). The Delgamuukw Supreme Court Decision offers an 'explicit recognition, on the national and constitutional level, of the reality of aboriginal title existing within the Canadian legal system' (Delgamuukw Gisday'wa National Process 2000). As a result, 'First Nations have the opportunity to begin planning for the future acknowledgement of their Aboriginal title' (Delgamuukw Gisday'wa National Process 2000) and the BC provincial government has commenced treaty negotiations with its First Nations.[21]

Vital in the claims to land title is the demand for self-determination or self-government. Tennant (1990, p. 14) quotes 1984 Nuu-chah-nulth Tribal Council leader George Watts expressing this desire as follows:

> We take the position that we are sovereign nations, that our existence stems from the fact that we were the first peoples here, that we have the aboriginal title to the land. But that sovereignty is one which could coexist along with the rest of Canada. We're not talking about being sovereign nations as far as having post offices, armed forces and monetary systems of our own. What we're talking about is having Indian governments within the Confederation of Canada.

A rights-based approach in Clayoquot Sound

As noted, Svendsen (2000) and Boutilier and Svendsen (2001) have provided a comprehensive analysis of the *process* by which the key actors in this case moved from conflict to collaboration and the case's lessons and implications for stakeholder theory. We believe there is a fundamental question to be answered about the Clayoquot Sound case and *why* these processes were successful. In this context, the application of a rights-based analysis begins to offer answers. We hope to demonstrate through our analysis that the actors in Clayoquot Sound were actually engaged in an implicit rights-based discourse. A 'rights-lens' to view a corporate–community conflict can provide an understanding and benchmark that can allow a managerial approach to be successful in resolving conflicts between a private company and its host communities.

While the national and provincial governments played a reluctant supportive role, the three critical actors in the conflict were the logging company, MacMillan Bloedel, the environmental NGOs and the Nuu-chah-nulth First Nations. The primary conflict was between the company and eNGOs while the First Nations found themselves in a more central position. This central position came about because of a number of factors. Svendsen (2000, p. 4) quotes the then Vice President of MacMillan Bloedel, Linda Coady:

> With a modern day Treaty process having begun in earnest in BC, the aboriginal peoples of Clayoquot Sound found themselves with the

moral authority to cast the swing vote in the whole controversy. They had the effective political power to either discredit Greenpeace's international market campaign or blow MB's defences to smithereens.

A rights-based analysis would suggest that this 'authority' arises from the acceptance and recognition by the other parties of the First Nations' rights – in this case the First Nations' right to ownership of land and resources and their right to self-determination. The First Nations' ability to discredit both the eNGOs and the company in the public's mind was possible because there was a wider recognition of the First Nations' rights over the resources and land in dispute – despite the fact that there was no legal recognition of their land rights.

On the one hand, the Nuu-chah-nulth First Nations had an interest in protecting their physical environment from logging and its effects on their livelihoods and cultural and spiritual life. On the other hand, some Nuu-chah-nulth individuals were directly or indirectly employed by the logging industry. Faced with poverty and its implications, especially in terms of health problems and an 85 per cent unemployment rate, the First Nations recognized the income of forestry as important for the community (Chow 2000, p. 3).

The First Nations were clear they wanted the conflict solved, and urged both the eNGOs and the logging company to 'sort it out'. They were also aware that without their support neither side would be able to win the conflict, and from this position of power, persuaded both sides to work towards a solution. Svendsen (2000, p. 4) quotes MB's Linda Coady: 'What this led to was a journey in which both MB and the environmental groups were like two convicts escaped from the chain gang manacled together. Like it or not, [we] had to work out a solution both could live with.'

Again this statement can be considered revealing when applying rights-based analysis. It acknowledges interdependence and implies an equality of position as both parties find themselves in the same circumstance and effectively having equal rights. With a position of equality accepted it helped both sides to understand each other's positions and find common ground. As they did so they were able to understand each other's values and began to see the differing emphasis they placed on different rights.

The final resolution of the conflict lies in a negotiated balancing of rights. Environmental organizations were concerned with the rights of indigenous peoples but they focused primarily on the protection of the environment – nature, forests, water, animals in forests and water. As the Friends of Clayoquot Sound write, 'FOCS works to protect the ecological integrity of the earth's most endangered forest type, the ancient temperate rainforest' (FOCS 2001f). However there was a balancing of rights to be achieved. The absolute rights of the environment – especially if these are interpreted as meaning absolutely no damage, were not compatible with the economic development rights of the Nuu-chah-nulth people or the legal rights of the logging companies.

The eNGOs theoretically recognized the land rights, cultural rights and environmental rights of First Nations – almost an ideological position of many environmental movements. However, this seeming ideological convergence is not necessarily borne out in practice, as Ali (2000) illustrated in his analysis of relations between mining companies in Australia and Canada. Ali found that the eNGOs and indigenous rights NGOs (INGOs) often had quite different agendas, as indeed there are frequently differences within the indigenous community. Similarly, in the Clayoquot Sound case, the right to self-determination, generally supported by environmental groups assuming that their perceptions and those of the indigenous peoples on environmental rights would intersect, proved to be something of a challenge to eNGOs. As Svendsen recounts:

> At the climax of one lengthy meeting attended by over 150 stakeholders, the First Nations elders asked everyone to stand up if they were willing to hand over decision making authority for Clayoquot Sound lands to the First Nations. The only people who did not stand up were the half dozen women leading the eNGOs. The MB representatives did stand. (Boutilier and Svendsen 2001, p. 13)

This anecdote suggests that at this point the eNGOs were not prepared to recognize the First Nations' traditional ownership rights and their right to self-determination. Consequently, the eNGOs could not even begin to balance the rights of the environment with the First Nations' rights.

MB also believed that they had rights; indeed they had rights that had been legally granted by the government of BC, via its Tree Farm License tenure, to log the area. There were related rights, such as those of MB's workers to livelihoods that were being curtailed by the actions of the eNGOs. These corporate and corporate related rights were also to be understood and debated.

Throughout the process of trust-building (Svendsen 2000), both agents negotiated their understanding of rights. The company accepted the cultural and environmental rights of the First Nations and the eNGOs came to accept the economic rights and right to development of the indigenous peoples. Svendsen notes that:

> The views of environmentalists ... changed. During the blockades, Greenpeace for example, took a very hard line on how the dispute might be resolved. They were not prepared to see any logging of old-growth forests. The agreement reached in the MOU deviated from this position and recognised the importance of socio-economic as well as environmental interests. Respondents in this study reported that the infusion of the First Nations' perspective and values into the dialogue was of central importance in the evolution of their thinking. (Svendsen 2000, p. 12)

We would suggest that it was more than the 'infusion of the First Nations' perspective and values' that led to the change in thinking – it was also an implicit recognition that the First Nations had rights in this situation and that these rights needed to be reconciled by the eNGOs with their articulation of the absolute rights that the environment held. By recognizing the right to self-determination of the First Nations, and examining what this meant for the First Nations – that is, accepting the full spectrum of rights – a compromise was possible. Moreover, through negotiations, the actors who were the furthest apart moved from moral and implicit *recognition* of indigenous people's rights to supporting the actual *enjoyment* of those rights via the establishment of the Iisaak joint venture.

Conclusion: rights and business–community relations

In summary, Svendsen (2000) and Boutilier and Svendsen (2001) list a number of reasons how and why the conflict was solved (mainly motivation, trust and mutual understanding), all of which we believe are important, if not crucial, to the actual solution of the conflict, and should be studied carefully by all proponents of managerial stakeholder theory and all those concerned with company–community conflicts. But in addition, we would stress the importance of the fact that both MB and eNGOs came to a position where they implicitly recognized the rights of First Nations, and by doing so conferred to them a power that was crucial in moving forward. We believe that the non-recognition of rights lies at the heart of many other unresolved community–corporate conflicts, and provides an explanation as to why certain conflicts remain unresolved, even though they have been the object of extensive and sophisticated stakeholder management processes.

For example, we have long tried to understand why the conflict between the Ogoni people in Nigeria and Shell had not moved beyond hostility (see Boele et al. 20001a,b; Wheeler et al. 2002), even though Shell has undergone significant changes since the height of the conflict. While Shell has gained a leadership position among corporations that are adopting stakeholder management strategies, both Shell and the Nigerian military government failed to acknowledge and honor basic rights in the oil-rich Niger Delta.[22] As we have argued when examining the Shell–Ogoni conflict (Boele et al. 2001b), applying a rights-based perspective on development may allow new insights into how conflicts over development of natural resources may arise and, by implication, may serve as a starting point for solving conflicts.

We believe a rights-based approach is a useful tool in stakeholder management, and while stakeholder management (see Freeman 1984 and Wheeler and Sillanpää 1997 for the concept of stakeholders) is a useful tool in solving community–corporate conflict, the rights of stakeholders must be acknowledged and recognized in full. Firms such as Shell, Rio Tinto and others may well exhibit increasingly stakeholder-responsive behaviors at the corporate, strategic level. Yet as we have argued elsewhere (Wheeler et al. 2002), a genuinely stakeholder-responsive model must be more than an instrumentalist management tool for managing troublesome groups in the service of conventional business goals. Stakeholder theory may fail, as we believe the Shell–Ogoni case shows, if the rights of all stakeholders are not respected and especially where they are negated. All stakeholders' rights must be acknowledged and recognized in order to begin the journey towards resolution and solution. Where there are competing rights a solution may only be possible where one or more parties surrender or exchange their rights freely and from a position of having the right to exercise a veto. Unless stakeholders are in a position to exercise their 'stake' and claim the respect of their rights, stakeholder management is in danger of being labeled a public relations exercise that fails a company's stakeholders more often than it succeeds.

There has been much academic debate in the corporate social responsibility area about the competing validity of normative versus managerial approaches towards stakeholder relations. In this chapter we have argued that the two approaches are not mutually exclusive, indeed a managerial approach can be significantly informed by the application of a rights-based perspective to stakeholder relations. In hindsight the application of a 'human rights lens' to the Clayoquot Sound case reveals a discourse between the stakeholders that was implicitly about rights – rights that were being curtailed, unrecognized and in competition with one another. If a rights-based approach had been taken from the beginning perhaps this conflict would have been able to move faster to the very innovative solutions that were eventually adopted.

Regardless of these issues, the importance of this case lies in its very existence. The legacy of Clayoquot Sound is that it shows us that the most heated corporate–community conflict can be solved if community rights are respected. This book contains a number of examples of negative impacts of transnational corporations on human rights. We hope some may benefit from studying the history of logging in Clayoquot Sound and the very powerful and positive role that mutual respect of human rights can play as both an end and a means for development.

Notes

1. This makes Clayoquot Sound about 8 per cent of Vancouver Island (FOCS 2001d).
2. The Biosphere declaration did not result in new protected areas or new environmental standards for Clayoquot Sound (FOCS 2001b).
3. The two protected valleys are Megin and Moyeha, located in Strathcona Provincial Park. The four unprotected pristine valleys are Sydney, Ursus, Bulson and Clayoquot (FOCS 2001d).
4. Tla-o-qui-aht (Clayoquot Sound) refers to both the area and the Nuu-chah-nulth band name and means 'people of other tribes'. The Tla-o-qui-aht are part of the Nootka linguistic group (Ministry of Aboriginal Affairs 2001).
5. It goes without saying that the impact of logging on indigenous rights has been significant too. Yet of utmost significance has been European and Canadian colonization. The legal situation of Canadian First Nations is complex. The Canadian Federal Government has 'fiduciary responsibility' for native peoples (while they are seen as 'dependent domestic nations' in the US). 'Several aboriginal groups in Canada have not ceded territory to the state by treaty ... These groups are judicially deemed to have "aboriginal title" to lands occupied since "time immemorial", but such title is an inferior status to Canadian sovereignty and has been by-passed relatively easy. Aboriginal title has been scant defence against industrial encroachments and the imposition of Euro-Canadian social institutions ... ' (Samson 2001, p. 389).
6. All forest land in British Columbia is owned by the government, with only a relatively small proportion privately owned. With most timber sold in BC originating in state-owned forests, timber revenue is an important income source (Drushka 1999, pp. 167–9). 'Provincially owned forest land is organized into two categories. Tree Farm Licences (TFLs) are relatively large areas leased to private firms and municipal bodies for the purpose of harvesting timber and growing future timber crops. The licence holders manage the land under terms and conditions prescribed by the government. The second and largest portion of BC-owned forest land is found in Timber Supply Areas (TSAs), which are managed by the Ministry of Forests in close collaboration with the forest industry. Timber from TSAs is sold to industry under a variety of leases and licences on an annual volume basis' (Drushka 1999, p. 19).

7. This decision came after a lengthy and vitally important legal process (detailed in Tennant 1990, pp. 220–4). The process was important in that it affirmed that Native Peoples in BC indeed had grounds to claim aboriginal title and that the province of BC should address these claims. Various injunctions were granted to put on hold other development projects on lands with uncertain claims. The injunctions prompted the major resource development corporations to consider whether their own interests would not be better served by the province's negotiating with the Indians (Tennant 1990, p. 225).

8. The remit of the panel was to devise recommendations on logging old-growth forests in a sustainable way rather than question whether to log them. Furthermore, the panel had to remain within the framework of the 1993 Clayoquot Land Use Decision, earmarking 74 per cent of the area's forest open for logging (FOCS 2001d). The main recommendations of the panel are: 1. To use an ecosystem-based instead of a volume-based approach to logging; 2. To establish a community-based planning process which utilizes scientific and traditional First Nations knowledge; 3. Restrict cutting of watershed areas; and 4. Increased tree retention in cutblocks (FOCS 2001d, p. 2).

9. Unlike MacMillan Bloedel, the Nuu-chah-nulth can increase their shareholding in the joint venture over time. Any of the Central Region First Nations may send an observer to the Iisaak board meetings to assure the interests of individual First Nations are respected (Iisaak 2000f).

10. MacMillan Bloedel held the Tree Farm License (TFL 44) on the west coast of Vancouver Island. Of this 452,826-hectare area, 101,009 hectares were in Clayoquot Sound (Chow 2000, p. 1). Iisaak now holds TFL 57, which comprises the Clayoquot Sound portion of TFL previously held by MB. The remainder of TFL 44 was left with MacMillan Bloedel (Chow 2000, p. 6).

11. The company has initiated a monitoring programme in partnership with the Long Beach Model Forest Society to monitor the results of the implementation of the Scientific Panel recommendations. These will be used to improve management plans and strategies through adaptive management (Iisaak 2000e, p. 2).

12. The memorandum does not cover the entire area of Clayoquot Sound, since some tenures are held by logging company Interfor, which did not join up to the memorandum.

13. The Forest Stewardship Council is an independent non-profit organization recognized internationally. It accredits and monitors independent forest product certifiers.

14. Although they did not oppose Iisaak's operations as such, they were unhappy with its decision to log old-growth forests.

15. In comparison, in 1993, at the height of the anti-logging campaign, a total of 456,000 cubic meters of wood was logged by all logging companies active in the area, already down from 959,000 in 1988. In 2000, the volume cut in Clayoquot Sound was 24,000 cubic meters (FOCS 2001d, p. 2)

16. The fact that they chose not to take sides in the battle between the eNGOs and MB does not mean they did not have an opinion, or were a passive group in this debate. The aboriginal people were fighting their own battle against logging on their land. The Nuu-chah-nulth were involved in a court action to regain land title (they submitted their land claim in 1983) and were instrumental in organizing the 1983 blockade of logging access to Mearnes

Island. For them, the logging itself was not the issue, indeed they had not expressed complaints about logging previously and many aboriginal people found employment in the forestry industry. Their protests against the logging companies stemmed directly from their land claims, and the protests aimed at protecting the lands until the claims could be settled.

17. Many logging companies prefer clearcutting – literally clearing all vegetation and cutting all trees across an entire area – over retention systems whereby a per- centage of trees are retained. Although environmental arguments and technological advances are brought forward in defense of more selective logging, economic and technical arguments are used by the companies to justify their preference for clearcutting. In announcing its policy change, MB became the first company to break the so-called 'Clearcutting Cartel'. It was significant that one logging company broke away from the clearcutting stand as this gave more voice and power to the retention argument.

18. The United Nations has undertaken specific work regarding the rights of indigenous peoples. Among others initiatives, a Draft United Nations Declaration on the Rights of Indigenous Peoples (which states in Article 30 that indigenous peoples have the 'right to determine and develop priorities and strategies for their development or use of their lands, territories or other resources') was initiated by the UN Working Group on Indigenous Populations.

19. Significantly, these new NGO alliances produced not only North–South, but also South–South alliances. Oilwatch, for example, is a network of organizations working against the effects of the oil industry based in Ecuador. Most of its member organizations are grassroots groups from areas where the oil industry is active, the majority based in the South, often in areas inhabited by indigenous people. Equally, the International Alliance of the Indigenous/Tribal Peoples of the Tropical Forests and the World Rainforest Movement bring together NGOs from around the globe (though mainly based in the South) to share information and strategies.

20. Except some treaties on Vancouver Island (arranged by James Douglas, chief official of the Hudson's Bay Company) and Treaty No. 8 arranged by the federal government in northeastern BC (Tennant 1990, p. 241).

21. As of September 2001, there were 49 First Nations in British Columbia participating in Treaty Negotiations. Only one of these is in the last stage of negotiations (see British Columbia Treaty Commission 2001a and 2001b). The Nuu-chah-nulth reached the initiation of stage 4 (out of 6) in their negotiations with the government in March 2001 (British Columbia Treaty Commission 2001c).

22. The Shell Nigeria and Ogoni case demonstrates that large corporations are capable of recognizing the value of rational, managerial processes of corporate social responsibility and stakeholder management – certainly at the corporate level. Since 1995, Shell International has taken significant steps to reorientate its business principles and literature in order to encourage a more accountable and dynamic set of relationships with key stakeholders. By supporting the Universal Declaration of Human Rights in 1996, Shell International has accepted and publicly acknowledged that the company is a significant human rights actor. The application of a rights-based approach to the Ogoni case may allow Shell to begin a deeper analysis of the company's

impacts on communities. This deeper understanding could then provide for the cognitive and attitudinal shifts which need to occur in Shell (most especially in Nigeria) in order finally to move forward and resolve their conflict with the Ogoni people (see Boele et al. 2001b).

References

Ali, Saleem H. 2000. 'Shades of Green: NGO Coalitions, Mining Companies and the Pursuit of Negotiating Power', in Jem Bendell, ed., *Terms for Endearment: Business, NGOs and Sustainable Development*. Sheffield: Greenleaf Publishing.

Barnes, Trevor J. and Roger Hayter (eds). 1997. *Trouble in the Rainforest: British Columbia's Forest Economy in Transition*. Canadian Western Geographical Series, Volume 33, Victoria: Western Geographical Press.

Bendell, Jem and David Murphy. 2000. 'Planting the Seeds of Change: Business–NGO Relations on Tropical Deforestation', in Jem Bendell, ed., *Terms for Endearment: Business, NGOs and Sustainable Development*. Sheffield: Greenleaf Publishing.

Boele, Richard, Heike Fabig and David Wheeler. 2001a. 'Shell, Nigeria and the Ogoni. A Study in Unsustainable Development I, The Story of Shell, Nigeria and the Ogoni People – Environment, Economy, Relationships: Conflict and Prospects for Resolution', *Journal of Sustainable Development* 9(2): 74–86.

Boele, Richard, Heike Fabig and David Wheeler. 2001b. 'Shell Nigeria and the Ogoni. A study in Unsustainable Development II, Corporate Social Responsibility and "Stakeholder Management" versus a Rights-Based Approach to Sustainable Development', *Journal of Sustainable Development* 9(3): 121–35.

Boutilier, Robert G. and Ann Svendsen. 2001. 'From Conflict to Collaboration: Stakeholder Bridging and Bonding in Clayoquot Sound', unpublished paper. Available at http://www.cim.sfu.ca.

British Columbia Treaty Commission. 2001a. 'About the Commission'. Available at http://www.bctreaty.net/files/bctreaty.html.

British Columbia Treaty Commission. 2001b. 'Policies and Procedures'. Available at http://www.bctreaty.net/files/policies.html.

British Columbia Treaty Commission, 2001c. 'First Nations – Nuu-chah-nulth Tribal Council'. Available at http://www.bctreaty.net/nations/nuuchahnulth.html.

Burger, Julian. 1987. *Report from the Frontier: the State of the World's Indigenous Peoples*. London: Cultural Survival and Zed Books.

Cassidy, Frank and Norman Dale. 1988. *After Native Claims? The Implications of Comprehensive Claims Settlements for Natural Resources in British Columbia*. Lantzville: Oolichan Books and Halifax: Institute for Research on Public Policy.

Chow, Victoria Y. 2000. 'Using Partnerships for Land Conservation, Yale School of Forestry and Environmental Services', Student Case Write-Ups (F&ES 882 Fall 1999). Available at http://www.yale.edu/yff/assets/images/chow.pdf.

Cowan, Jane K., Marie-Bénédicte Dembour and Richard A. Wilson. 2001. *Culture and Rights: Anthropological Perspectives*. Cambridge: Cambridge University Press.

Delgamuukw Gisday'wa National Process. 2000. 'Delgamuukw News and Events – A Backgrounder', Delgamuukw Gisday'wa National Process. July 2000. Available at http://www.delgamuukw.org/news/news.htm.

Drushka, Ken. 1999. *In the Bight: the BC Forest Industry Today*. Madeira Park (BC): Harbour Publishing.

Elkington, John. 1997. *Cannibals with Forks, the Triple Bottom Line of 21st Century Business*. Oxford: Capstone.

Estes, Ralph. 1996. *Tyranny of the Bottom Line: Why Corporations Make Good People Do Bad Things*. San Francisco: Berrett-Koehler Publishers.

FOCS (Friends of Clayoquot Sound). 2001a. 'Clayoquot Sound Campaign'. Available at http://ancientrainforests.org/campaigns/clayoquot/clayoquot_campaign.html.

FOCS (Friends of Clayoquot Sound). 2001b. 'Is There Hope in the Biosphere Reserve?'. Available at http://ancientrainforests.org/campaigns/clayoquot/biosphere_reserve.htm.

FOCS (Friends of Clayoquot Sound). 2001c. 'What is Clayoquot Sound and What are Ancient Temperate Rainforests?'. Available at http://ancientrainforests.org/campaigns/clayoquot/what_is_clayoquot.htm.

FOCS (Friends of Clayoquot Sound). 2001d. 'Temperate Rainforest Fact Sheet and Clayoquot Sound Update'. Available at http://ancientrainforests.org/logging_updates/fact_sheet.html.

FOCS (Friends of Clayoquot Sound). 2001e. 'Iisaak and Interfor: Not in the Same League'. Available at http://ancientrainforests.org/campaigns/clayoquot/iisaak_and_interfor.htm.

FOCS (Friends of Clayoquot Sound). 2001f. 'Our Campaigns'. Available at http://ancientrainforests.org/home.htm.

Forest Futures. 2001. 'First Nations Rights'. Available at http://www.forestfutures.org/weyer_firstnations.html.

Fowler, Penny and Simon Heap. 2000. 'Bridging Troubled Waters: the Marine Stewardship Council', in Jem Bendell, ed., *Terms for Endearment: Business, NGOs and Sustainable Development*. Sheffield: Greenleaf Publishing.

Freeman, R.E. 1984. *Strategic Management: a Stakeholder Approach*. New York: Basic Books.

Gandhi, M. 1997. 'The Quest for Simplicity: My Idea of Swaraj', in M. Rahmena and V. Bawtree, eds, *The Post-Development Reader*. London: Zed Books.

Haynes, Patricia H. 1991. 'The Race to Save the Planet: Will Women Lose?', *Women's Studies International Forum* 14(5): 473–8.

Hitchcock, Robert K. 1997. 'Indigenous Peoples, Multinational Corporations and Human Rights', *Indigenous Affairs* (April/May/June): 6–11.

Iisaak (Iisaak Forest Resources). 2000a. 'Welcome'. Available at http://www.iisaak.com/index.html. Last updated 27 September 2001.

Iisaak (Iisaak Forest Resources). 2000b. 'Historic Agreements'. Available at http://www.iisaak.com/historicagreements.html.

Iisaak (Iisaak Forest Resources). 2000c. '2000 Operations'. Available at http://www.iisaak.com/operations.html.

Iisaak (Iisaak Forest Resources). 2000d. 'The Clayoquot Sound Scientific Panel'. Available at http://www.iisaak.com/sciencepanel.html.

Iisaak (Iisaak Forest Resources). 2000e. 'Monitoring'. Available at http://www.iisaak.com/monitoring.html.

Iisaak (Iisaak Forest Resources). 2000f. 'Questions and Answers'. Available at http://www.iisaak.com/QuestionsandAnswers.html.

Iisaak (Iisaak Forest Resources). 2001. 'Iisaak Achieves Forest Stewardship Council (FSC) Certification for Forestry Operations in Clayoquot Sound', press release. 27 July 2001. Clayoquot Sound. Available at http://www.iisaak.com/PRJuly24.htm.

Marchak, Patricia. 1983. *Green Gold: the Forest Industry in British Columbia*. Vancouver: University of British Columbia Perss.

Ministry of Aboriginal Affairs. 2001. 'Tla-o-qui-aht (Clayoquot)'. Available at http://www.aaf.gov.bc.ca/nations/nuuchah/660.stm.

Morris, G. 1992. 'International Law and Politics: Toward a Right to Self-Determination for Indigenous Peoples', in M.A. Jaimes, ed., *The State of Native America: Genocide, Colonization and Resistance*. Boston: South End Press.

Murphy, David F. 1997. 'Responsible International Trade: Key Issues and Best Practice', New Academy of Business, London.

Murphy, David F. and Jem Bendell. 1997. *In the Company of Partners: Business Environmental Groups and Sustainable Development Post-Rio*. Bristol: The Policy Press.

Murphy, David F. and Gill Coleman. 2000. 'Thinking Partners: Business, NGOs and the Partnership Concept', in Jem Bendell, ed., *Terms for Endearment: Business, NGOs and Sustainable Development*. Sheffield: Greenleaf Publishing.

Nuu-chah-nulth Tribal Council. 2001. 'Looking Ahead'. Available at http://nuuchahnulth.org/trees.htm.

ODI (Overseas Development Institute). 1999. 'What Can We Do with a Rights-Based Approach to Development', London: ODI. Available at http://www.odi.org.uk/briefing/3_99.html.

Plant, Christopher and Judith Plant. 1991. *Green Business: Hope or Hoax?* Gabriola Island: New Society Publishers, and Devon: Green Books.

Porter, M. and C. van der Linde. 1996. 'Green and Competitive: Ending the Stalemate', in R. Welford and R. Starkey, eds, *The Earthscan Reader in Business and the Environment*. London: Earthscan

Rival, Laura. 1993. 'Confronting Petroleum Development in the Ecuadorian Amazon: the Huaorani, Human Rights and Environmental Protection', *Anthropology in Action* 16: 14–15.

Samson, Colin. 2001. 'Rights as the Reward for Simulated Cultural Sameness: the Innu in the Canadian Colonial Context', in Jane K. Cowan, Marie-Bénédicte Dembour and Richard A. Wilson, eds, *Culture and Rights: Anthropological Perspectives*. Cambridge: Cambridge University Press.

Saro-Wiwa, Kenule. 1995. *A Month and A Day – A Detention Diary*. London: Penguin Books.

Sen, Amartya. 1999. *Development as Freedom*. Oxford: Oxford University Press.

Shanin, T. 1997. 'The Idea of Progress', in M. Rahnema and V. Bawtree, eds, *The Post-Development Reader*. London: Zed Books.

Stafford, Edwin R. and Cathy L. Hartman. 2001. 'Greenpeace's "Greenfreeze" Campaign": Hurdling Competitive Forces in the Diffusion of Environmental Technology Innovation', in K.P. Green Groenewegen and P.S. Hofman, eds, *Ahead of the Curve: Cases of Innovation in Environmental Management*. Dordrecht: Kluwer Academic Publishers.

Stafford, Edwin R., Michael Jay Polonski and Cathy L. Hartman. 2000. 'Environmental NGO–Business Collaboration and Strategic Bridging: a Case Analysis of the Greenpeace–Foron Alliance', *Business Strategy and the Environment* 9: 122–35.

Svendsen, Ann. 2000. 'From Conflict to Collaboration: the Evolution of Corporate–Stakeholder Relationships in the Forest Sector', unpublished paper. Available from author via: svendsen@sfu.ca.

Tennant, Chris. 1994. 'Indigenous Peoples, International Institutions and the International Legal Literature', *Human Rights Quarterly* 16(1): 1–57.

Tennant, Paul. 1990. *Aboriginal Peoples and Politics: the Indian Land Question in British Columbia 1849–1989*. Vancouver: University of British Columbia Press.

UNHCHR (United Nations High Commissioner for Human Rights). 2001a. 'Human Rights in Development – What is a Rights-Based Approach to Development?' Available at http://www.unhchr.ch/development/approaches-04.html.

UNHCHR (United Nations High Commissioner for Human Rights). 2001b. 'Human Rights in Development – What is Development from a Human Rights Perspective?' Available at http://www.unhchr.ch/development/approaches-02.html.

UNHCHR (United Nations High Commissioner for Human Rights). 2001c. 'Human Rights in Development – How do Rights-Based Approaches Differ and What Is The Value Added?' Available at http://www.unhchr.ch/development/approaches-07.html.

UNHCHR (United Nations High Commissioner for Human Rights). 2001d. 'Human Rights in Development – What are the Main Development Concerns of Indigenous Peoples?' Available at http://www.unhchr.ch/development/approaches-08.html.

UNHCHR (United Nations High Commissioner for Human Rights). 2001e. 'Human Rights in Development – Development as a Right'. Available at http://www.unhchr.ch/development/right-01.html.

UNTCMD (United Nations Transnational Corporations and Management Division). 1993. 'Transnational Investments and Operations on the Lands of Indigenous Peoples', Report to the Working Group on Indigenous Populations of the Sub-Commission on Prevention of Discrimination and Protection on Minorities. New York: UNTCMD.

Vogel, David. 1978. *Lobbying the Corporation: Citizen Challenges to Business Authority*. New York: Basic Books.

Wayne Dunn Associates. 2001. 'The Changing Resource Development Paradigm – Maximising Sustainable Local Benefits from Resource Development', Prepared for the Government of British Columbia, Ministry of Community Development Cooperatives and Volunteers, Mill Bay (BC): Wayne Dunn Associates.

Weir, Anne. 2000. 'Meeting Social and Environmental Objectives through Partnership: the Experience of Unilever', in Jem Bendell, ed., *Terms for Endearment: Business, NGOs and Sustainable Development*. Sheffield: Greenleaf Publishing.

Wheeler, David and Maria Sillanpää. 1997. *The Stakeholder Corporation: a Blueprint for Maximizing Stakeholder Value*. London: Pitman Publishing.

Wheeler, David, Richard Boele and Heike Fabig. 2002. 'Paradoxes and Ethical Dilemmas for Stakeholder Responsive Firms in the Extractive Sector – Lessons from the Case of Shell and the Ogoni', *Journal of Business Ethics* 39(3): 297–318.

Wilson, Richard (ed.). 1997. *Human Rights, Culture and Context, Anthropological Perspectives*. London: Pluto Press.

Young, Elspeth. 1995. *Third World in the First: Development and Indigenous Peoples*. London and New York: Routledge.

Index